I0810248

IMAGES
*of America*

# OLD YORK BEACH
## VOLUME II

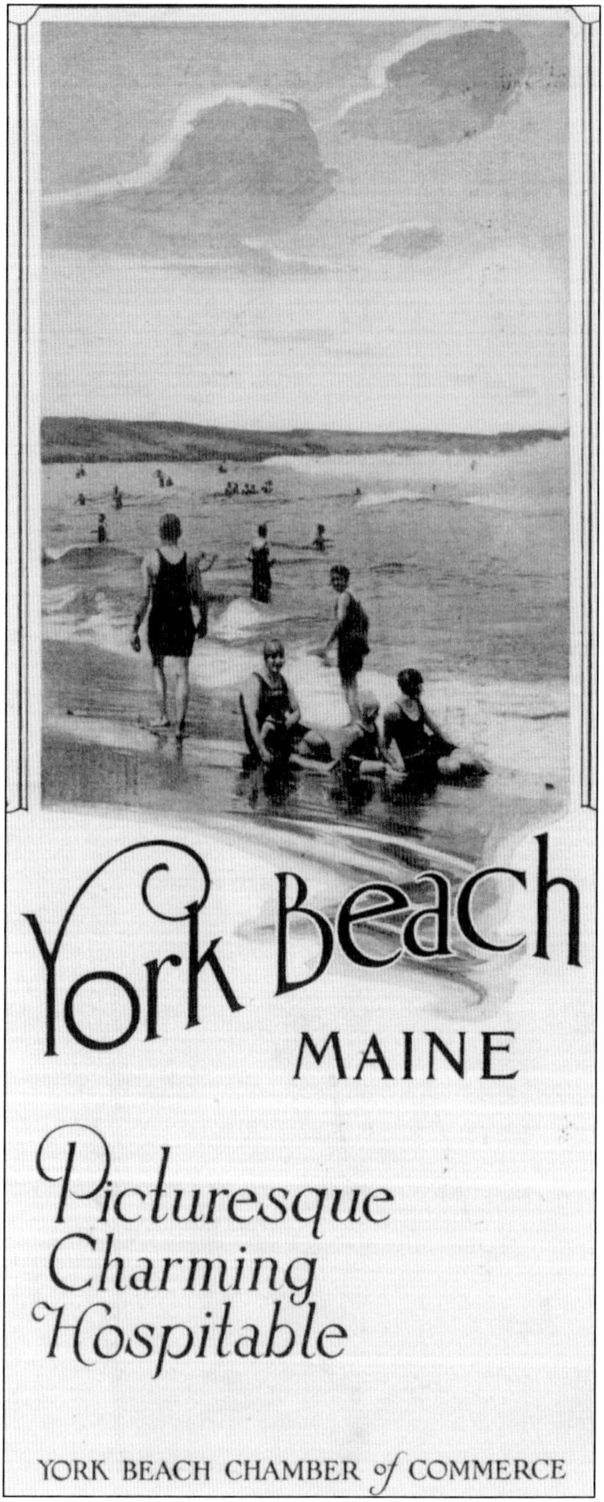
York Beach
MAINE
Picturesque
Charming
Hospitable
YORK BEACH CHAMBER of COMMERCE

IMAGES
*of America*

# OLD YORK BEACH
# VOLUME II

John D. Bardwell

ARCADIA
PUBLISHING

ISBN 978-0-7385-6286-5

Published by Arcadia Publishing
Charleston, South Carolina

Printed in the United States of America

Library of Congress Catalog Card Number: 2003107151

For all general information contact Arcadia Publishing at:
Telephone 843-853-2070
Fax 843-853-0044
E-mail sales@arcadiapublishing.com
For customer service and orders:
Toll-Free 1-888-313-2665

Visit us on the Internet at www.arcadiapublishing.com

OTHER PUBLICATIONS BY JOHN D. BARDWELL:
*The Diary of the Portsmouth, Kittery and York Electric Railroad* (1986)
*A History of the Country Club at York, Maine* (1988)
*The Isles of Shoals: A Visual History* (1989)
*A History of York Harbor and the York Harbor Reading Room* (1993)
*Old York Beach* (1994)
*Old York* (1994)
*Ogunquit-by-the-Sea* (1994)
"Greece: An Archaeological Treasure Chest," from *American Photographers at the Turn of the Century: Travel and Trekking* (1994)
*Old Kittery* (1995)
*The York Water District: One Hundred years of Community Service* (1996)

PUBLICATIONS BY JOHN D. BARDWELL AND RONALD P. BERGERON:
*Images of a University: A Photographic History of the University of New Hampshire* (1984)
*The White Mountains of New Hampshire: A Visual History* (1989)
*The Lakes Region of New Hampshire: A Visual History* (1989)

PUBLICATIONS BY JOHN D. BARDWELL AND PETER A. MOORE:
*A History of the York Beach Fire Department: 1890–1990* (1990)

# Contents

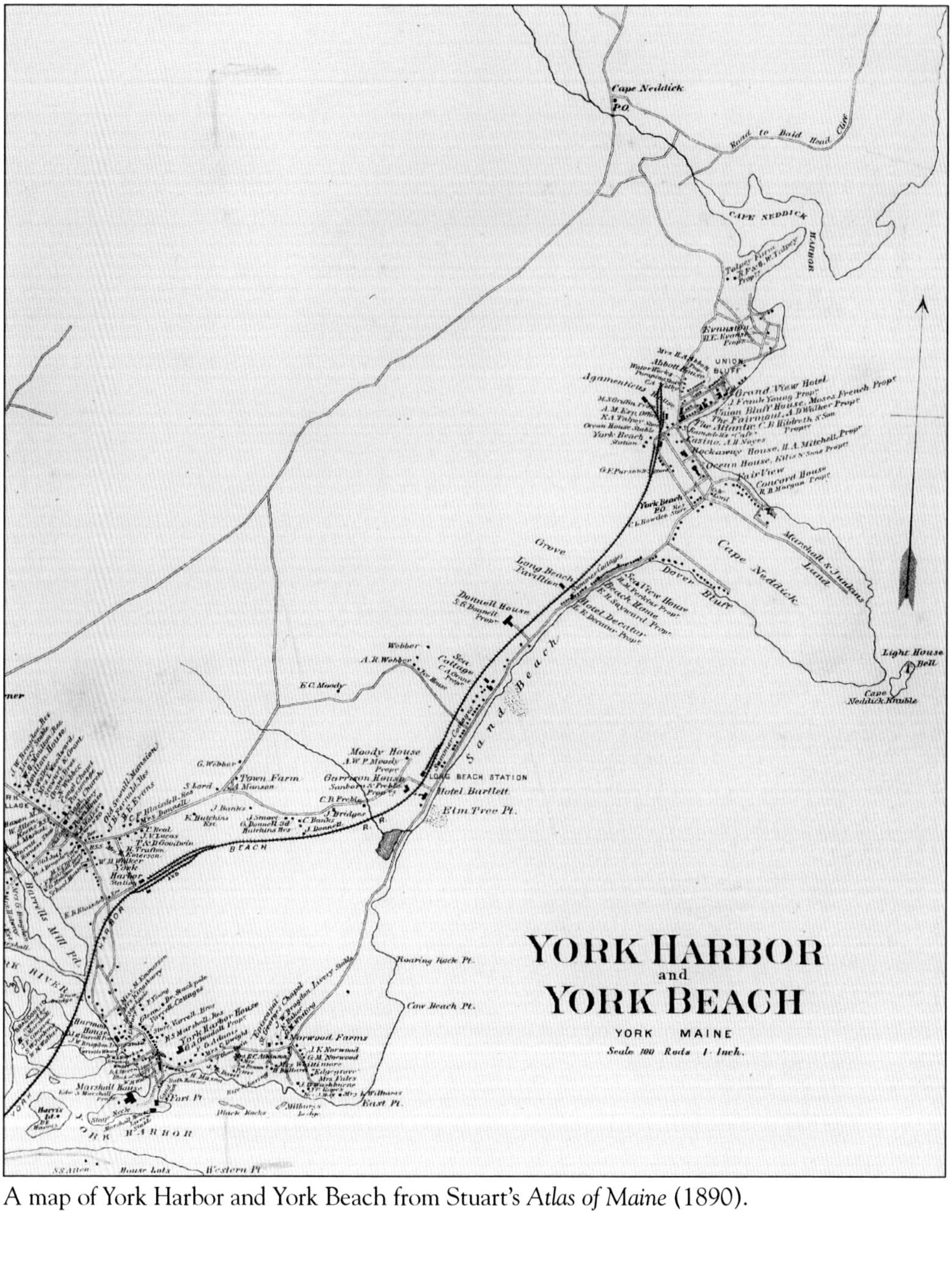


A map of York Harbor and York Beach from Stuart's *Atlas of Maine* (1890).

# Introduction

In 1994, I wrote *Old York Beach*, the first of a series of photographic histories that have been published by Arcadia Publishing. Since that time I have accumulated a number of additional images documenting the history of York Beach. *Old York Beach Volume II* was born when the publishers saw these images and urged me to consider publishing another collection of York Beach photographs, postcards, and ephemera. Elephants walking down Railroad Avenue, a sailing party on the boat of Charles "Oz" Freeman, a view of York Beach from Hildreth's Hill in 1892, stereo views of Union Bluffs and Concordville, an aerial view of the Nubble in the 1940s, an aerial view of Turner's airfield near the intersection of Broadway and Church Streets, the York Beach Casino, the Fairview, and views of York Cliffs are just a few of the images that motivated me to put together this new collection of photographs.

The area around Short Sands Beach was once part of Cape Neddick. However, the explosion of tourism after 1865 created the community now known as York Beach. Over five hundred and fifty summer dwellings were built in the next fifty years along with hotels, guest houses, amusement parks, and summer businesses. Cape Neddick, like York Corner, was no longer a business or municipal center and was eclipsed by the development of the summer colonies. York Beach became a village corporation: the corporation became its winter identity, but in the summer it was a vacation resort and its business was tourism.

In the early 1900s improved transportation changed the vacation habits of the summer residents and York Beach adapted to people arriving by train, trolley, bus, and automobile. The evolution of the Sea Cottage to the Anchorage Hotel and then to the Anchorage Motel is an example of how the facilities met the changing needs of new generations of tourists. Dance halls at Saint Aspinquid Park, the Gay White Way, and the York Beach Casino were replaced by lounges in hotels and restaurants. Cabins became motels and tenting grounds became trailer parks. The Goldenrod continued to make kisses, candy, and ice cream, but the tea room was closed when the end of prohibition gave new meaning to the word "tea." Parking lots replaced train stations and Railroad Avenue needs to be renamed. There is no airport near Airport Drive and Saint Aspinquid Park is now the site of the sewer treatment plant.

The history of York Beach is relatively short but very fascinating. Fortunately, the community evolved after the invention of photography, and people tend to take photographs when they are on vacation. It is my hope that the images I have selected for this volume will bring back memories and increase your understanding of the history of Old York Beach.

John D. Bardwell

# Dedication

To Elizabeth Ehret Bardwell,
my favorite daughter-in-law and a lover of good books.

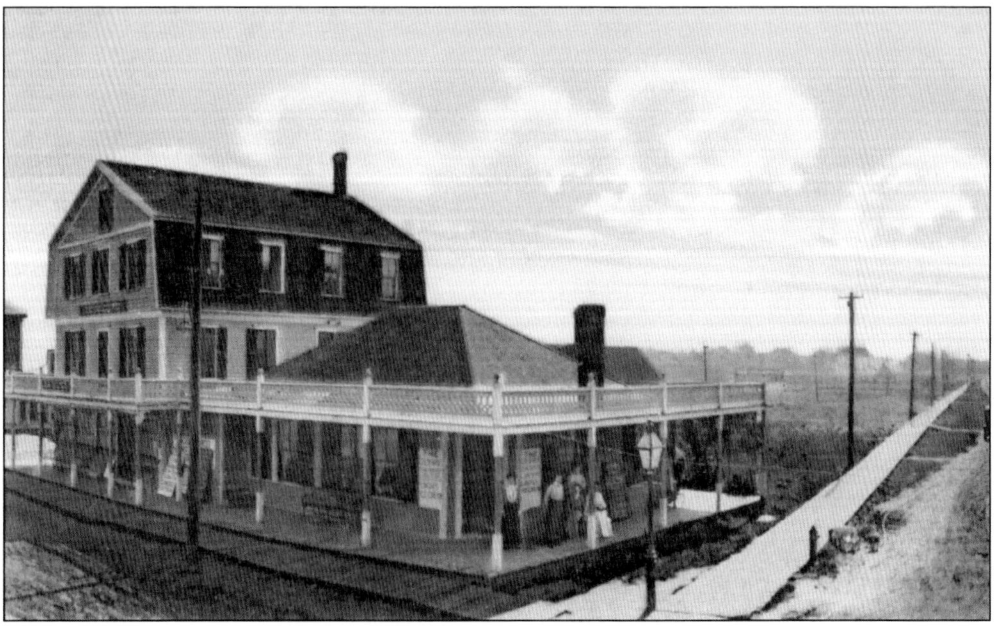

# *One*

# Early Times

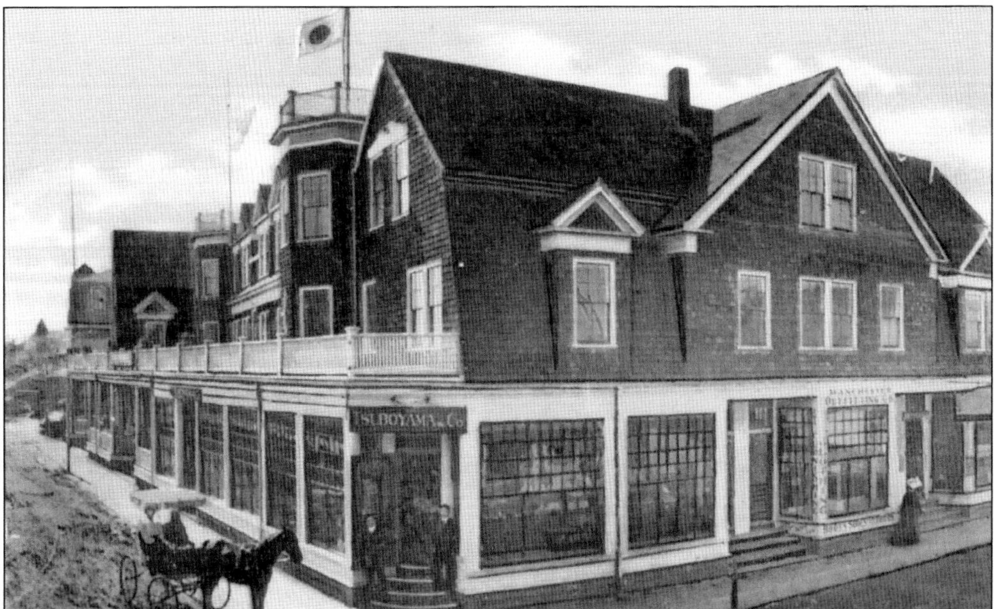

Intersection of Main Street and Ocean Avenue. The Goldenrod is on the left and the Kearsarge Hotel is on the right.

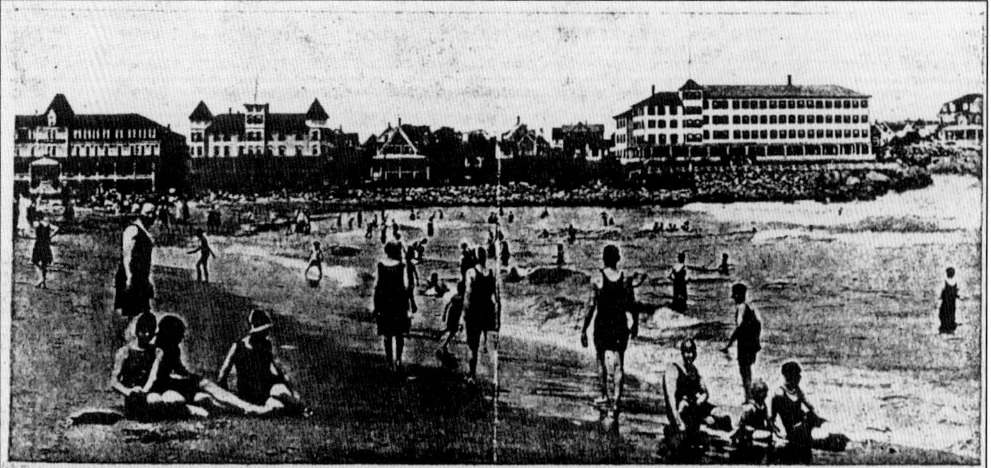

THE scenic beauties of the Pine Tree State have a magic appeal that is found in no other part of the country. The wonderful combination of fragrant pine woods and the sparkling blue ocean dashing restlessly upon the rocks or curling into picturesque breakers along the white expanse of beach is a sight that thrills all who are privileged to see it.

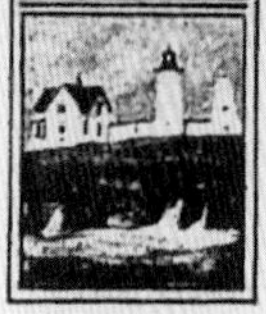

Vacationists and tourists from every state in the nation are quick to tell of the picturesque beauty of the Maine Coast. It's fame as a vacation resort is nation-wide, and every summer more people make this beautiful state their vacation ground.

York Beach combines all the charming features of the wonderful Maine Coast. The fragrant odor of evergreen pines, the tang of the salt air, the beauty of curling surf, the delightful beach for bathing, strolling or reclining on the clean white sand—all these attractions make York Beach an ideal spot for a real vacation.

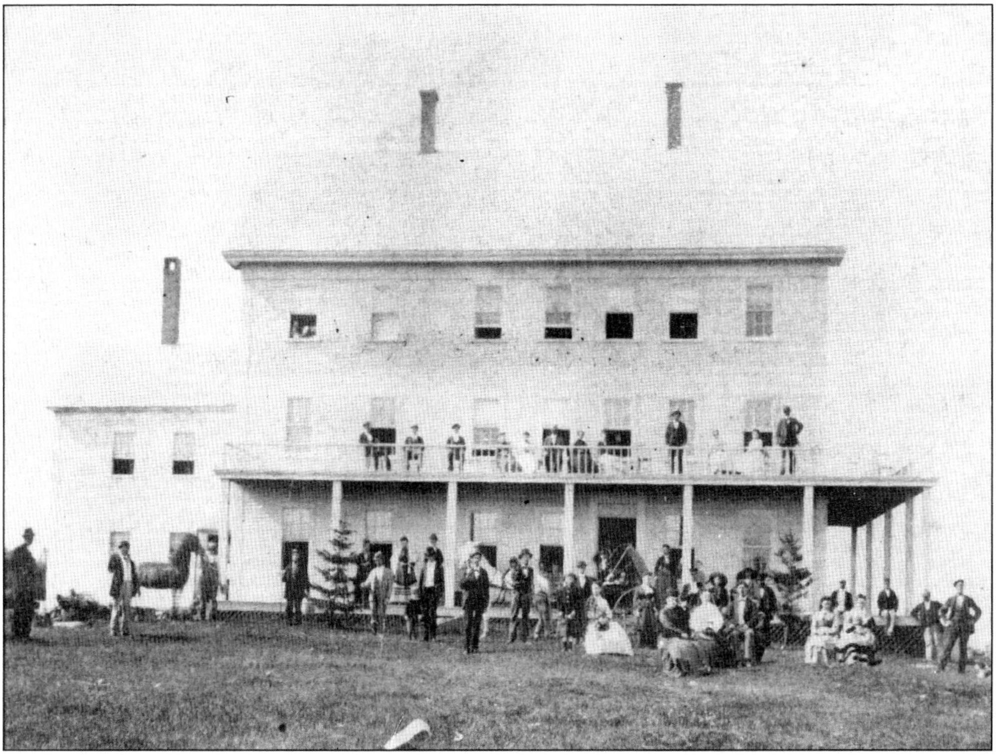

The Bowden House was the first hotel in York. Built in 1879 and destroyed by fire in 1883, it was located at the junction of Church Street and Long Beach Avenue.

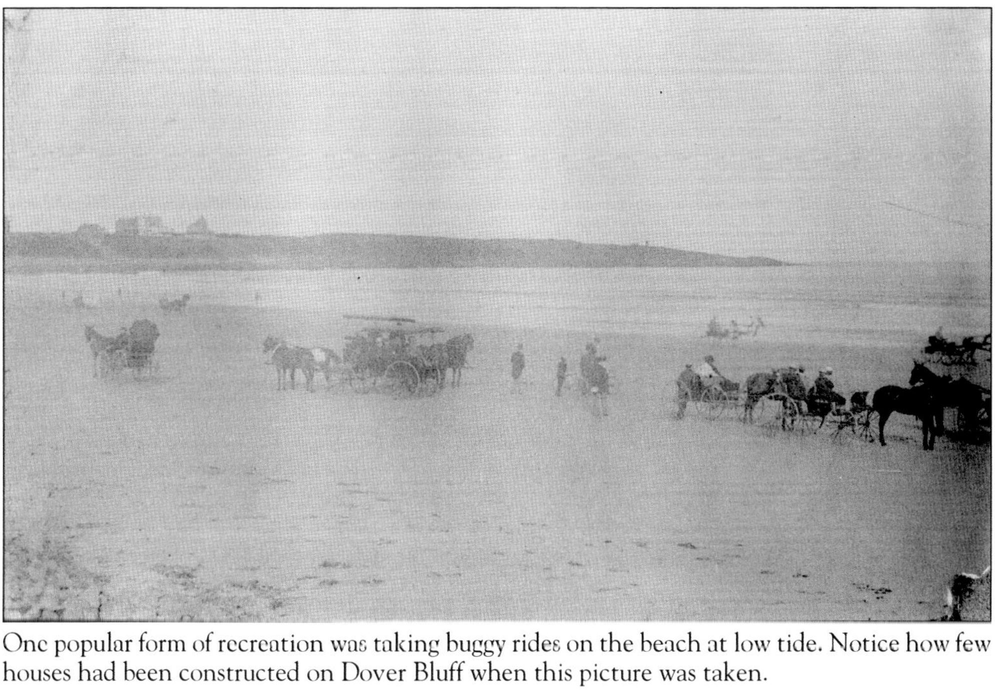

One popular form of recreation was taking buggy rides on the beach at low tide. Notice how few houses had been constructed on Dover Bluff when this picture was taken.

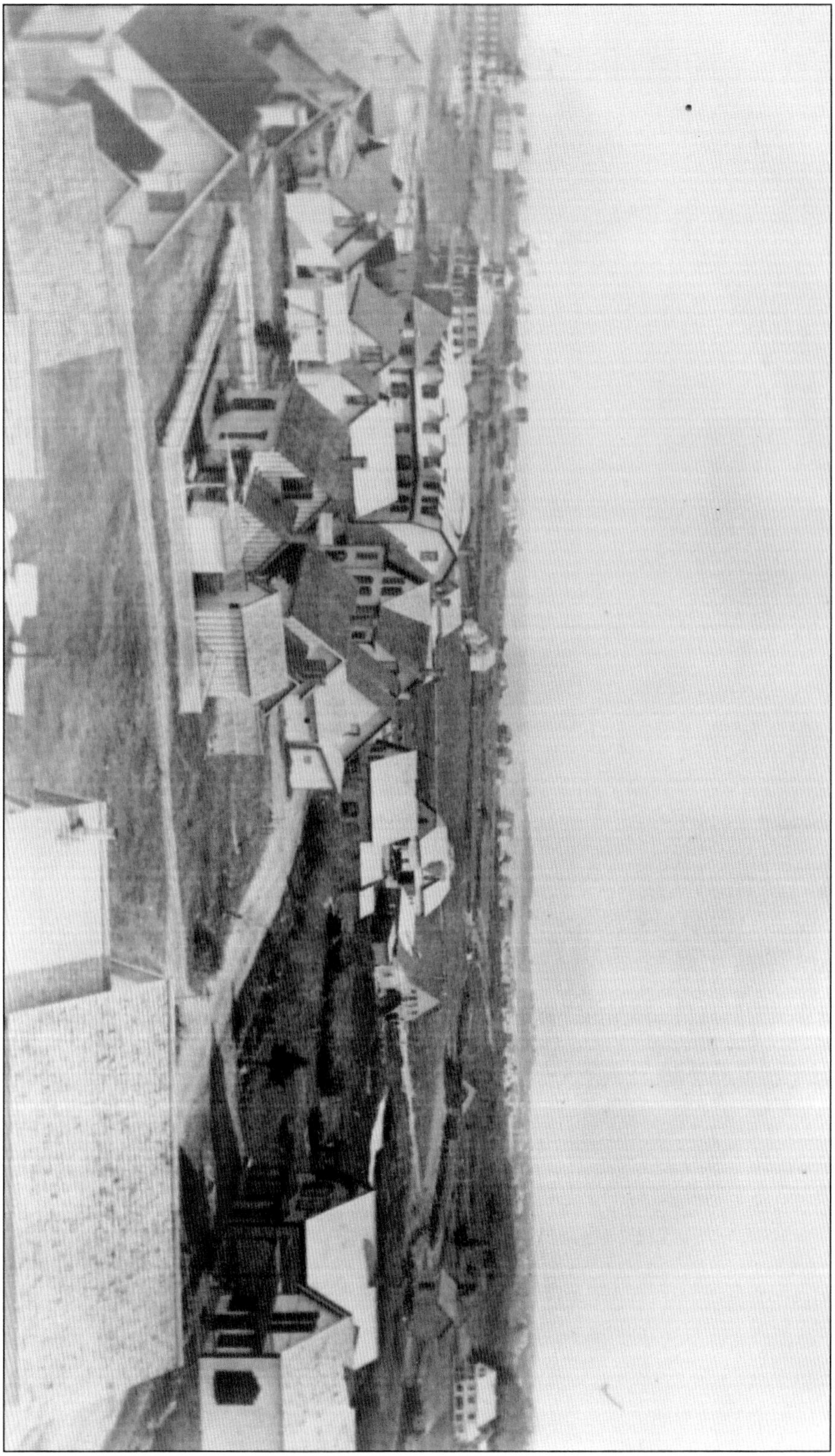

A view of York Beach from Hildreth's Hill in 1892.

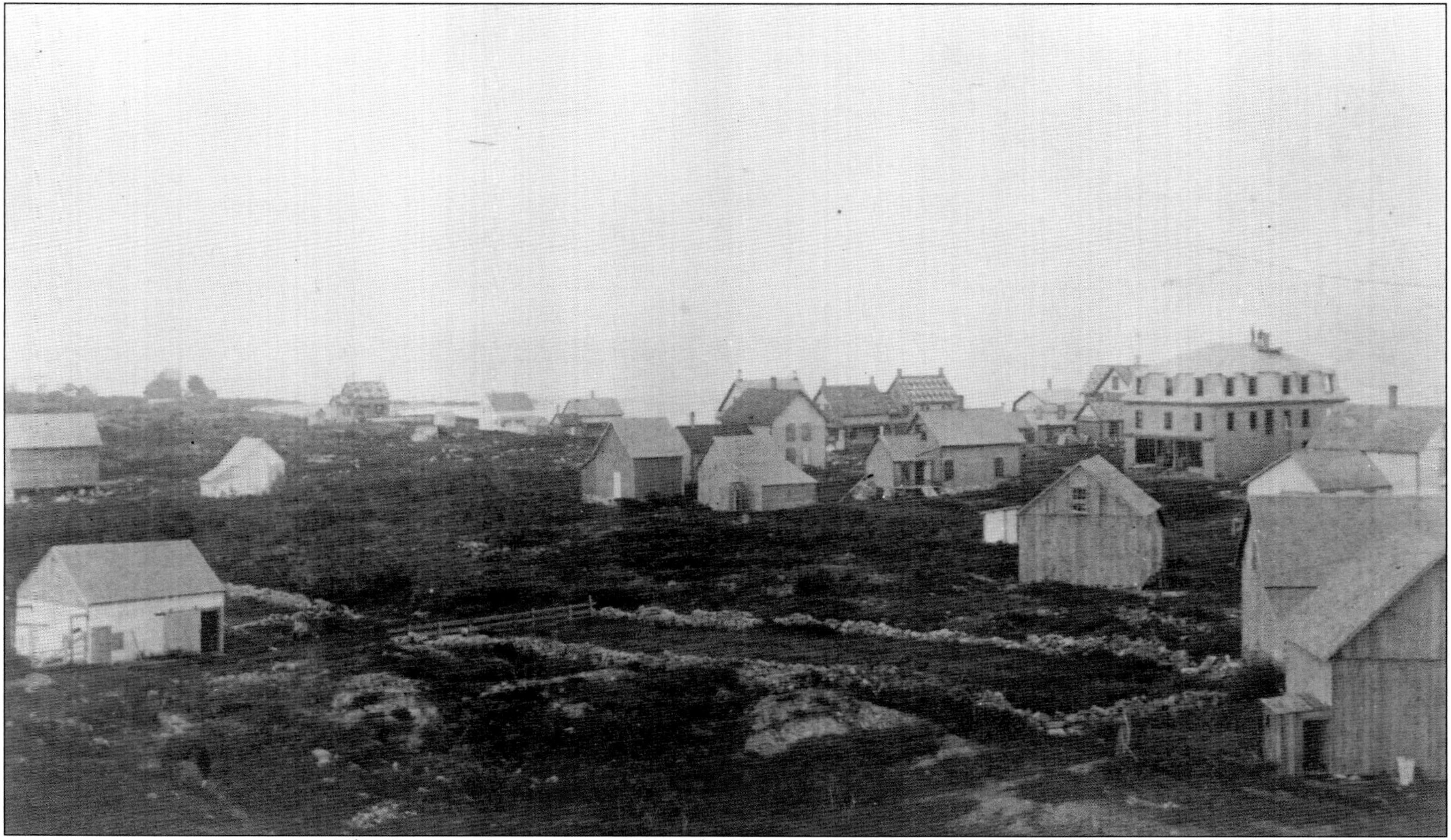

The Freeman Street area in 1892. The Hastings-Lyman Hotel is on the right.

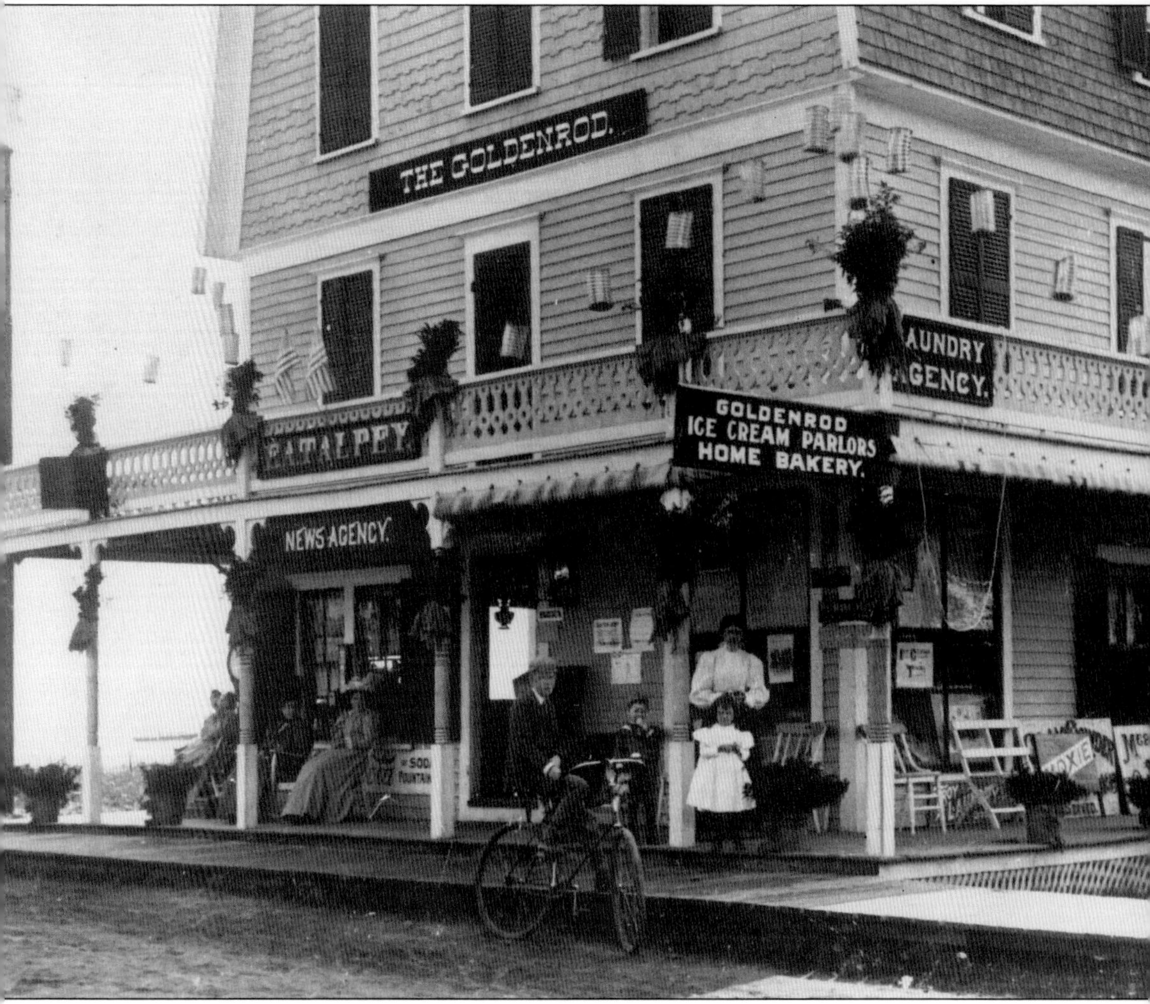


The Goldenrod advertised an ice cream parlor, a home bakery, a news agency, and a laundry agency. Note the boardwalks and the unpaved roads.

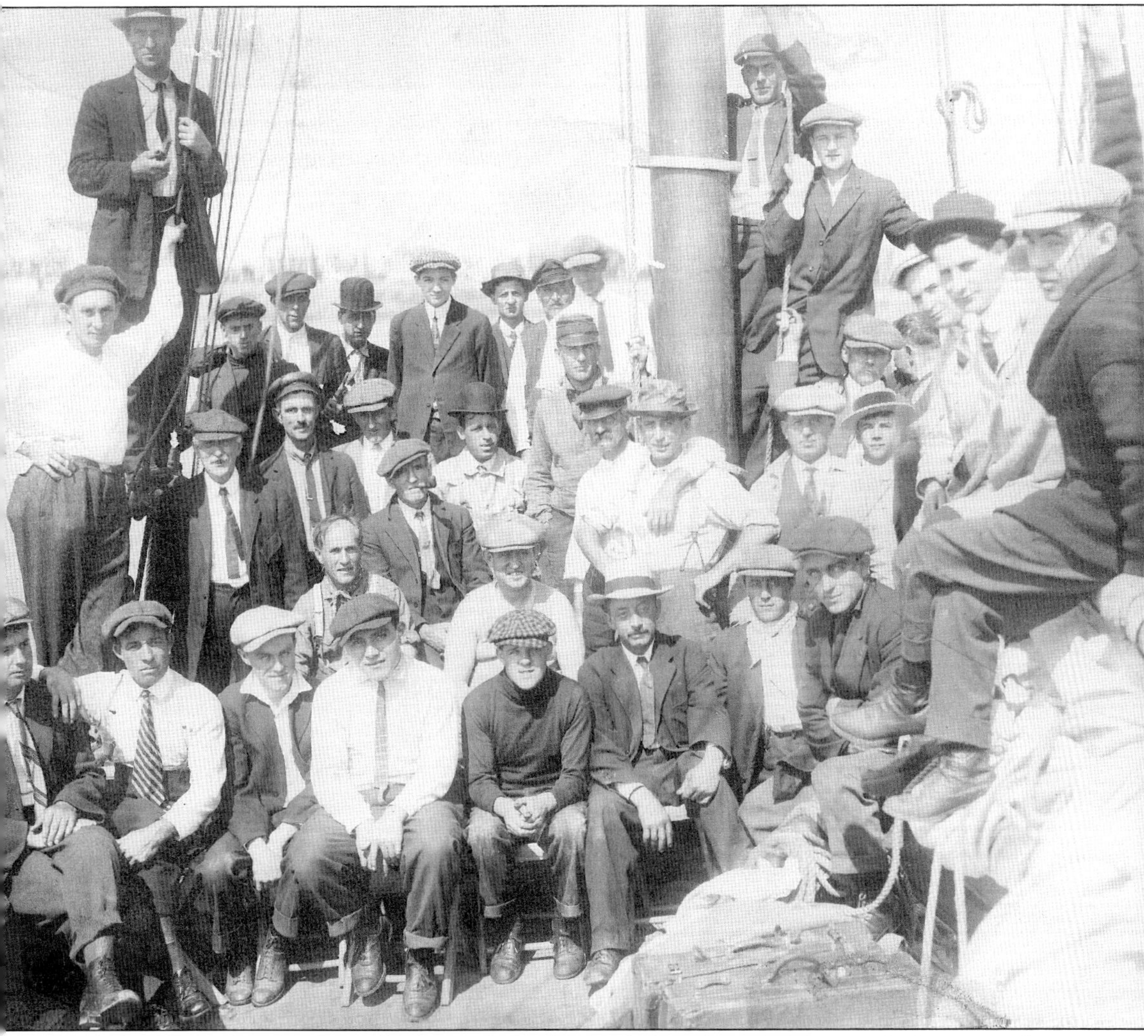

A sailing party on the boat of Captain Charles "Oz" Freeman, the man with the mustache standing by the mast. A newspaper reported that Captain Freeman of the *Comet* took a party of seventeen people out for a night's fishing and they caught about 800 pounds of fish.

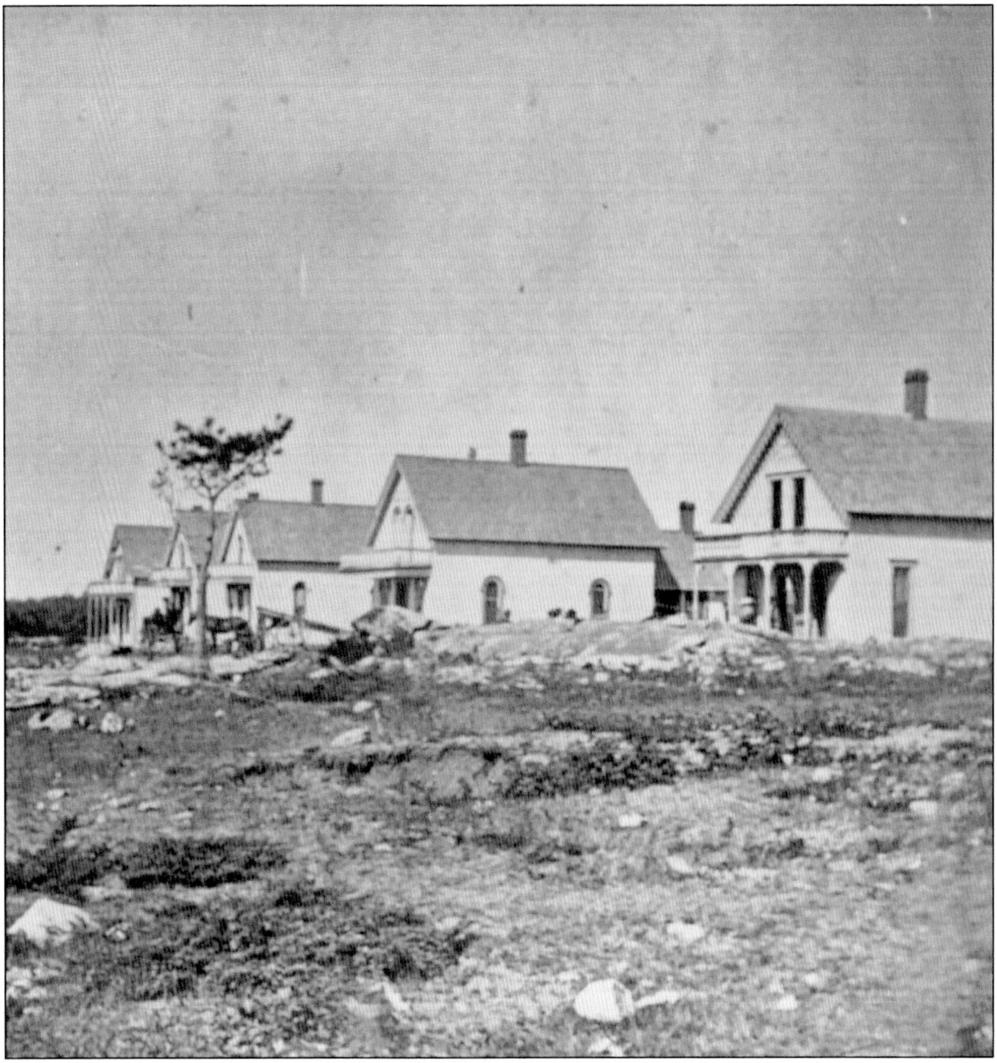
This image was taken from a stereographic view card of Union Bluff.

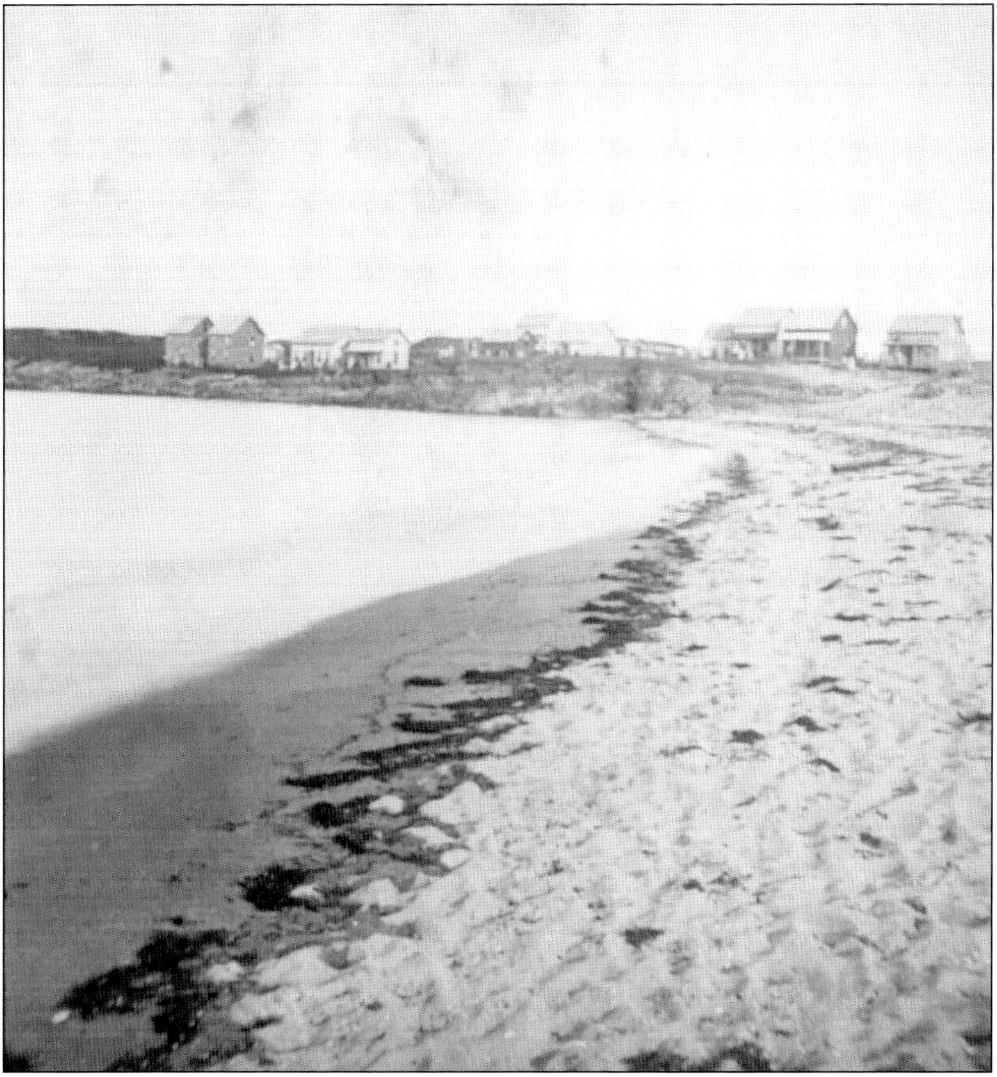
This half of a stereographic print shows Concordville and Short Sands Beach.

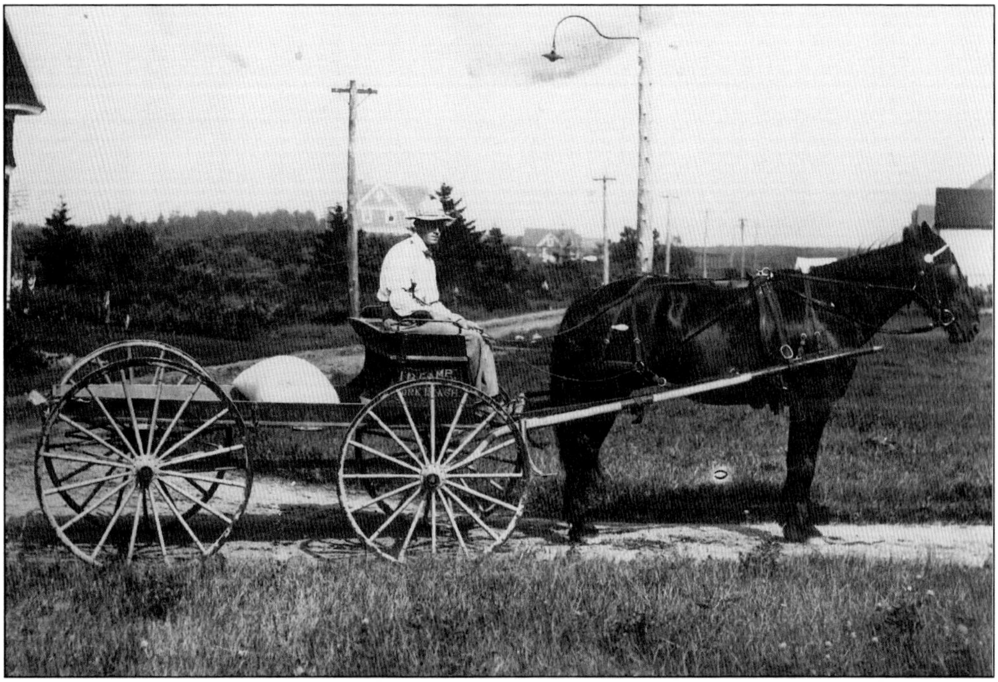

George S. Freeman is driving I.B. Camp's team to deliver a bag of grain.

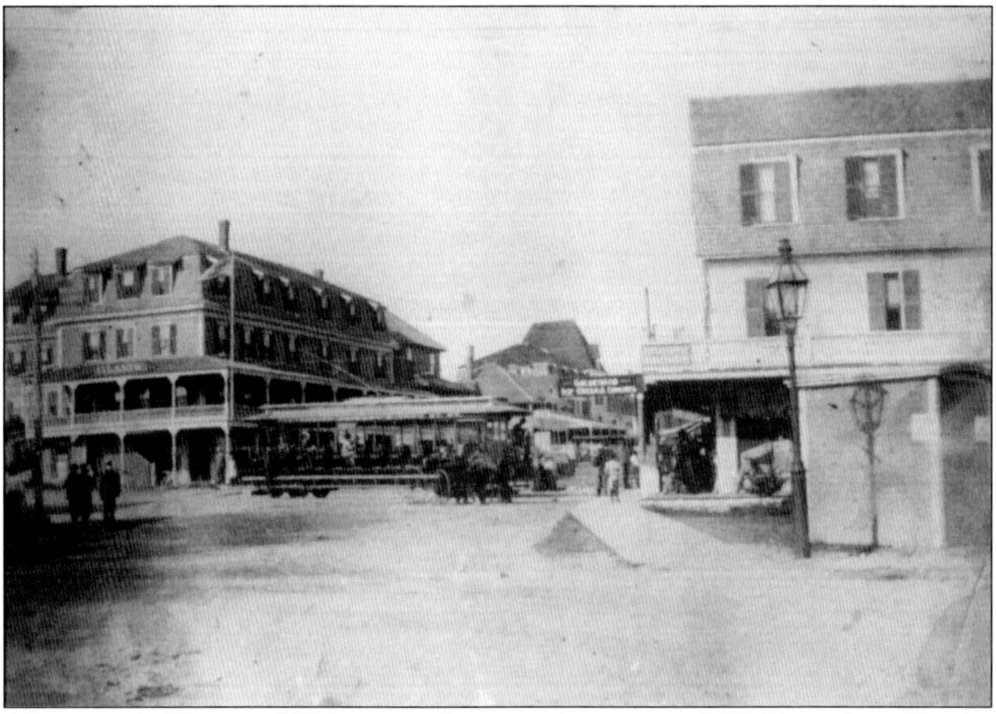

A Portsmouth, Kittery, and York open trolley car in the square, *c.* 1900. The Atlantic Hotel is on the left and the Goldenrod is on the right. Note the streetlight by the Goldenrod.

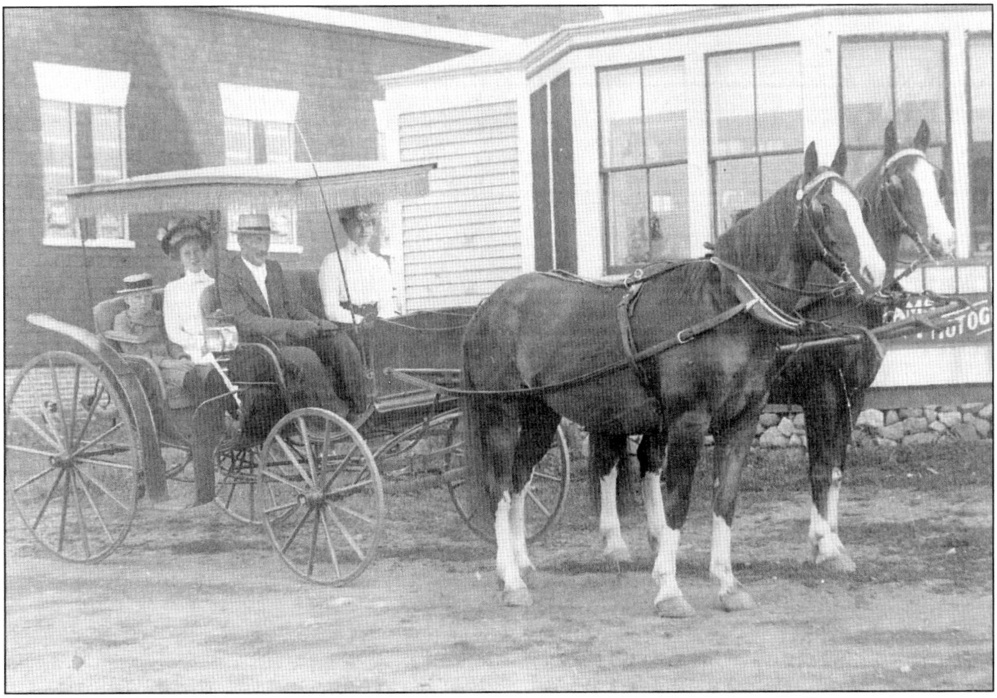

Raymond O. Weare and Bertha Weare are in the rear, with Moses and Kate Weare up front. Their team is in front of the W.N. Gough photographic studio and the Union Congregational Church.

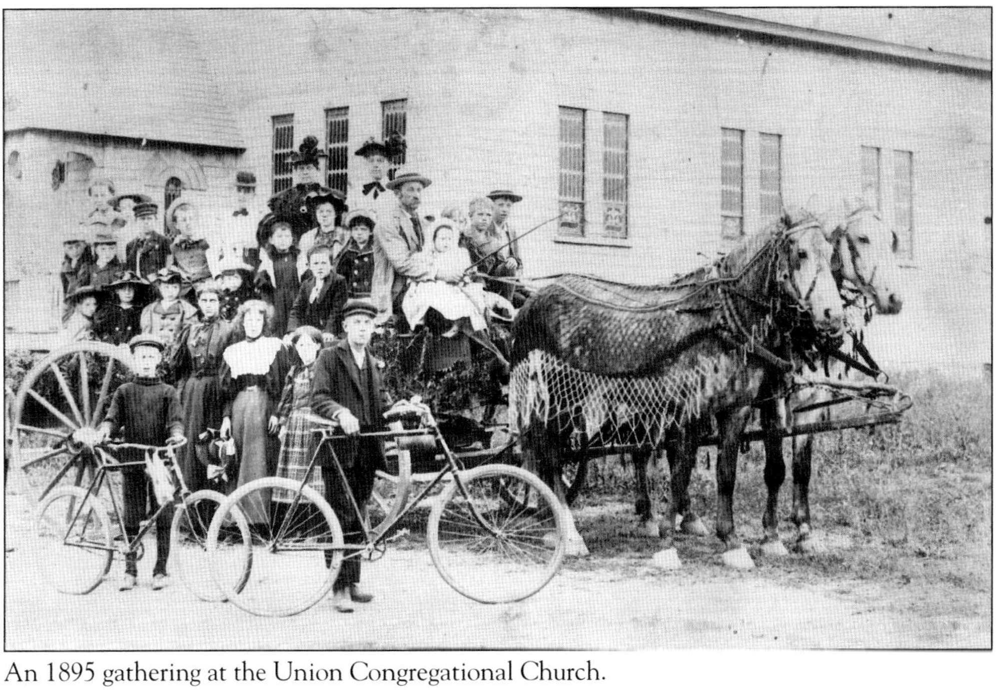

An 1895 gathering at the Union Congregational Church.

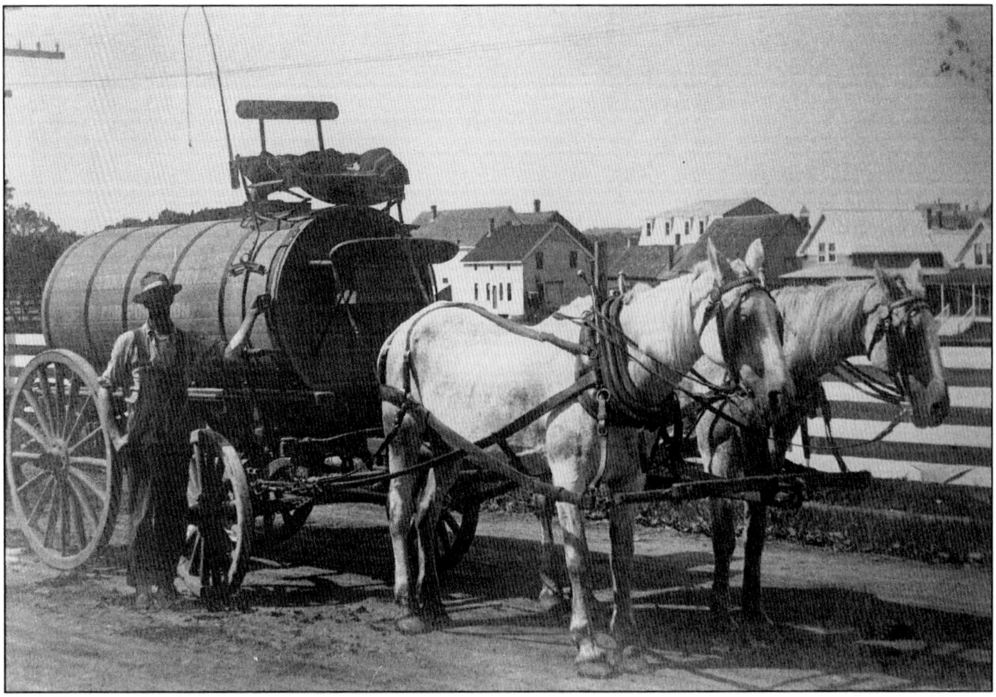

This water wagon was used to "lay the dust" on the streets. It is shown here on Church Street near the ball field.

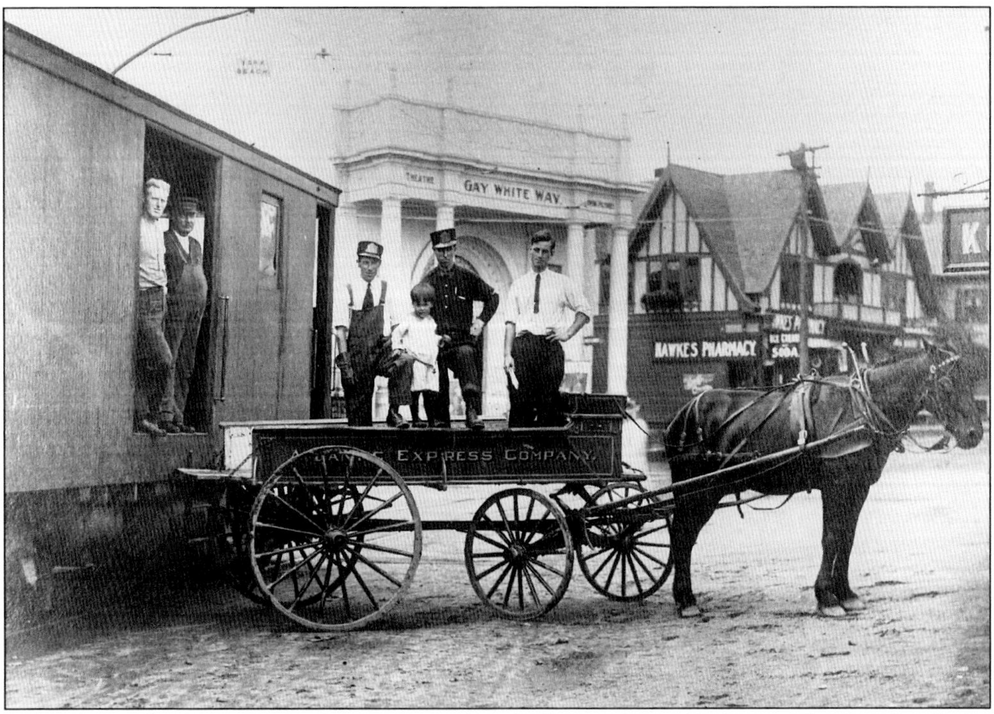


A freight car for the Portsmouth, Kittery, and York Electric Street Railway unloading freight for the American Express Company in York Beach Square.

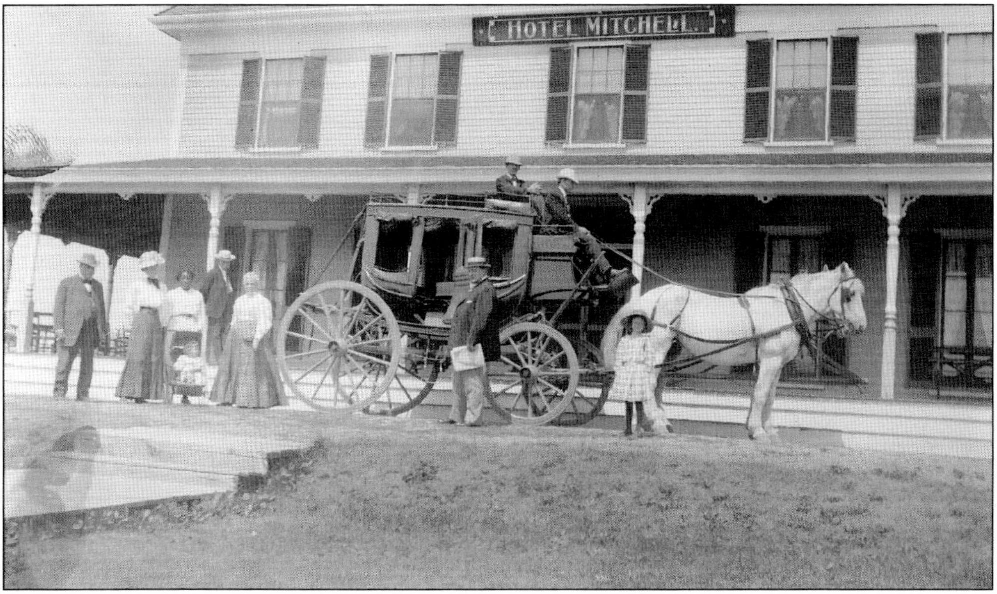


E.E.E. Mitchell, proprietor of the Mitchell House on Long Sands Beach, at the reins of the stagecoach that met the trains from Portsmouth.

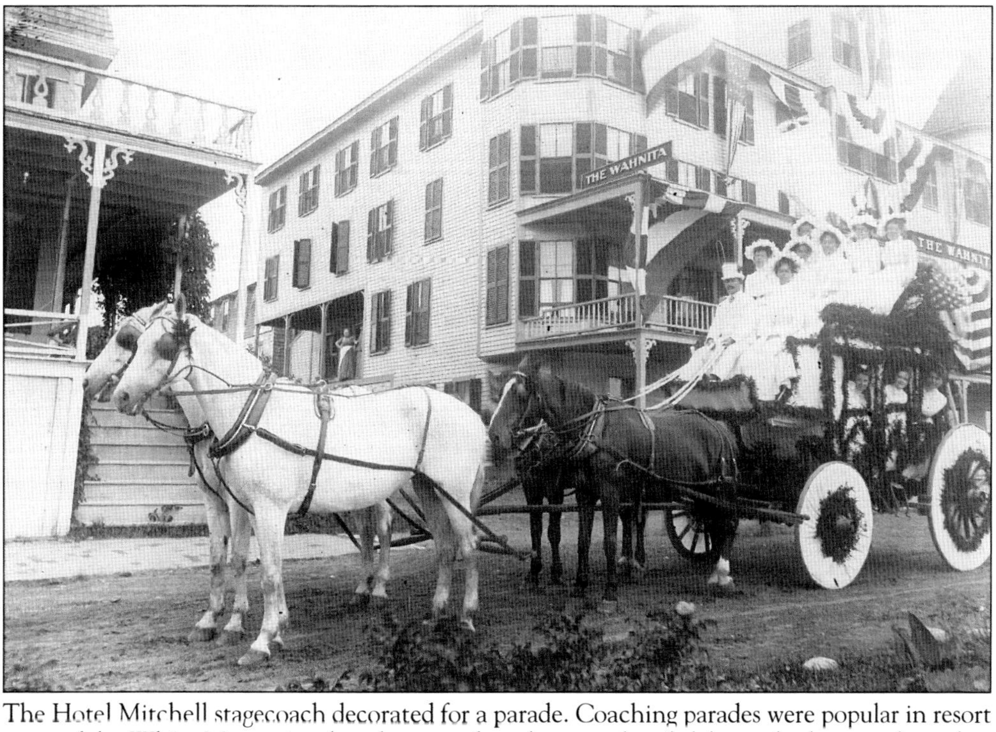


The Hotel Mitchell stagecoach decorated for a parade. Coaching parades were popular in resort areas of the White Mountains, but there are few photographs of elaborately-decorated coaches from this area.

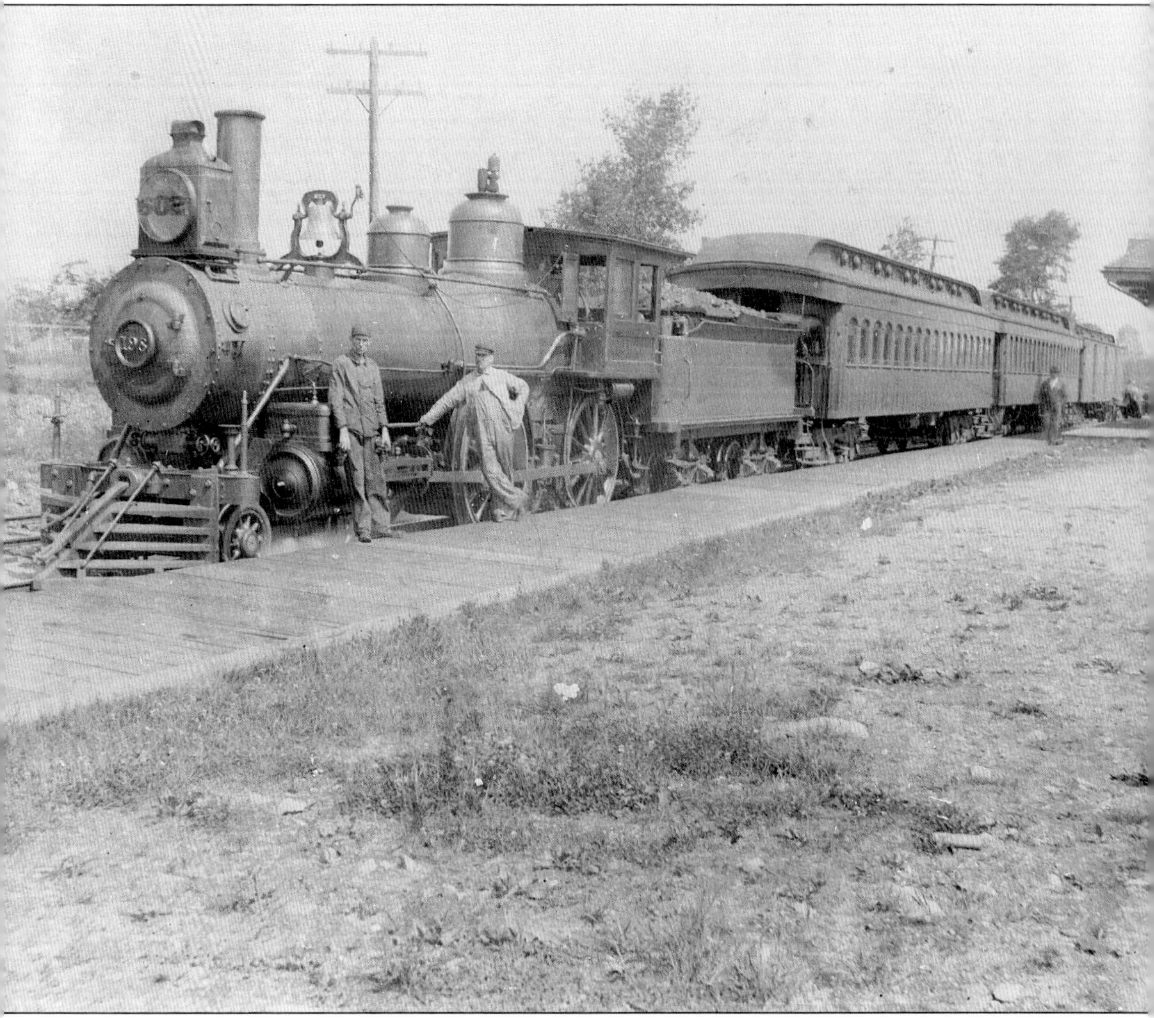

The York Harbor & Beach steam train at the York Beach depot. Thomas B. Emery, the first engineer on the line, is shown here with an unidentified fireman.

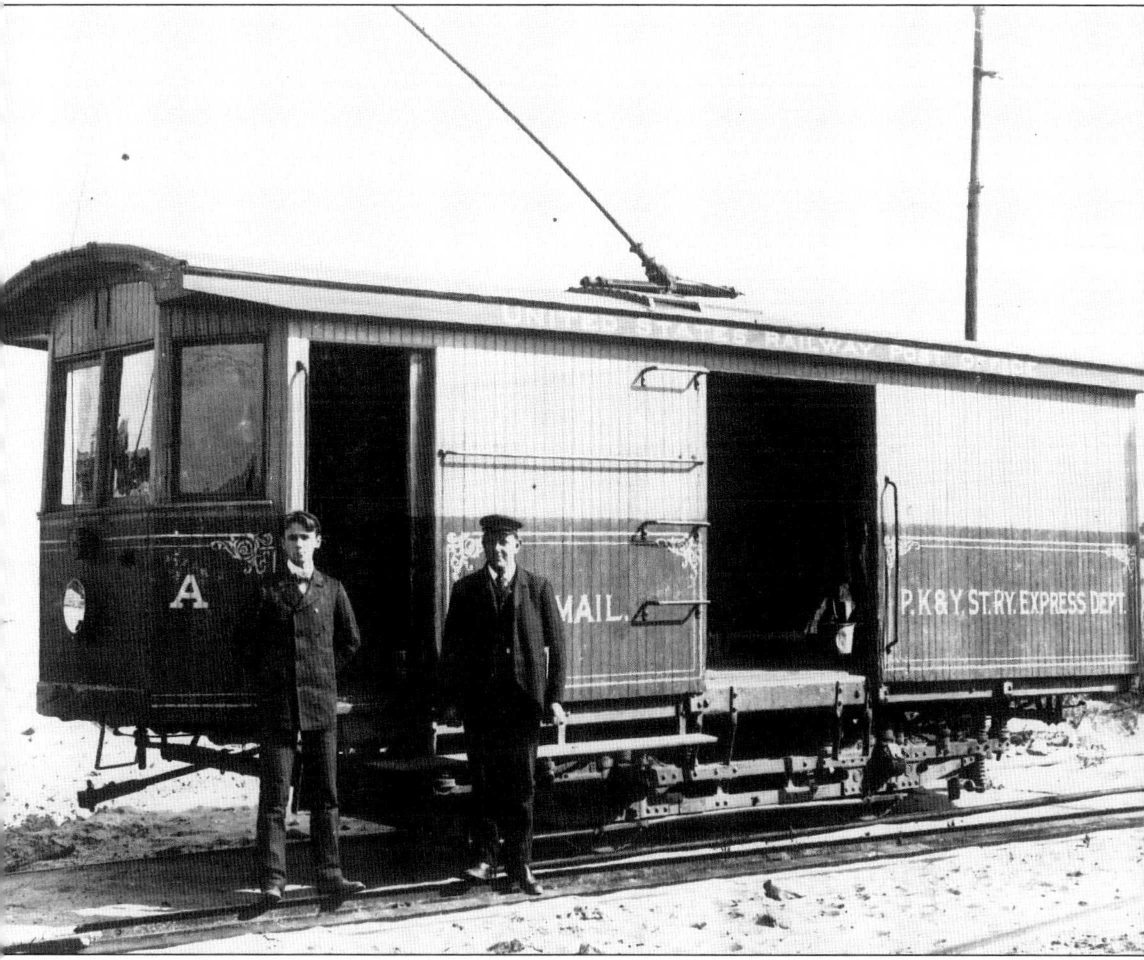


Mail car A of the P.K. & Y. This was the original mail car that began operation in 1898. The young man on the left is Charlie Davis. His companion is George Woodward.

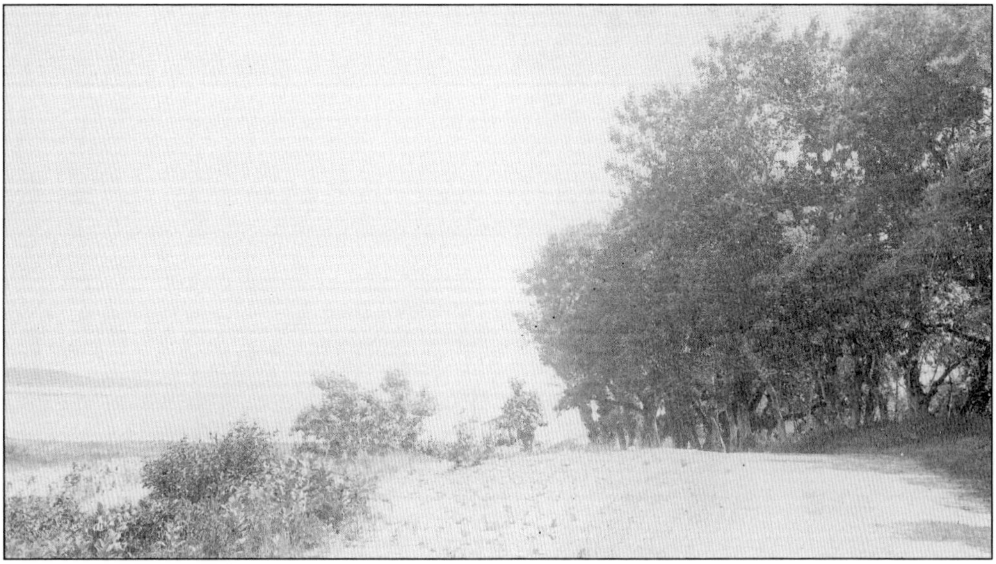

A W.N. Gough photograph of The Willows at the entrance to Short Sands. In this early photograph, the road is lined with willow trees and there are no cottages.

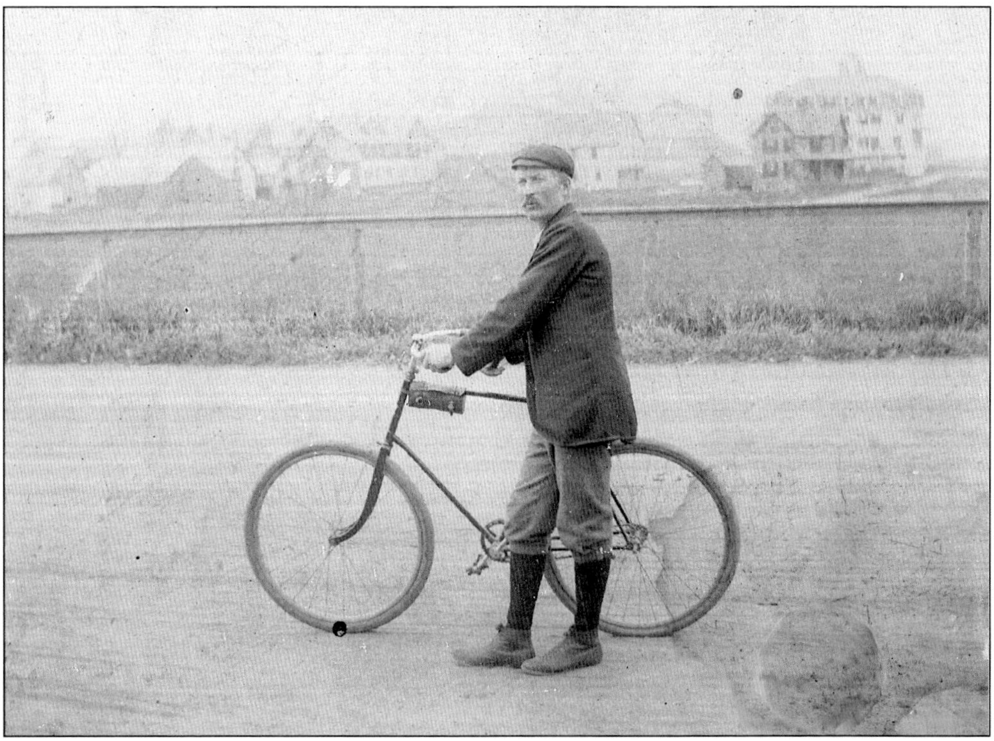

Thomas B. Emery poses with his bicycle in front of the family home on Church Street, *c.* 1897.

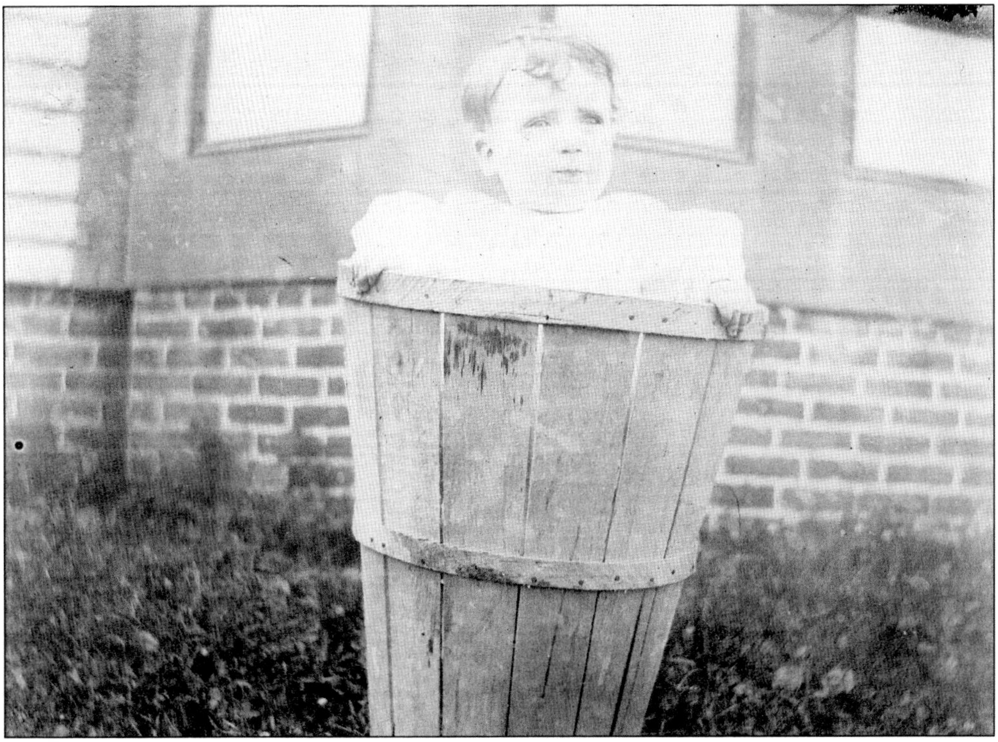

This photograph of a baby in a peach basket was taken in June 1897. The photographer used great creativity to keep the young man still while the film's lengthy exposure time elapsed.

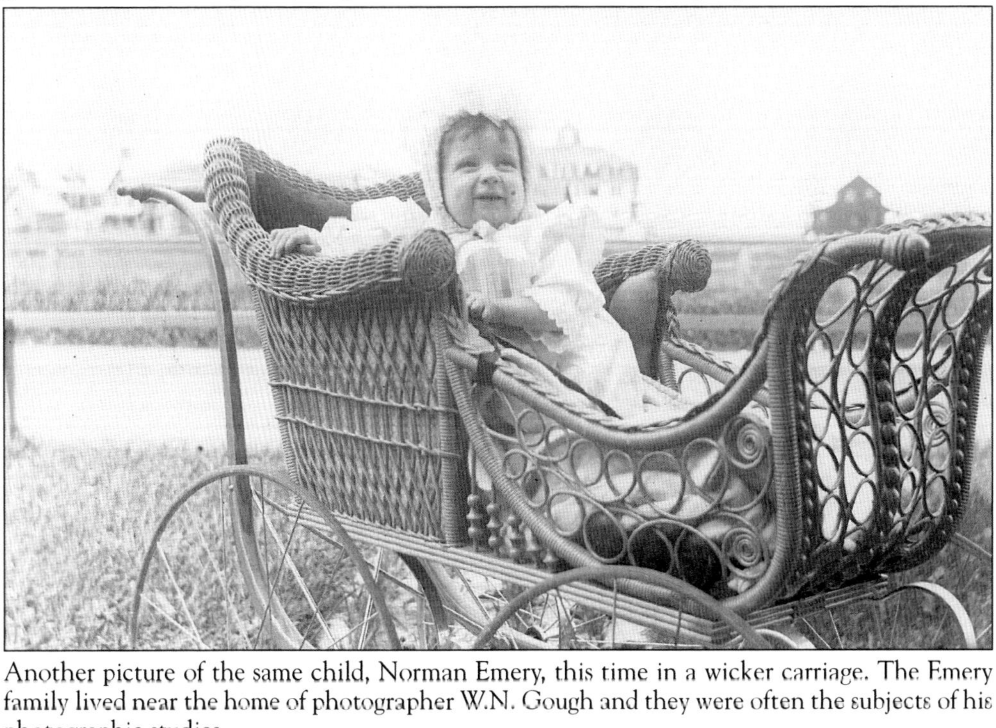

Another picture of the same child, Norman Emery, this time in a wicker carriage. The Emery family lived near the home of photographer W.N. Gough and they were often the subjects of his photographic studies.

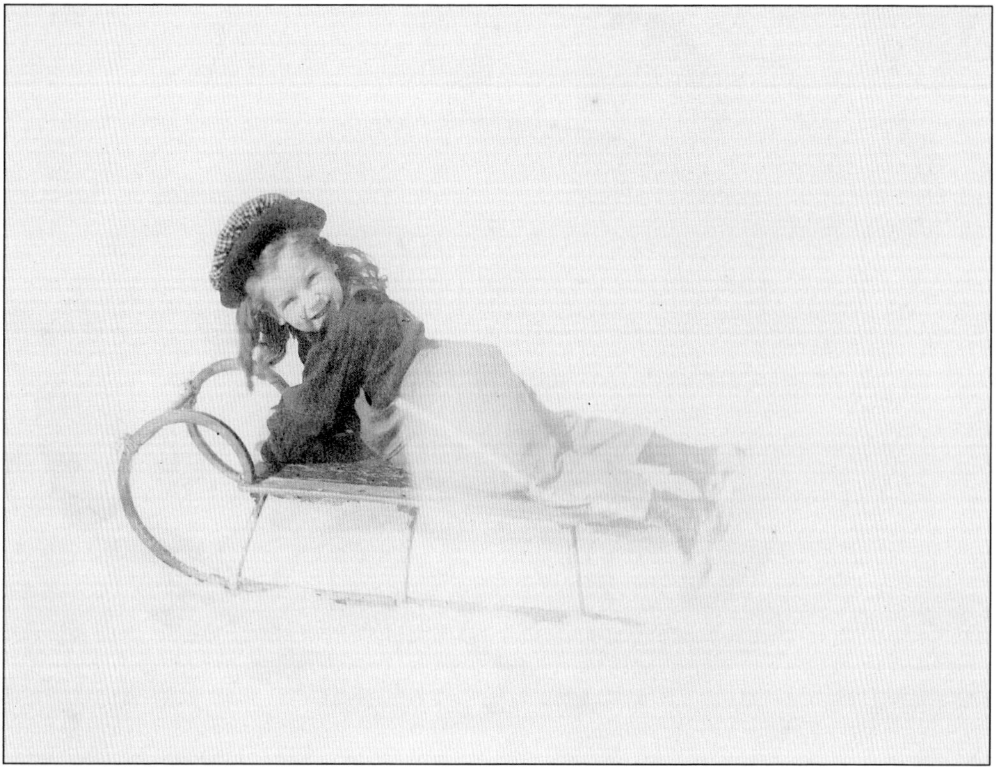

Young Norman Emery on his sled in 1900. The removal of a boy's curls was a traumatic experience for mothers of this period. This haircut marked an important phase in a young boy's growing up, and the timing of the event was not to be taken lightly.

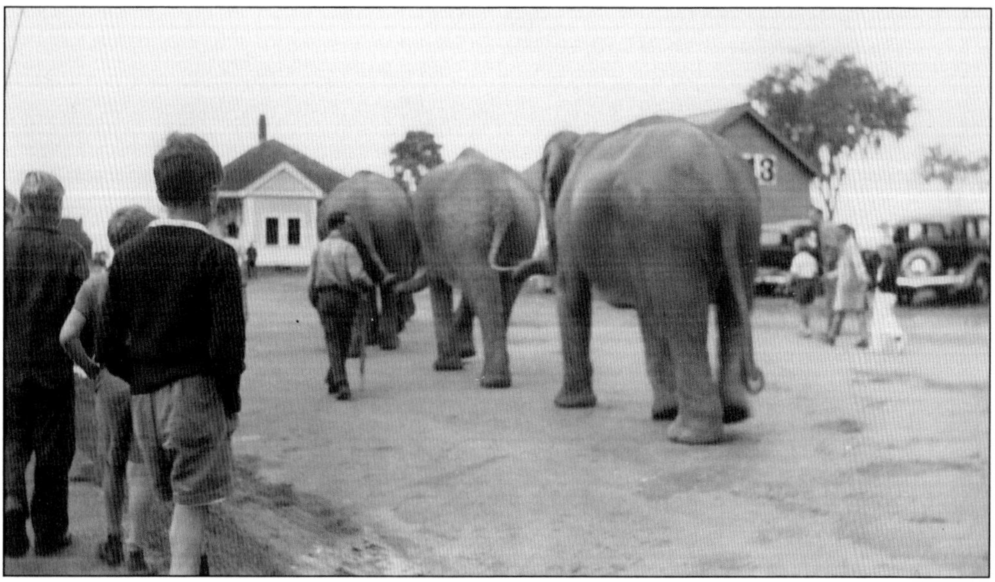

People gather to watch the circus elephants parade down Church Street toward the railroad station. The arrival of the circus or carnival was a major summer event.

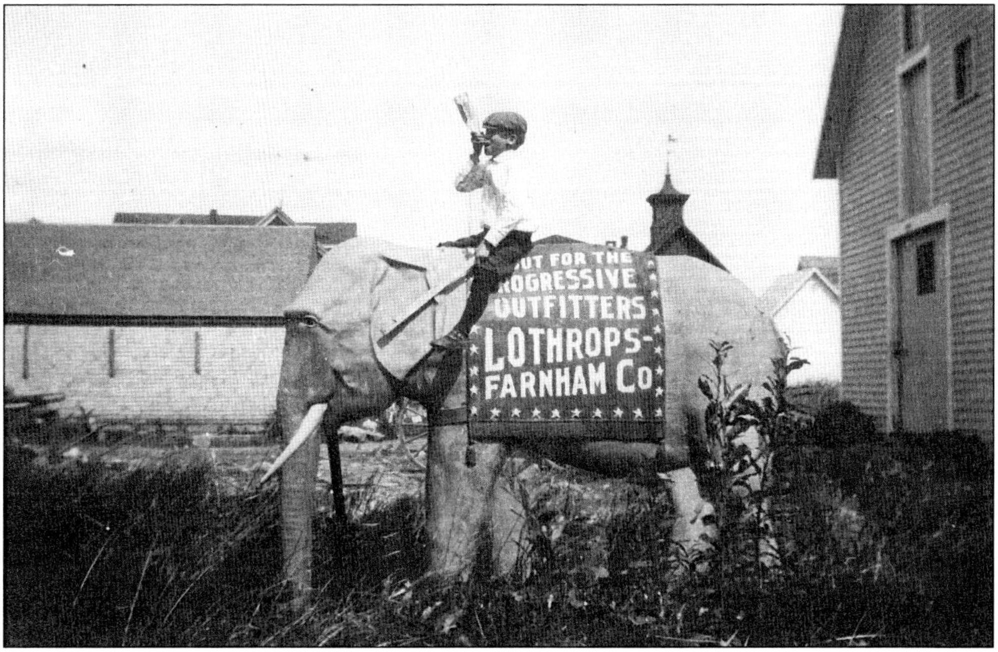


The Lothrops and Farnham Company did some advertising while a small boy got his picture taken on the elephant.

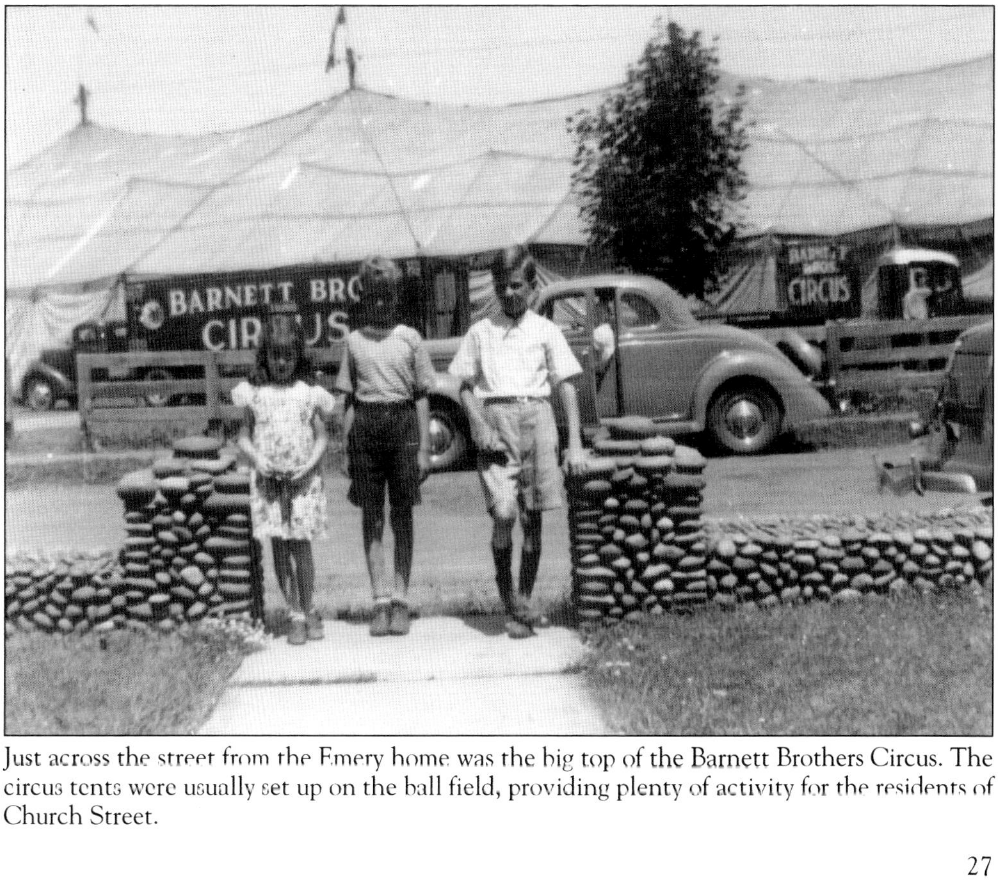


Just across the street from the Emery home was the big top of the Barnett Brothers Circus. The circus tents were usually set up on the ball field, providing plenty of activity for the residents of Church Street.

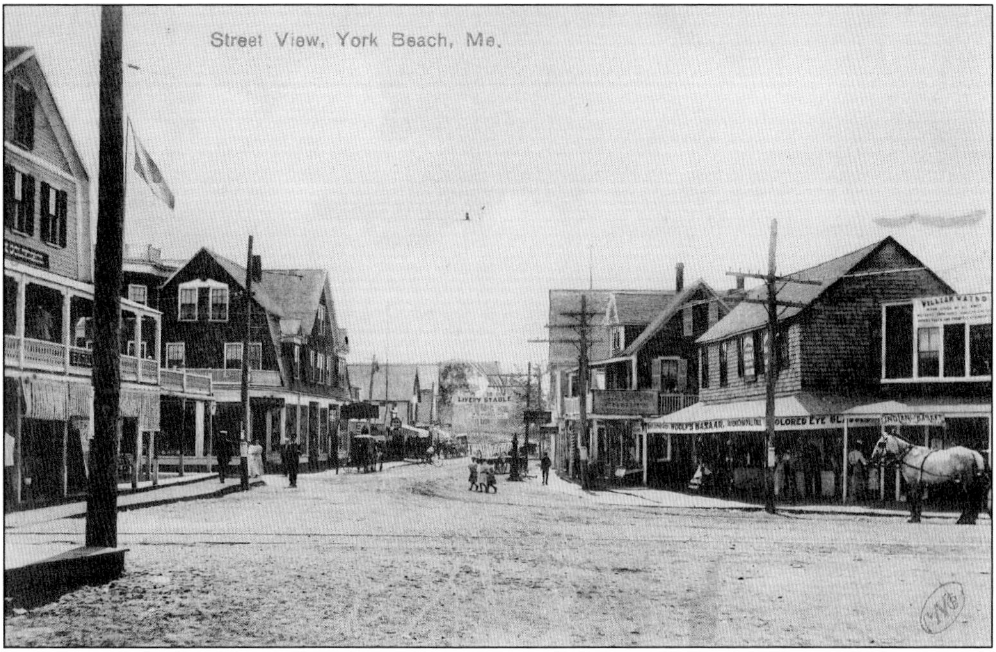


An early street view of York Beach at the turn of the century. There are no motorized vehicles, but the trolley tracks mean this is a post-1897 view.

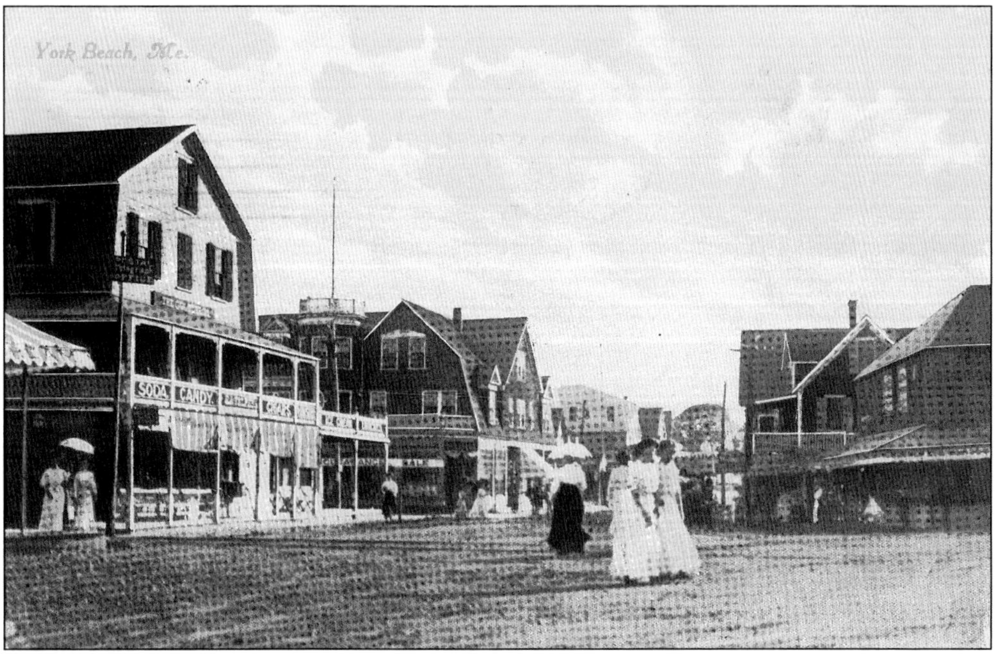


Ladies in white summer dresses crossing the unpaved square in front of the Goldenrod. This postcard was mailed approximately one hundred years ago.

# *Two*

# Downtown York Beach

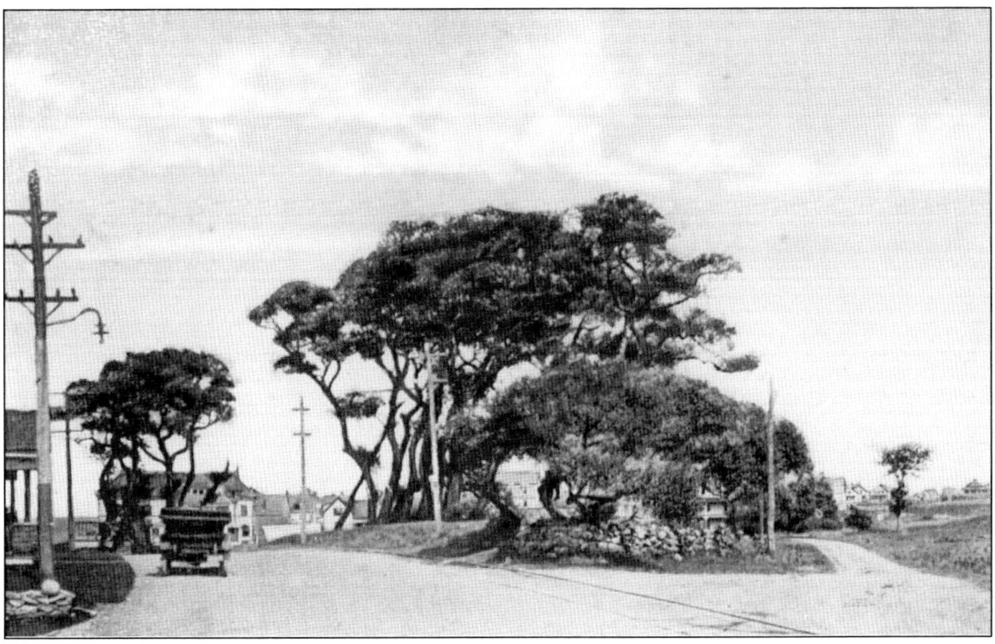

The Willows at the entrance to Short Sands Beach. There are trolley cars, motor cars, and electric lights. Sadly, the willow trees have been reduced in number. The postcard message reads: "*Am spending a week here at Yorke Beach and it is fine . . .*"

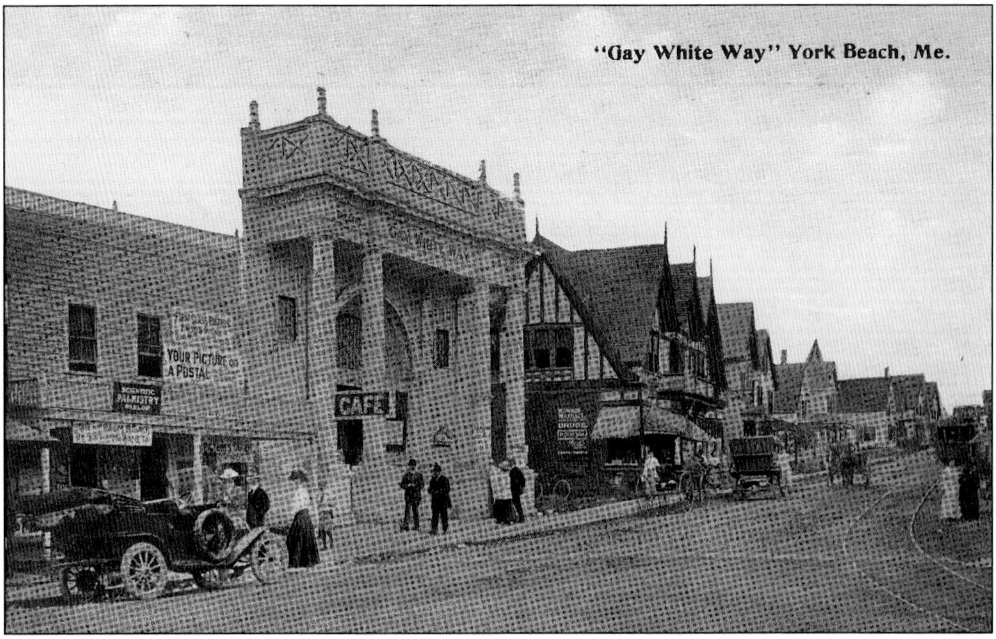


Motor cars appear in this view up Hildreth's Hill from the square. The popular Gay White Way, with its impressive facade, is on the left.

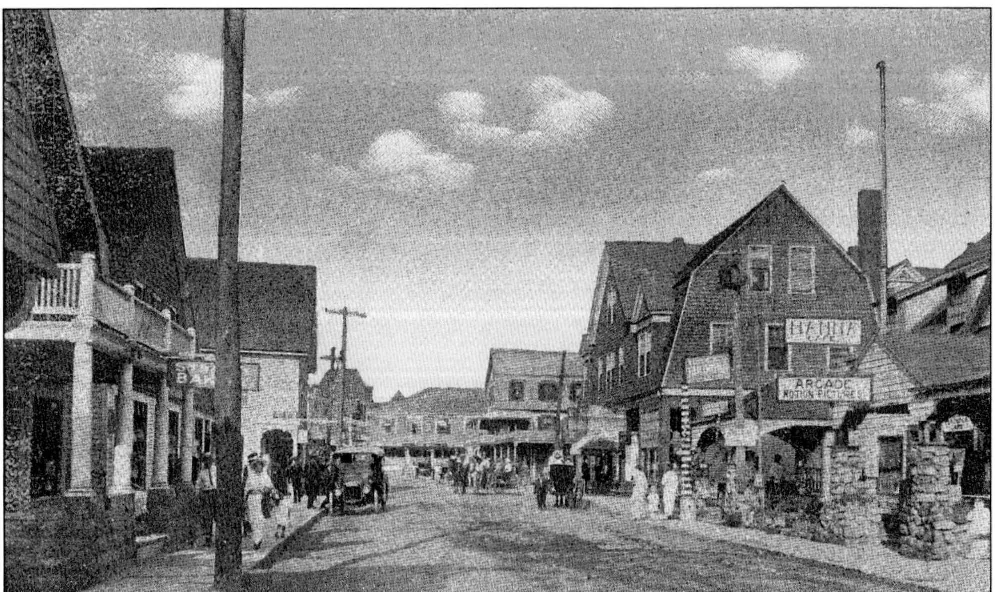


Railroad Avenue as it appeared during the same period. This was before the Arcade and Weare's Market, shown here on the right, were destroyed by fire.

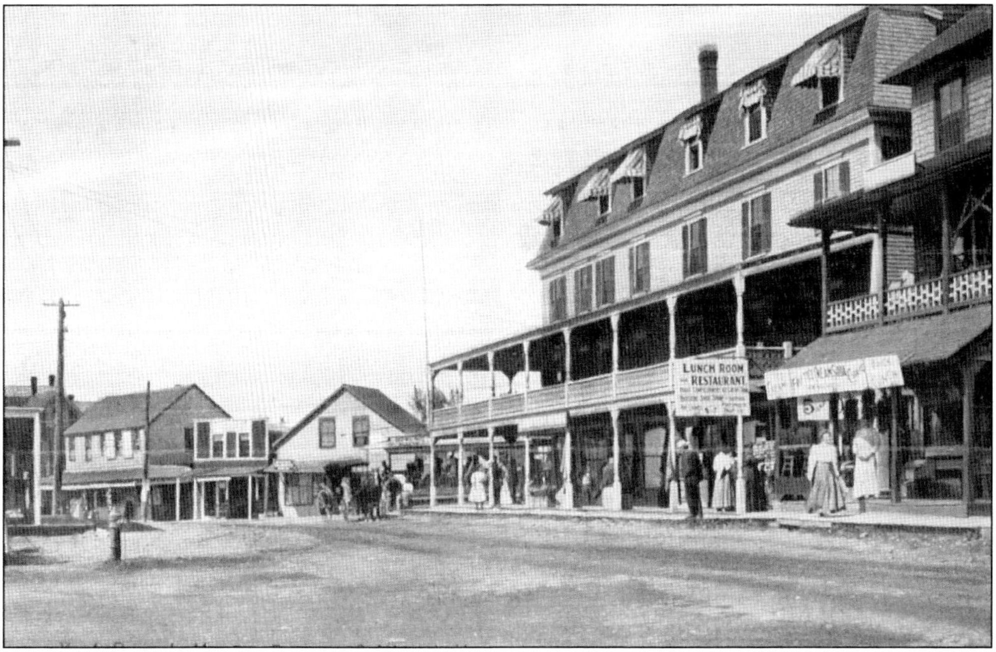

The Atlantic House in 1909.

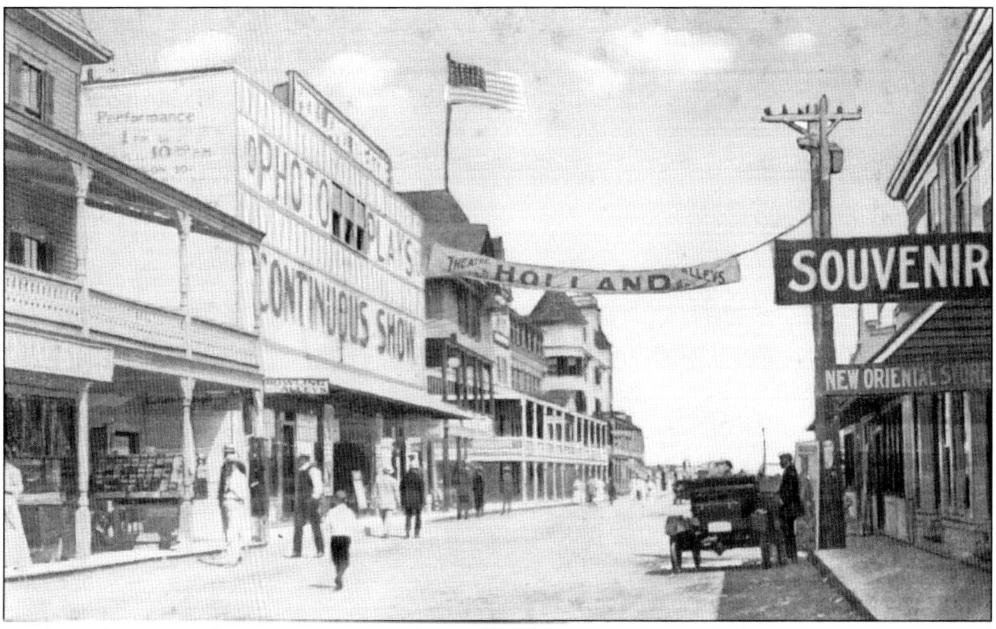

Looking down Beach Street in 1917. The Holland Theater featured *Photo Plays*. The postcard message reads: "*Stopped here for ice cream. Having a fine time. Everybody well . . .*"

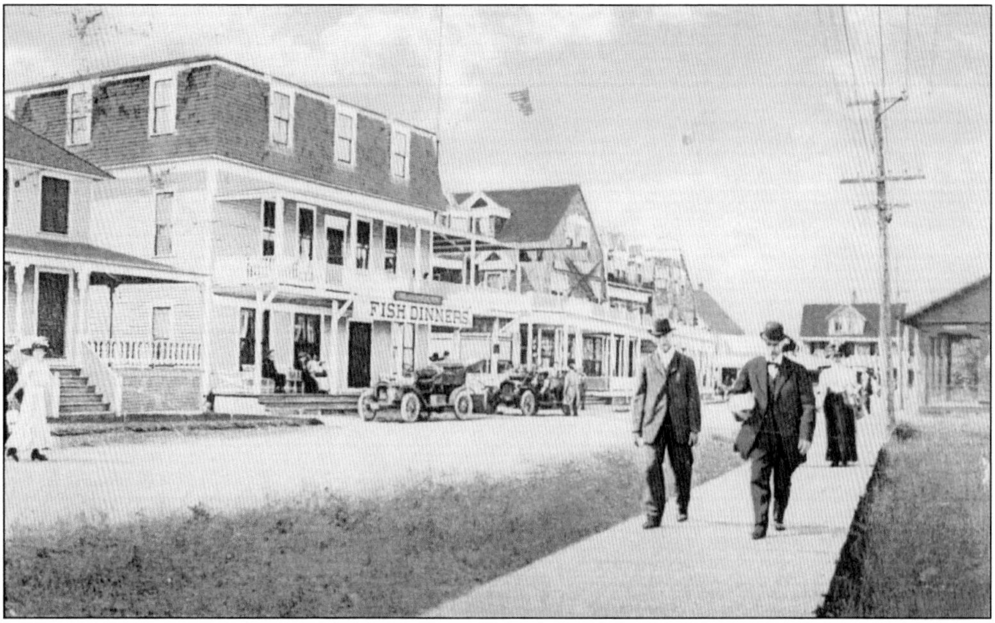


The Algonquin and Kearsarge Hotels in 1917. On the back of this postcard is written: "*Spending day at York Beach. This is the place where we are stopping . . .*"

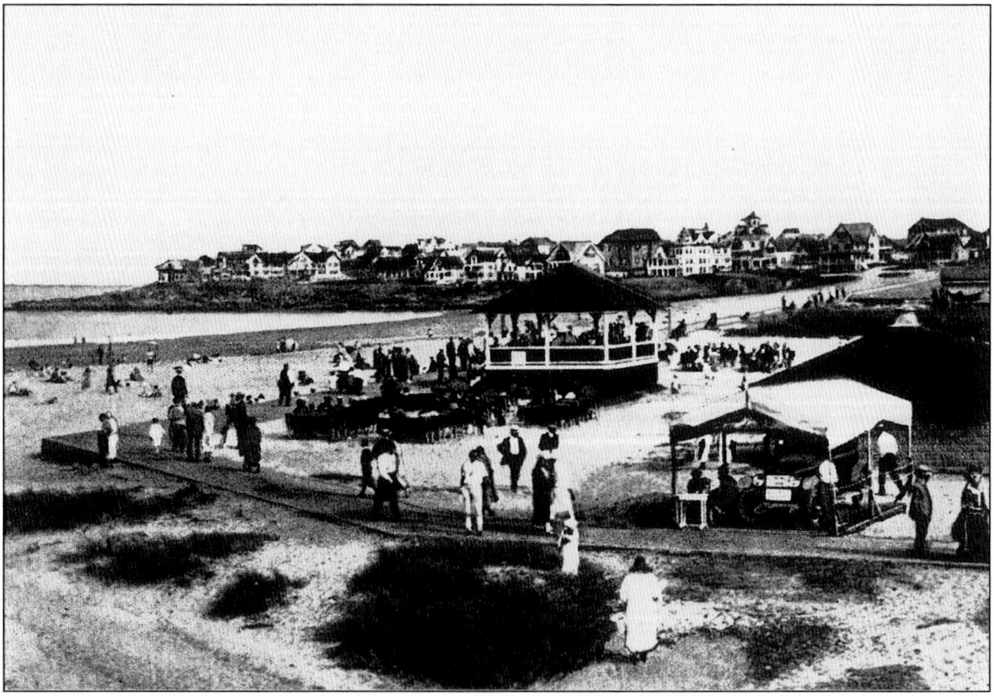

The boardwalk, bandstand, and beach at Short Sands. On the right is an automobile that was raffled off by the Chamber of Commerce to help finance its promotional activities. Tickets were 25¢ each or five for $1. The vehicle was parked near the rest rooms because almost everyone passed by there eventually.

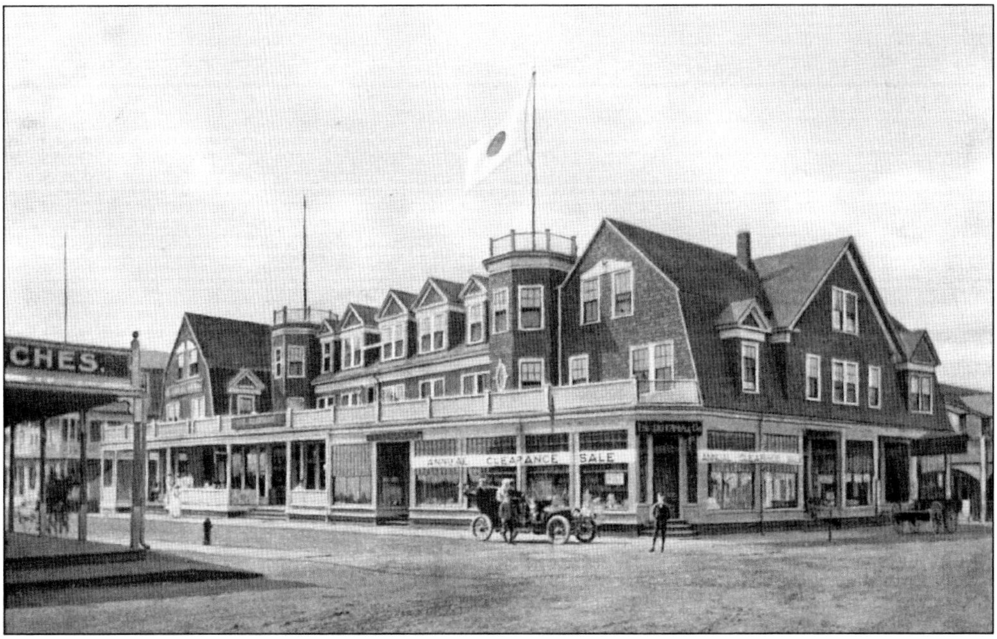

The Kearsarge Hotel flew a Japanese flag to advertise the store of T. Tsubayama. Japanese imports were popular during this period and there were several Japanese shops in the area.

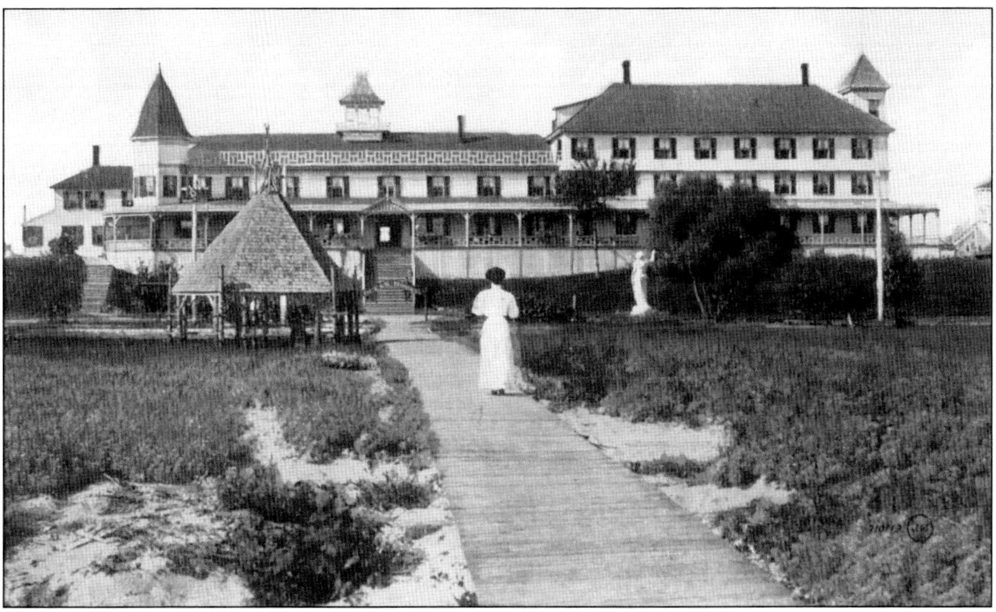
The Ocean House, operated by members of the Ellis family, was located on a ridge overlooking Short Sands Beach. A boardwalk led directly to the beach. The land between the hotel and the beach had bathhouses, tennis courts, and a gazebo.

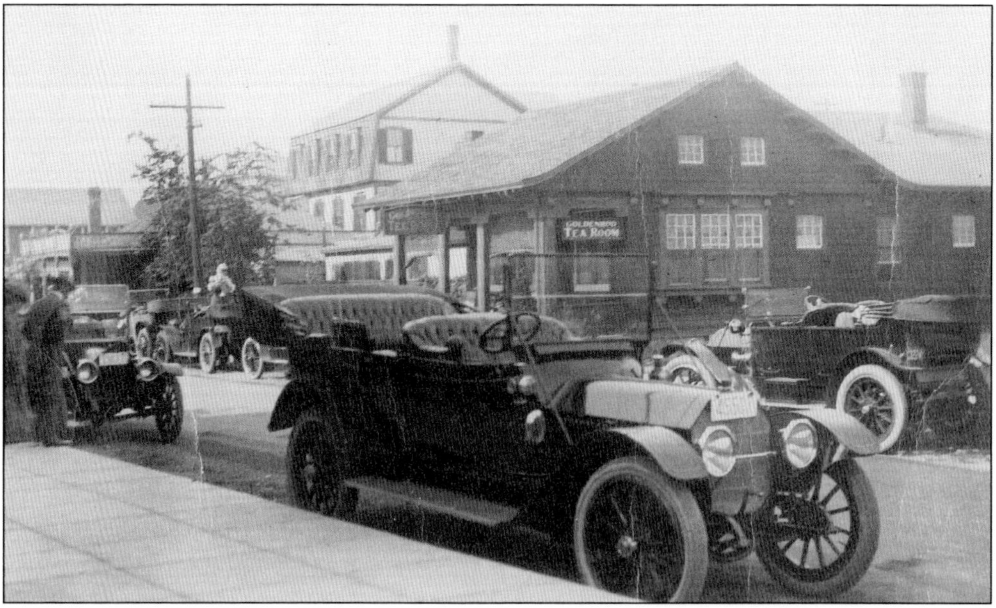


The Goldenrod tearoom catered to York Harbor and York Cliffs residents who considered afternoon tea to be a necessary element of their social routine. They could order chowder, small sandwiches, and bakery products. The "Sultana Roll" was a particular favorite.

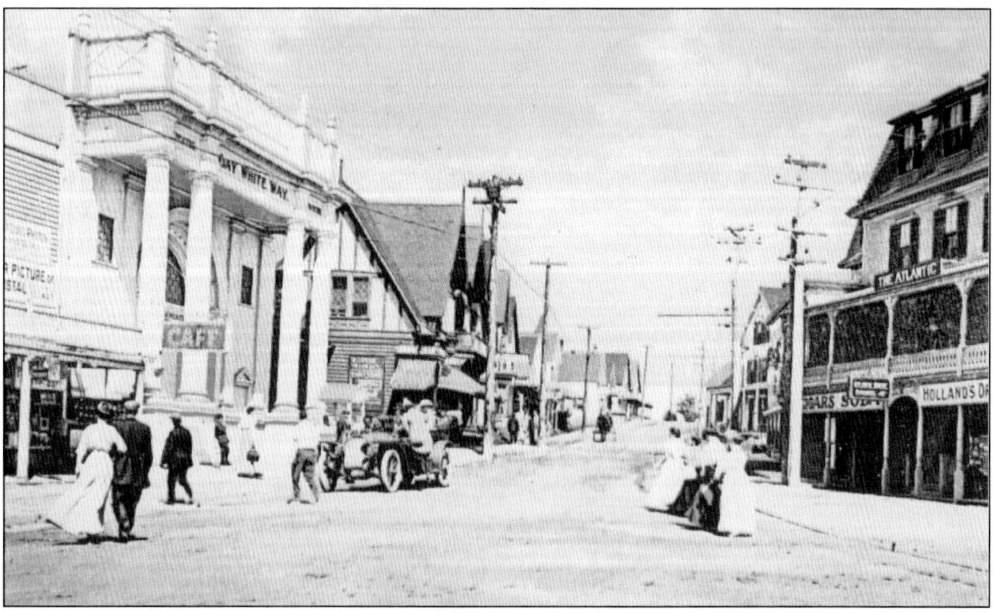


High Street looking north up Hildreth's Hill in 1900. The Atlantic Hotel is on the right.

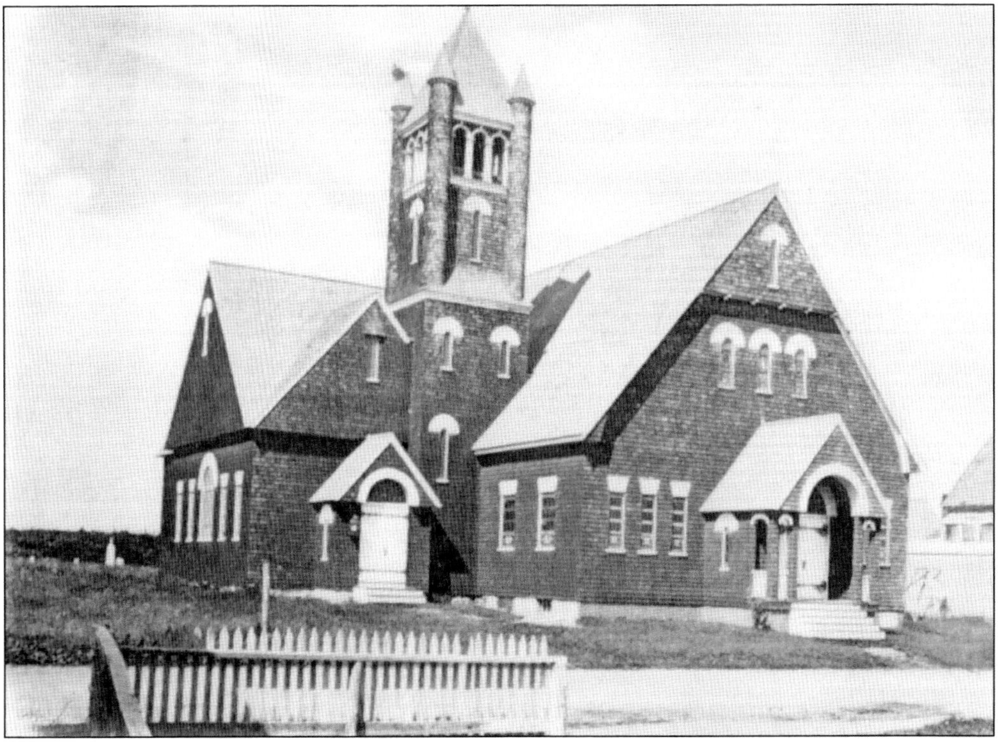

The Union Congregational Church celebrated its 100th anniversary in 1995. The church was designed by Edward B. Blaisdell and constructed by volunteers. Its cornerstone was put in place on May 28, 1895, and a praise service was held in the new church on June 5.

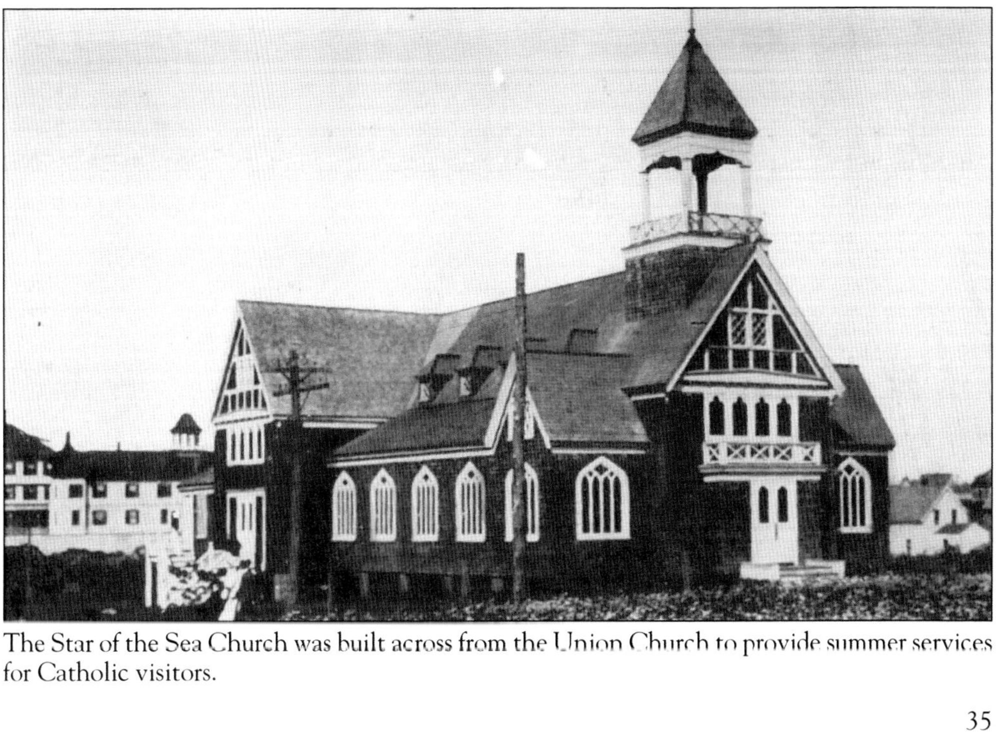

The Star of the Sea Church was built across from the Union Church to provide summer services for Catholic visitors.

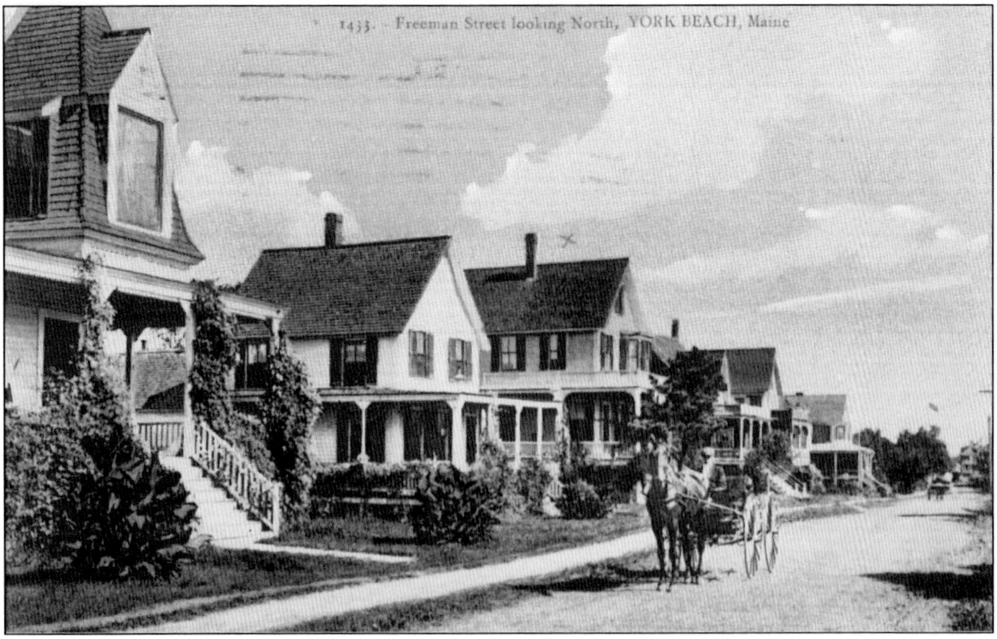


Freeman Street in 1922.

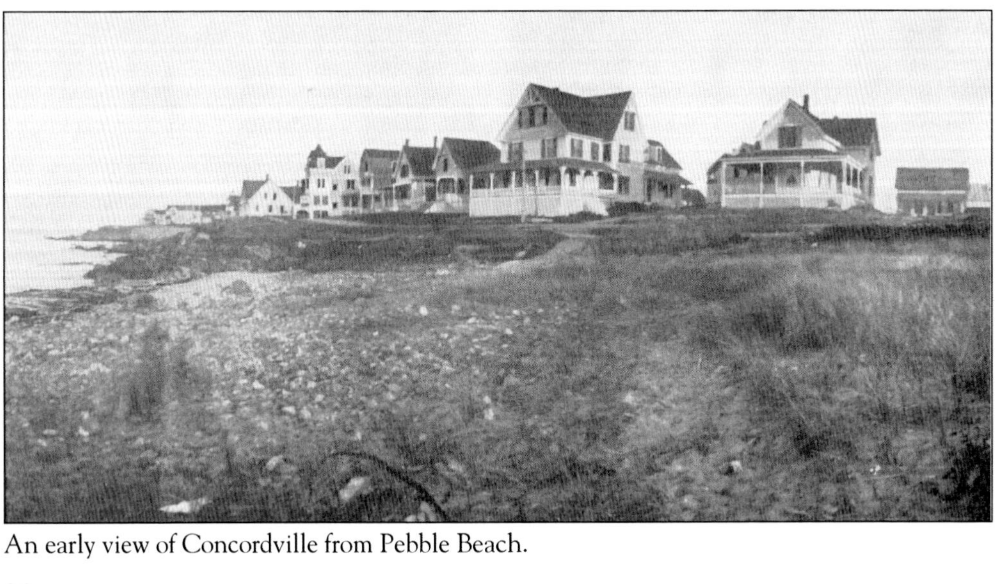

An early view of Concordville from Pebble Beach.

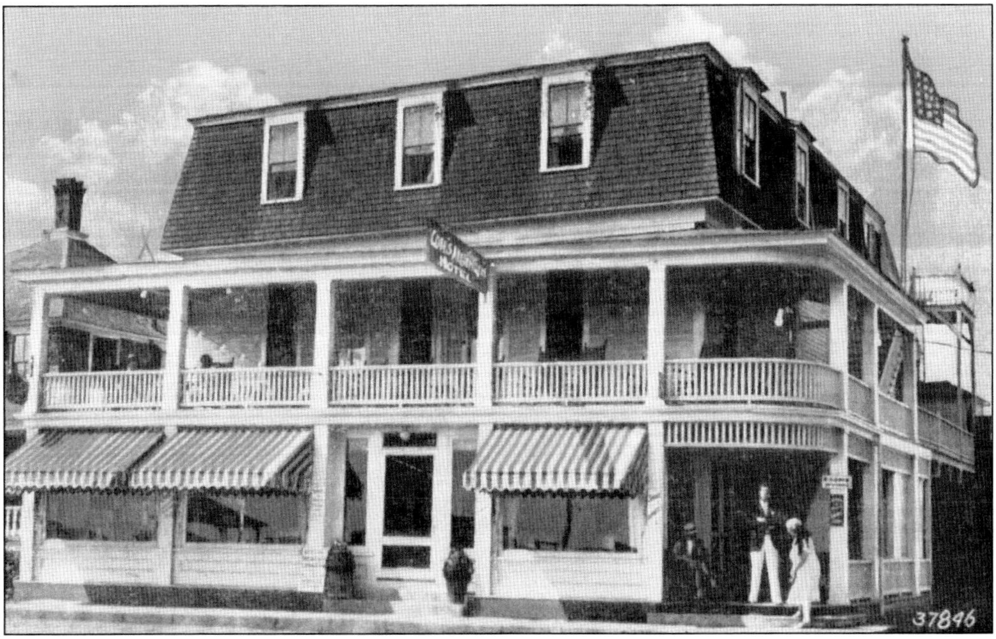


Cobb's Algonquin Hotel. A visitor wrote: "*Very misty past three days. A Great Place. Very nice here. You should see your father eat . . .*"

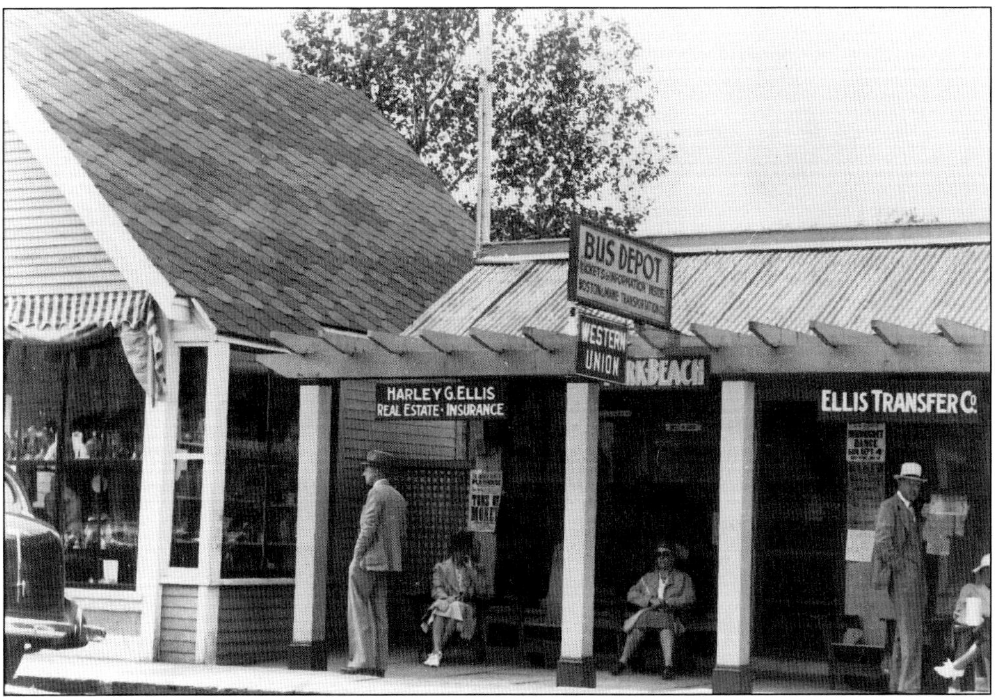


The York Beach Bus Depot on Railroad Avenue near the York Beach Fish Market. At a time when many vacationers traveled by bus, the ticket office and waiting station provided many vital services.

WAITING ROOMS AND TICKET OFFICES

BOSTON, MASS.

Consolidated Coach Terminal, 3 Providence Street, Park Square, opposite New Statler Hotel (Tel.—Kenmore 1025)

Travel Bureau, North Station (Tel.—Porter 5000)

New Statler Hotel (Tel.—Hancock 5007)

PORTLAND, ME.

Boston & Maine Railroad City Ticket Office, 602 Congress Street (Tel.—Forest 113-114-115)

Columbia Hotel (Tel.—Forest 2037)

BIDDEFORD, ME.

Morin's Drug Store (Tel.—Biddeford 177)

KENNEBUNK, ME.

Bowdoin's Drug Store (Tel.—Kennebunk 8039)

OGUNQUIT, ME.

Clark's Restaurant (Tel.—Wells 8064-12)

YORK BEACH, ME.

Ellis Transfer Station (Tel.—York 189-W)

PORTSMOUTH, N. H.

Boston & Maine R. R. Station for Boston & Portland Motor Coaches. Green's Drug Store, Market Square, for all other lines.

HAMPTON, N. H.

Lamie's Restaurant (Tel.—Hampton 8198)

Boston & Maine Transportation Co.

PORTSMOUTH DIVISION

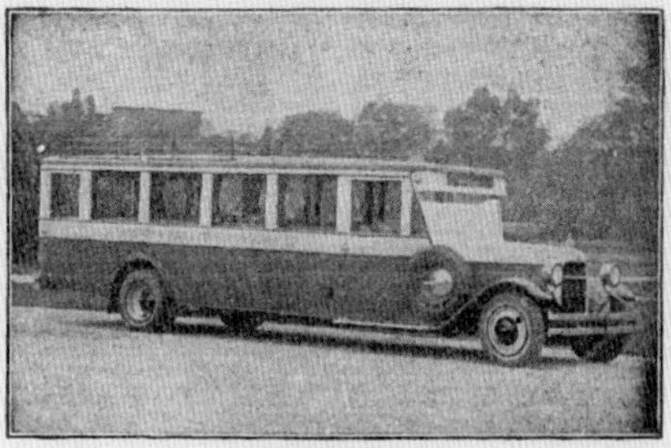

*Effective April 24, 1927*

ALL TIMES SHOWN AS

EASTERN STANDARD TIME

(one hour earlier than daylight saving time)

Schedules between

BOSTON AND PORTLAND
HAMPTON BEACH AND EXETER
PORTSMOUTH—RYE BEACH AND LITTLE BOARS HEAD
PORTSMOUTH AND YORK BEACH
DOVER AND DURHAM
PORTSMOUTH PLAINS AND CHRISTIAN SHORES

PHONE OUR OFFICE . PORTSMOUTH 33

WHEN YOU WANT TO CHARTER
A COACH FOR A SPECIAL PARTY

BOSTON & MAINE TRANSPORTATION COMPANY

For Additional Motor Coach Service Consult
Boston and Maine R.R. Time Table Form 1

R. J. LITTLEFIELD, Mgr.,
Lechmere Square
E. Cambridge, Mass.

E. A. CHASE, Supt.,
Portsmouth, N. H.
Tel. Portsmouth 33

Buses ran on a regular schedule, providing transportation services to all the seacoast resorts.

## *EASTERN STANDARD TIME*

### BOSTON AND PORTLAND

*Daily*

**Leave BOSTON, MASS.**

**Consolidated Coach Terminal, 3 Providence Street, Park Square** . . . . . . . . **1.00 p.m.**

Opposite New Statler Hotel.

**North Station** . . . . . . . . **1.15 p.m.**

**Leave PORTLAND, ME.**

**Boston & Maine City Ticket Office, 602 Congress Street** . . . . . . . . **1.00 p.m.**

Stops at Columbia Hotel to pick up passengers.

### SPECIAL RATES

**Boston to:—**

| | |
|---|---|
| Hampton, N. H. | $1.75 |
| Portsmouth, N. H. | 1.75 |
| York Beach, Me. | 2.00 |
| Ogunquit, Me. | 2.00 |
| Wells, Me. | 2.15 |
| Kennebunk, Me. | 2.25 |
| Biddeford, Me. | 2.25 |
| Portland, Me. | 2.50 |

**Portland to:—**

| | |
|---|---|
| Wells, Me. | $1.25 |
| Ogunquit, Me. | 1.50 |
| York Beach, Me. | 1.75 |
| Portsmouth, N. H. | 2.00 |
| Hampton, N. H. | 2.00 |
| Newburyport, Mass. | 2.25 |
| Boston, Mass. | 2.50 |

**Round trip fare** between Boston and Portland . . . . . . . . 4.00

### RESERVATIONS

**At Boston:—**

Consolidated Coach Terminal, 3 Providence Street, Park Square (Tel. Kenmore 1025 or Circle 1239)

Travel Bureau, North Station (Tel. Porter 5000)

New Statler Hotel (Tel. Hancock 5007)

**At Portland:—**

Boston & Maine Railroad City Ticket Office, 602 Congress Street (Tel. Forest 113-114-115)

Columbia Hotel (Tel. Forest 2037)

**EASTERN STANDARD TIME**

**PORTSMOUTH TO YORK BEACH**

**Weekdays**

| | a.m. | a.m. | p.m. | p.m. | p.m. |
|---|---|---|---|---|---|
| **Lv. Portsmouth** | ...... | 10.00 | 4.40 | ...... | 6.00 |
| **Lv. Navy Yard** | ...... | ...... | ...... | ‡4.20 | ...... |
| **York Village** | ...... | 10.30 | 5.10 | ...... | 6.30 |
| **York Harbor** | ...... | 10.35 | 5.15 | ...... | 6.35 |
| **Ar. York Beach** | ...... | 10.55 | 5.30 | ...... | 6.50 |
| **Lv. York Beach** | ‡6.00 | ...... | ...... | ...... | ...... |
| **Ar. Cape Neddick** | ‡6.10 | ...... | ...... | ‡5.00 | ...... |

**YORK BEACH TO PORTSMOUTH**

**Weekdays**

| | a.m. | a.m. | p.m. | p.m. | p.m. |
|---|---|---|---|---|---|
| **Lv. Cape Neddick** | ‡6.15 | ...... | ...... | ‡5.00 | ...... |
| **Ar. York Beach** | ‡6.25 | ...... | ...... | ‡5.10 | ...... |
| **Lv. York Beach** | ‡6.25 | 8.00 | 12.20 | ...... | 5.10 |
| **York Harbor** | ‡6.35 | 8.10 | 12.30 | ...... | 5.20 |
| **York Village** | ‡6.40 | 8.15 | 12.35 | ...... | 5.25 |
| **Navy Yard** | ‡7.00 | ...... | ...... | ...... | ...... |
| **Ar Portsmouth** | ‡7.10 | 8.50 | 1.10 | ...... | 5.55 |

**NO SUNDAY SERVICE**

**FARE LIMITS**

Portsmouth and Rogers Road, 10c
Rogers Road and Durgin Park, 10c
Durgin Park and York Corner, 10c
York Corner and York Harbor, 5c
York Harbor and Eatons' Camp Ground, 5c

Eatons' Camp Ground and Oceanside, 5c
Oceanside and York Beach, 5c
York Beach and Cape Neddick, 10c
Minimum Fare, 10c

**REFERENCES**

‡—Except Holidays.

**DOVER TO DURHAM**

**Weekdays**

| | a m | a.m. | a.m. | a.m. | p.m. | p.m. | p.m. | p.m. | p.m. | p.m. |
|---|---|---|---|---|---|---|---|---|---|---|
| **Lv Dover** | 6 25 | 7.35 | 8.35 | 9 40 | 12.30 | 2.00 | 3 20 | 4 30 | 6.00 | 9 45 |
| **Ar. Durham** | 7 00 | 8.00 | 9 00 | 10.05 | 12.55 | 2 25 | 3 45 | 4 55 | 6.25 | 10.10 |

**Sundays**

| | a.m. | p.m. | p.m. | p.m. | p.m. | | | | | |
|---|---|---|---|---|---|---|---|---|---|---|
| **Lv. Dover** | 9 00 | 12 30 | 4 00 | 6 00 | 9.45 | ..... | ..... | ..... | ..... | ..... |
| **Ar. Durham** | 9.25 | 12 55 | 4.25 | 6.25 | 10.10 | ..... | ..... | ..... | ..... | ..... |

**DURHAM TO DOVER**

**Weekdays**

| | a.m. | a.m. | a.m. | p.m. | p.m. | p.m. | p.m. | p.m. | p.m. | p.m. |
|---|---|---|---|---|---|---|---|---|---|---|
| **Lv. Durham** | 7.00 | 8.00 | 9.00 | 12.00 | 1.00 | 2 30 | 4 00 | 5 05 | 6.30 | 10 10 |
| **Ar. Dover** | 7.25 | 8.25 | 9 25 | 12.25 | 1.25 | 2.55 | 4.25 | 5.30 | 6.55 | 10 35 |

**Sundays**

| | a.m. | p.m. | p.m. | p.m. | p.m. | | | | | |
|---|---|---|---|---|---|---|---|---|---|---|
| **Lv. Durham** | 9.30 | 1 00 | 5 00 | 7.00 | 10.10 | ..... | ..... | ..... | ..... | ..... |
| **Ar. Dover** | 9.55 | 1.25 | 5 25 | 7.25 | 10 35 | ..... | ..... | ..... | ..... | ..... |

**FARE—25 cents**

Long-distance travelers could ride to Boston or Portland and transfer to other bus lines or trains destined for more distant locations. Harley Ellis also sold real estate, insurance, and operated a Western Union Telegraph office.

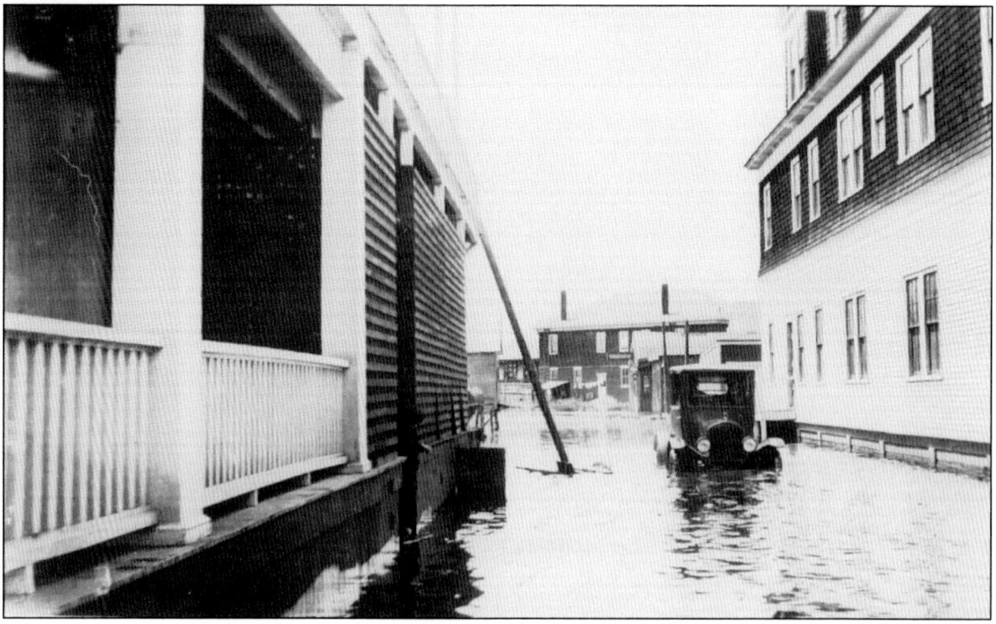

Over the years there have been several significant floods in York Beach. These usually occurred after intense storms released more rain than could be carried away by storm drains. This car was trapped between the Algonquin and the Kearsarge in 1922.

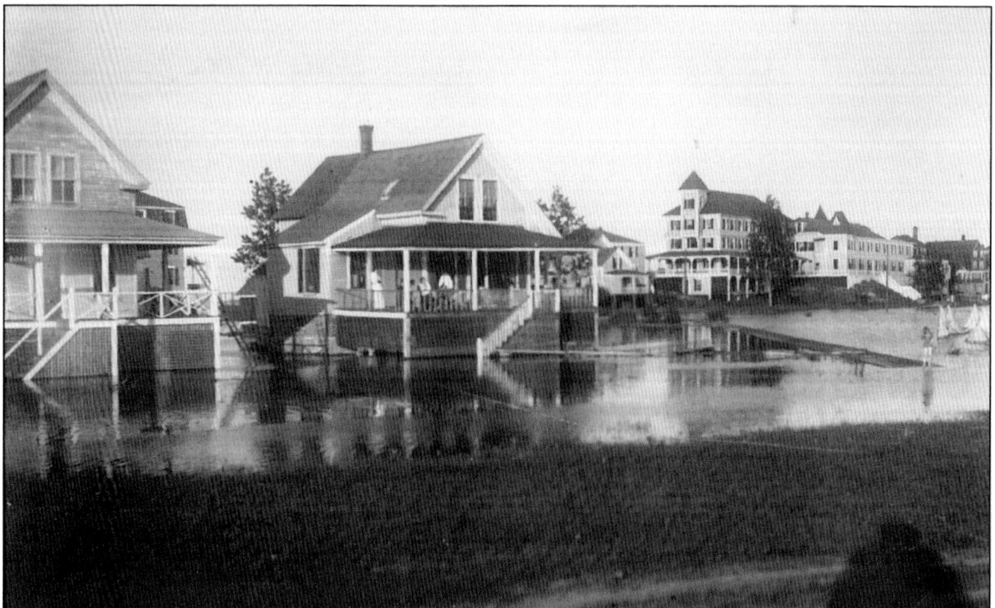

This 1915 flood behind the Ocean House isolated several cottages that had been built in a marshy area.

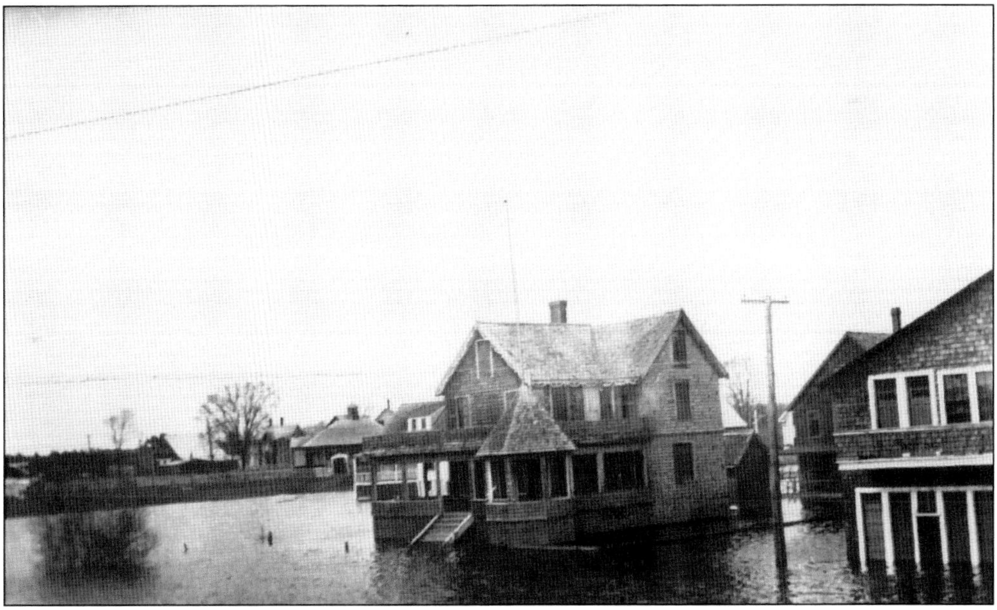

Most of the business district was built on marshland and the natural drainage areas were filled as the resort expanded. This is another flood scene in 1922.

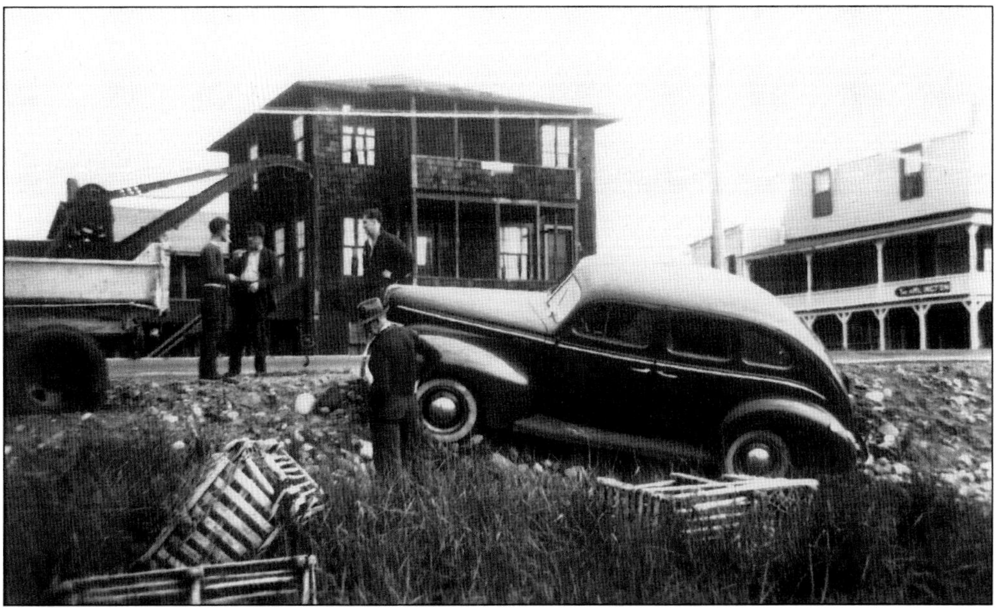

As automobile traffic increased on Long Beach Road, so did the number of accidents. This wrecker is about to pull a 1940s-vintage vehicle from a jumble of abandoned lobster traps and other debris.

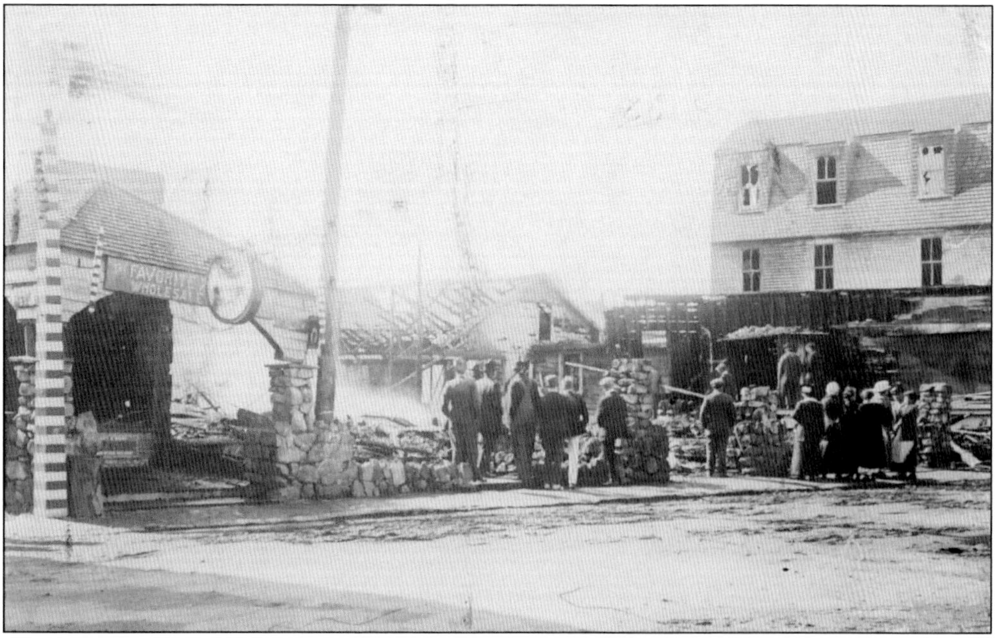

A serious fire, probably electrical, destroyed the Arcade Block owned by Mrs. Samuel Stringer on September 25, 1916. Weare's Market, the Arcade Theater, Proctor's Livery Stable, Avery's Barber Shop, Tsubayama's Store, and the York Beach Fire Station were also demolished. Damaged were J.H. Paul's Store, the Ellis Garage, the Kearsarge Hotel, the Algonquin Hotel, and the Rockaway Hotel.

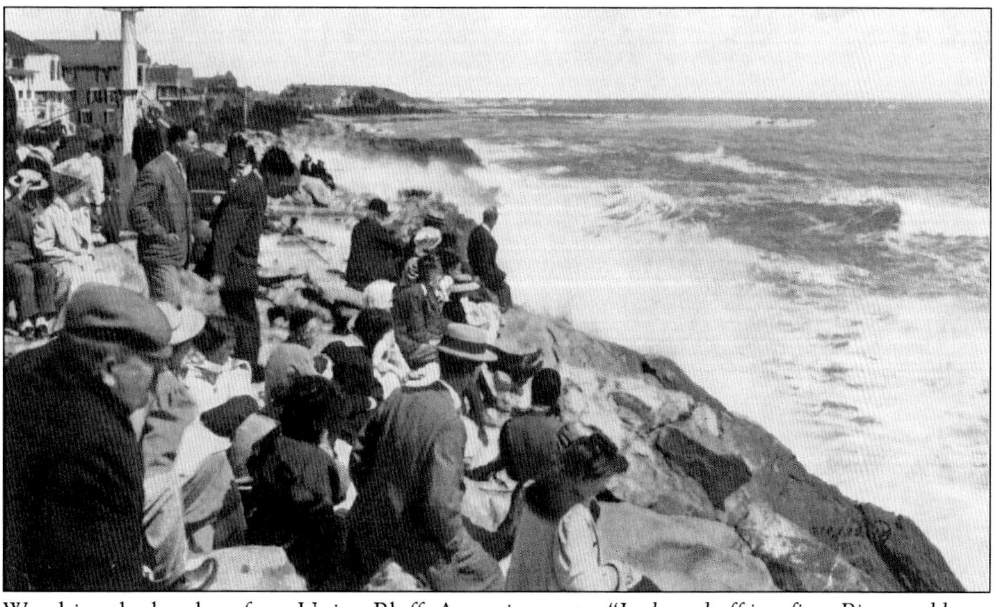

Watching the breakers from Union Bluff. A tourist wrote: "*It cleared off just fine. Big crowd here. Am fixed all right with room and board. Can stand it for a week all right . . .*"

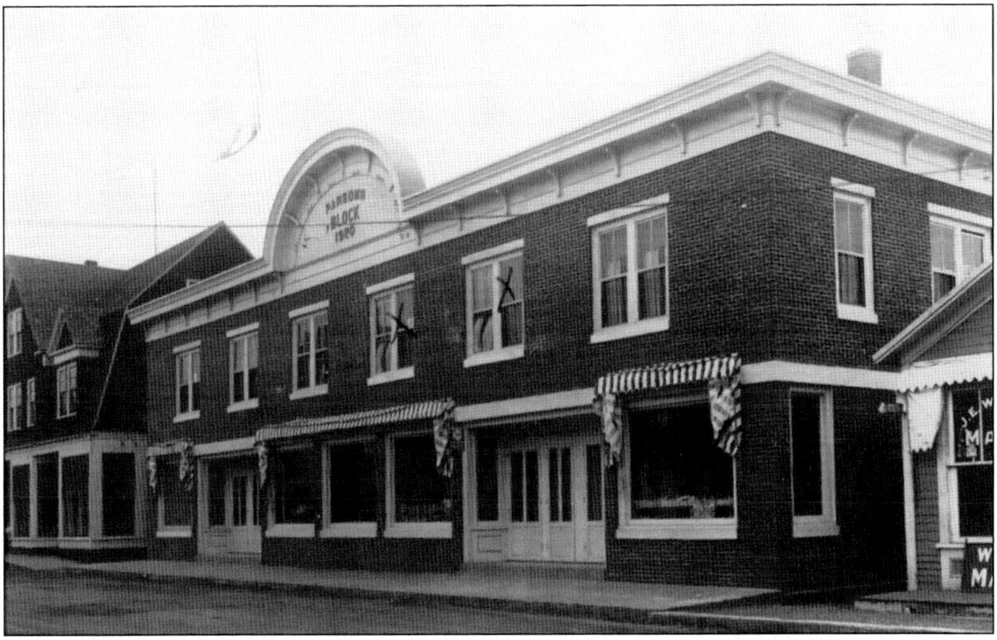


The Parsons block was built on the site of the Arcade Block and Weare's Market after they were destroyed by fire.

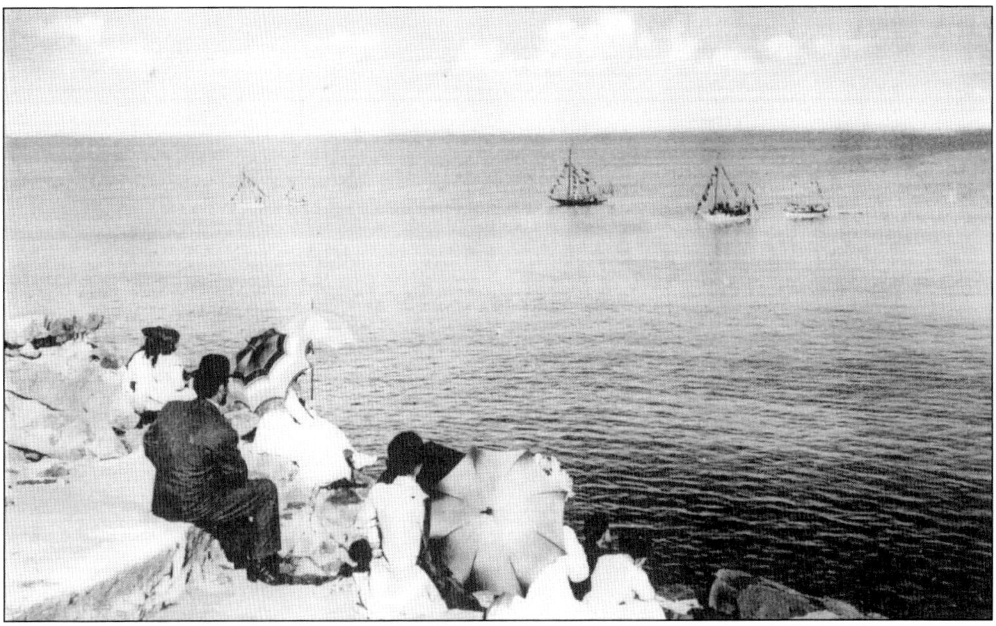

On the rocks at Union Bluff. "*We expect to be here another week anyway. We are keeping Edith out of school on account of the Infantile Paralysis. It looks like too serious a thing to take chances with . . .*"

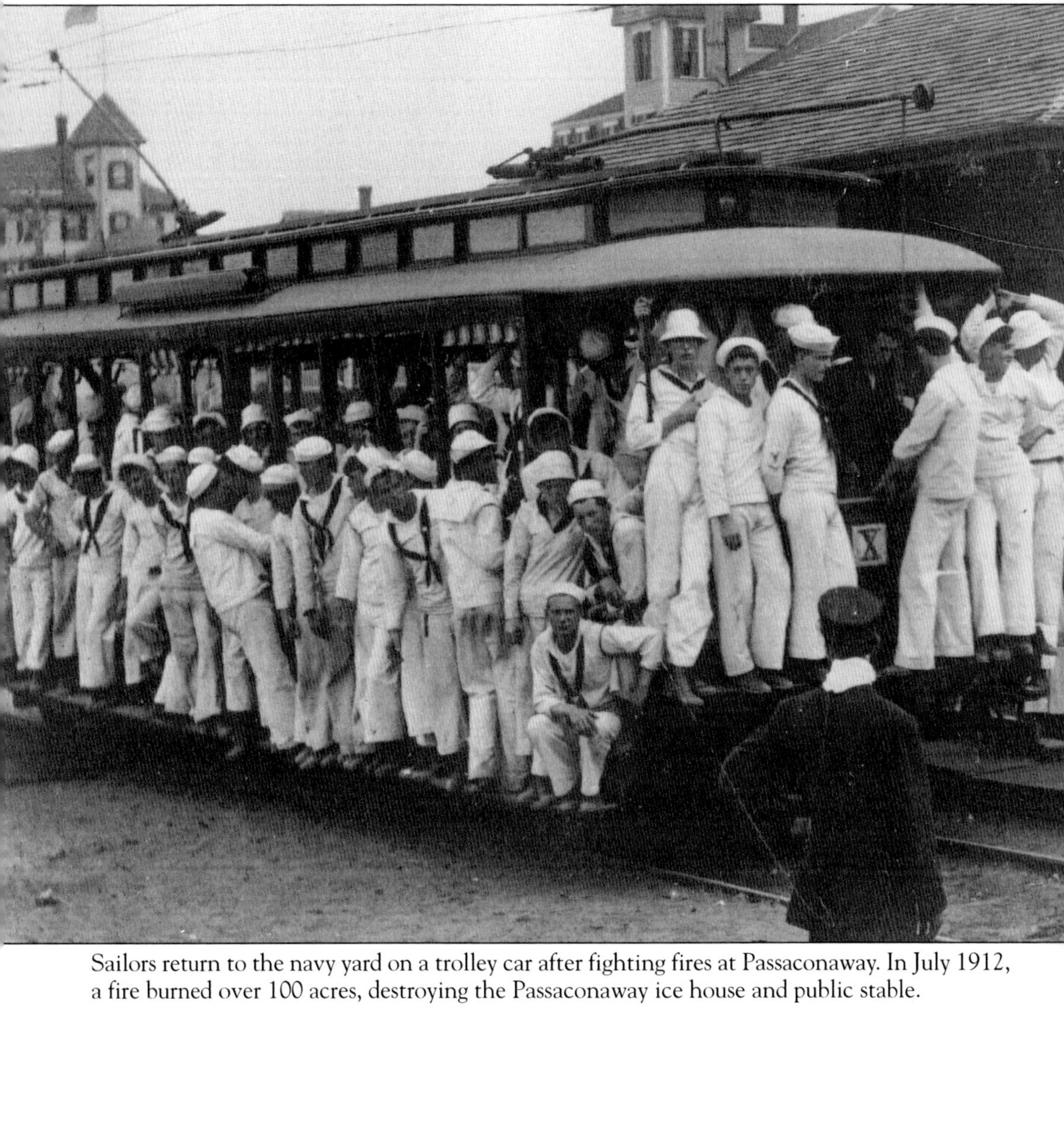

Sailors return to the navy yard on a trolley car after fighting fires at Passaconaway. In July 1912, a fire burned over 100 acres, destroying the Passaconaway ice house and public stable.

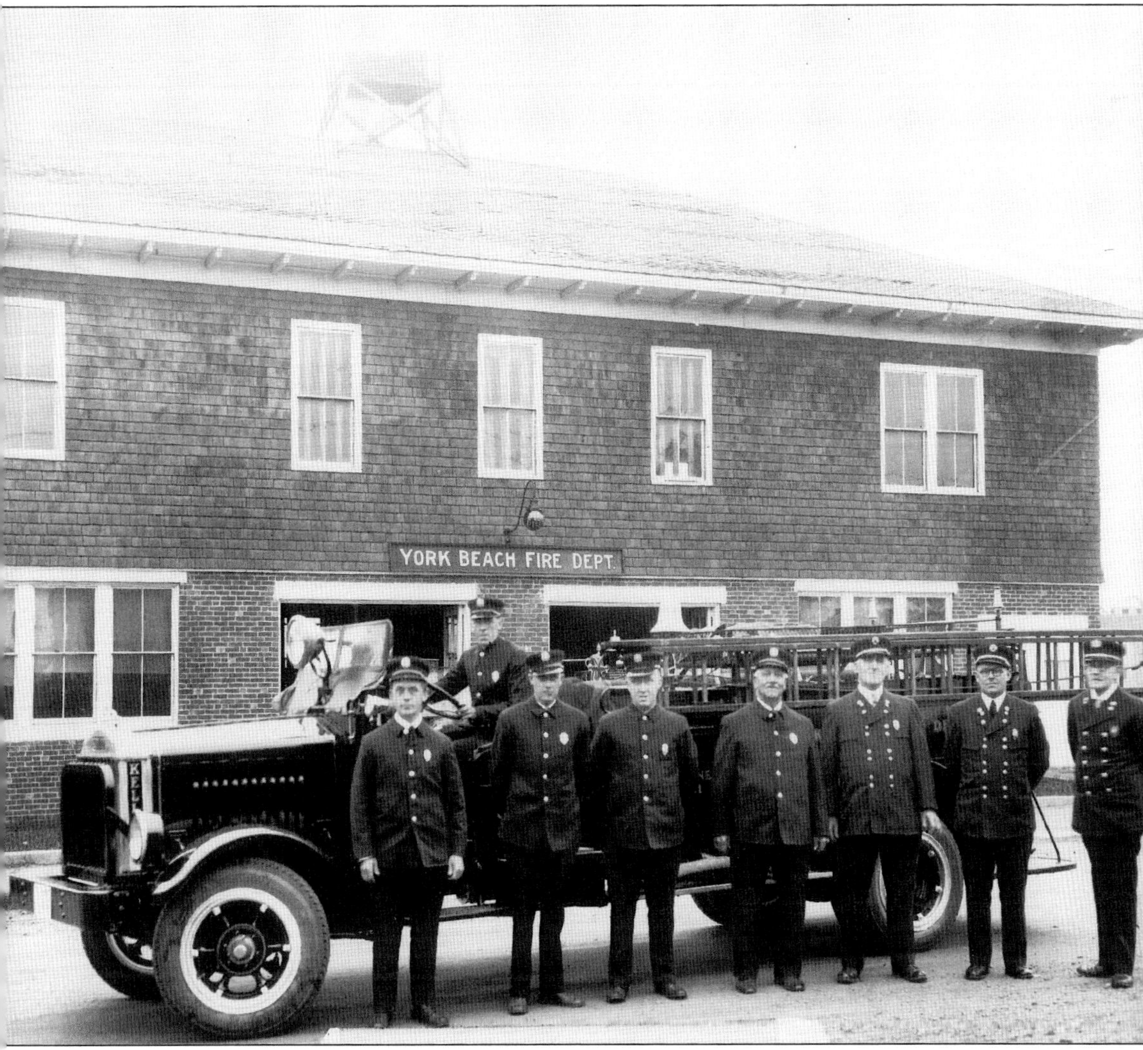


York Beach firefighters with their 1928 Kelly-Springfield 400-GPM pumper. The driver is Maurice Chase. Standing from left to right are: Paul Norton, Ben Armstrong, Arthur Chase, Fred Frisbee, Caleb Bowden, Harley Ellis, and Will Hildreth.

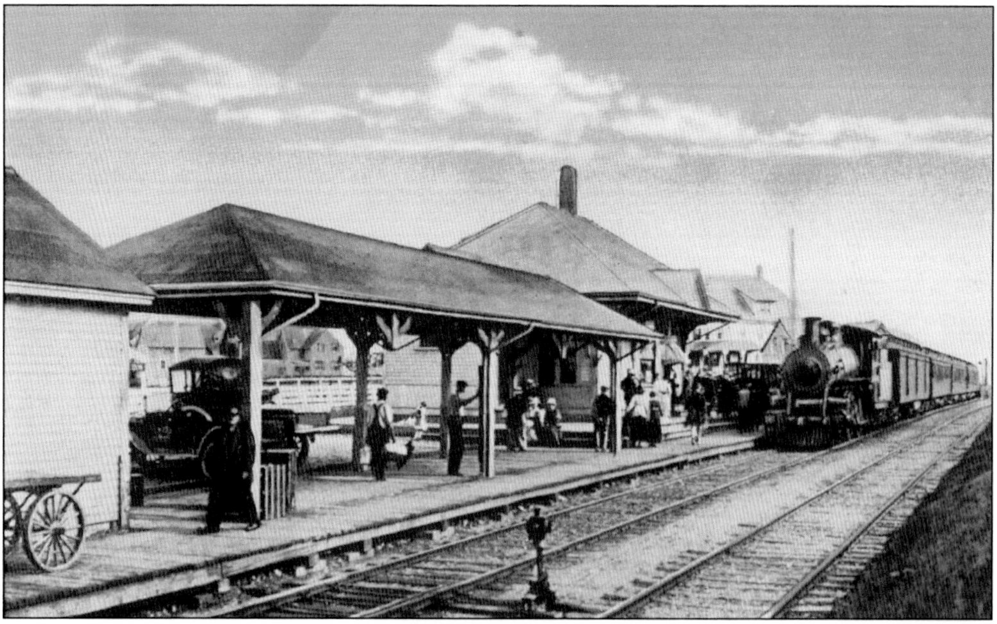

The first scheduled train over the York Harbor & Beach Railroad tracks ran on August 8, 1887. It arrived with a second locomotive on the rear of the train because York Beach was the end of the line and the roundhouse was not yet operational.

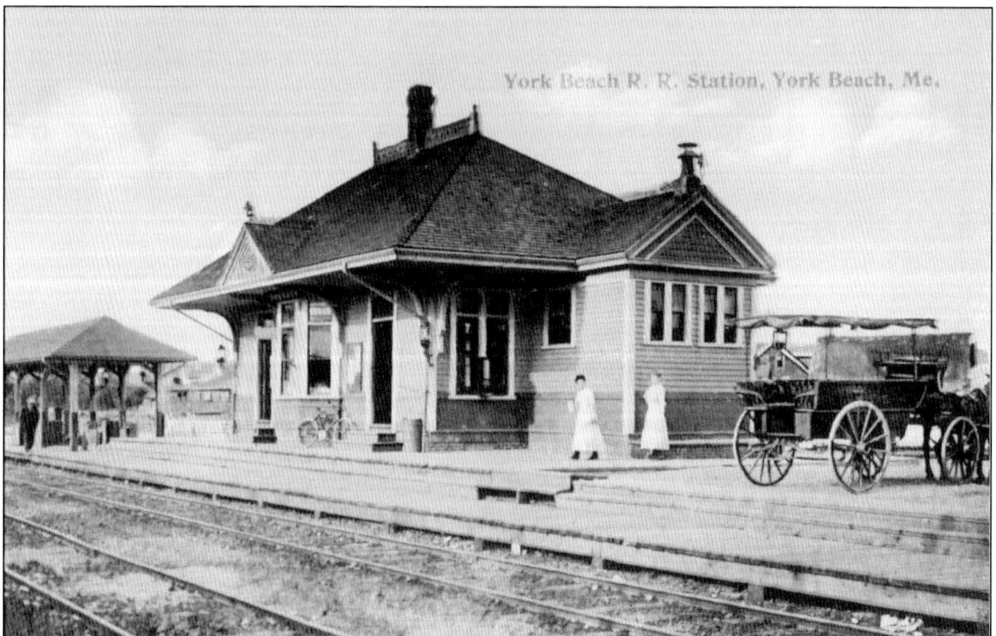


York Harbor & Beach operated under an agreement with Frank Jones's Boston & Maine Railroad that provided the rolling stock and access to the Portsmouth depot over B & M tracks.

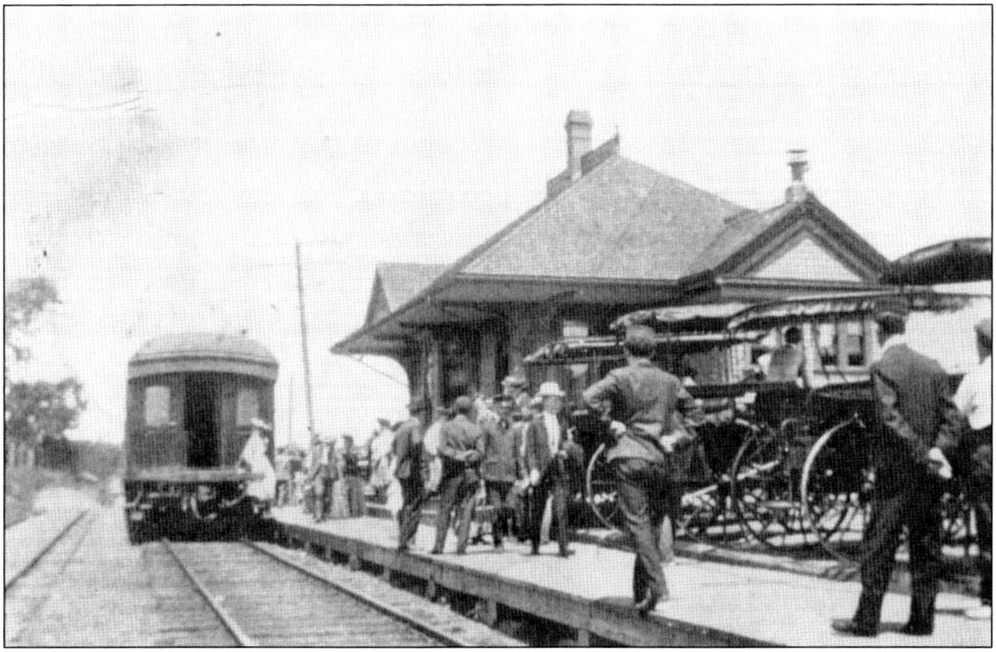

The design of most of the stations on the Y.H. & B. was very similar. York Beach was the northernmost station, located 11 miles from Kittery Junction. Other stations of similar design were at the Kittery Navy Yard, Kittery Point, York Harbor, and Long Beach. This photograph was taken c.1912.

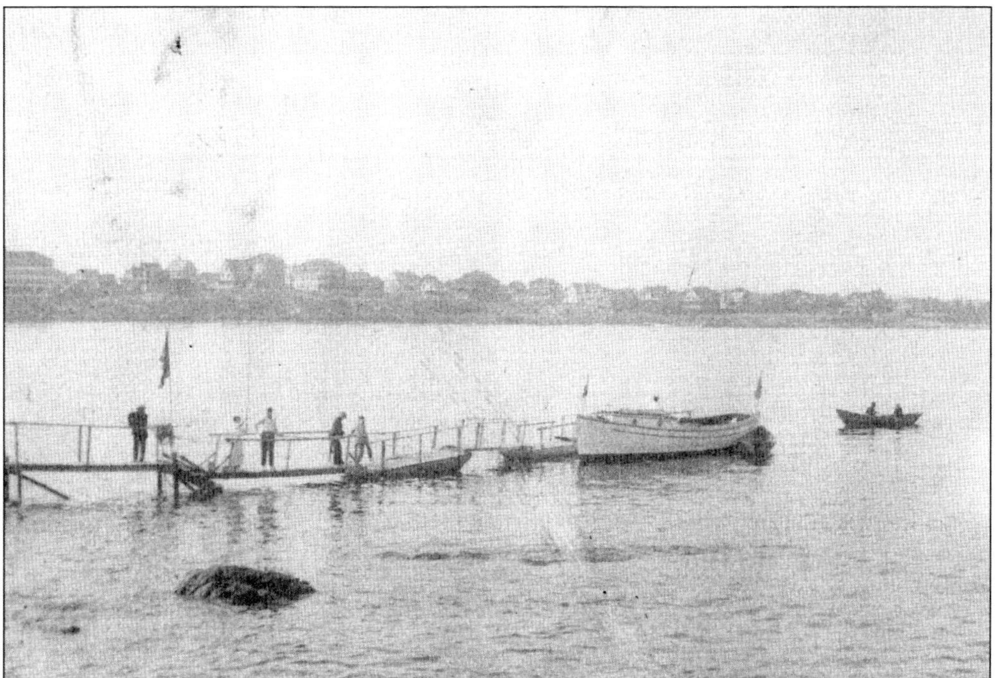

A pier and landing at Short Sands near Concordville enabled fishing parties to board sailing vessels that anchored just off shore.

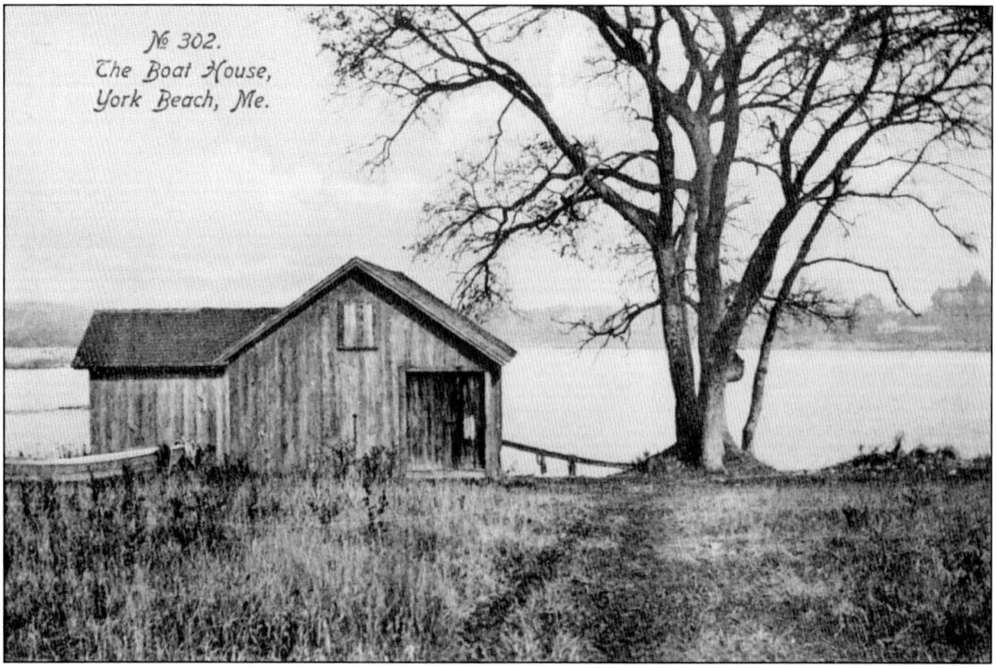

The boathouse of the Bay Haven Yacht Club. The club was organized in 1910 to promote boating and yachting at York Beach and Cape Neddick. It had two hundred members and was active in promoting York Beach as a summer resort.

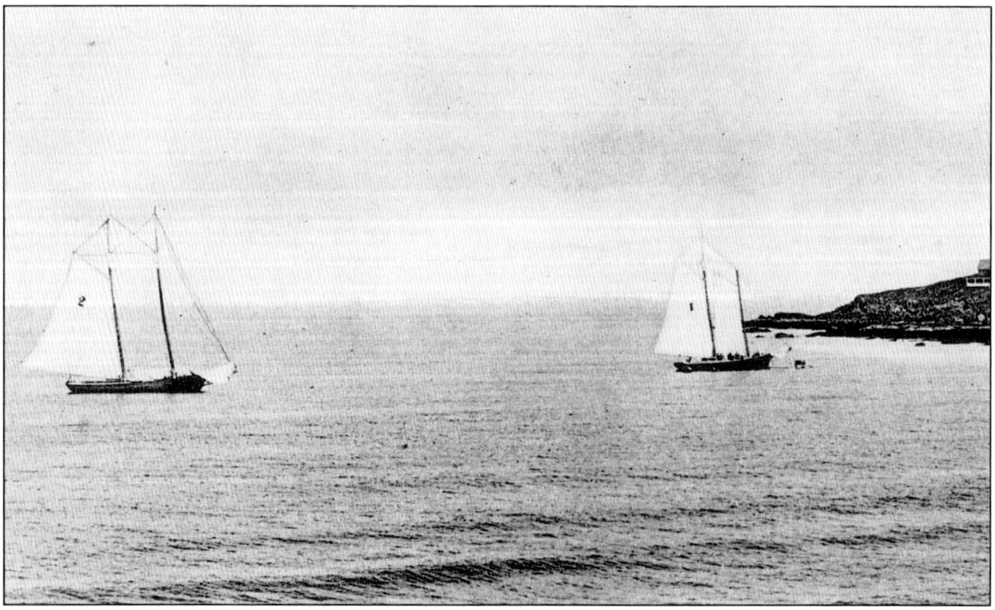
Schooners 1 and 2 at York Beach. They came from Portland each summer to serve as charter boats for deep-sea fishing parties. The distinctive numbers are visible on their sails.

Back from fishing. The message reads: "*This card represents Bert coming in from fishing yesterday. He is as bad as ever holding hands and hugging the girls, but no leg pulling as yet . . .*"

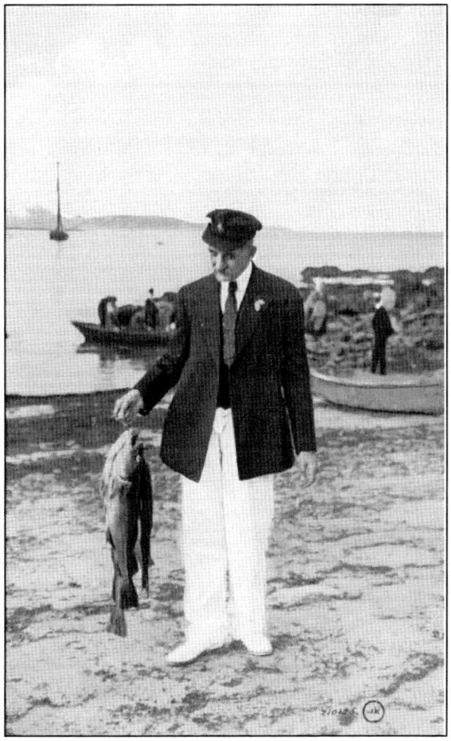

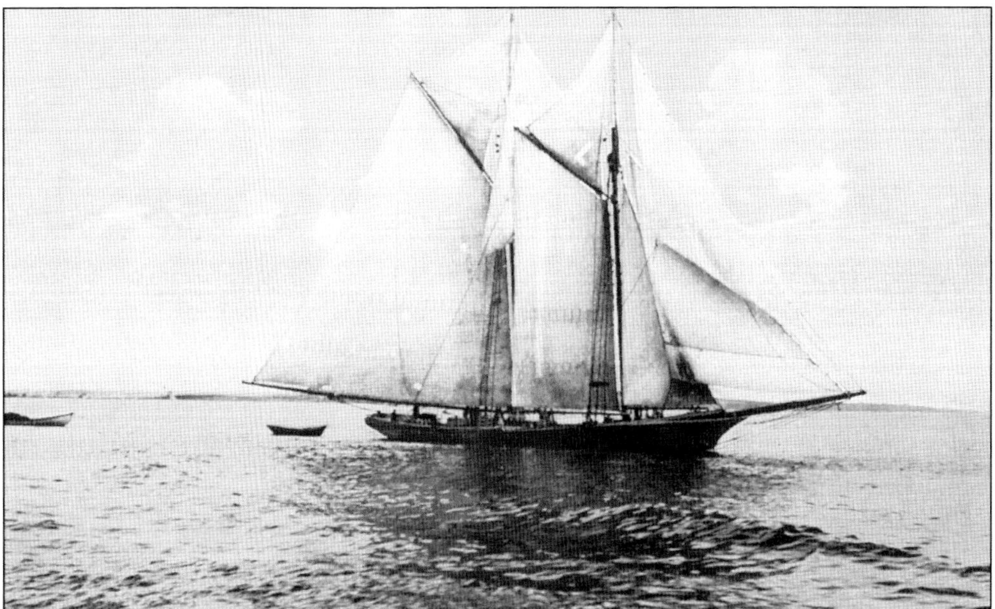

Custom decreed that the first two or three fish caught were the property of the ship, to be cleaned on the spot and plunged into the pot for a noon-day chowder. Each boat had a barrel of pilot crackers that were round, 6-inches in diameter, and substantial enough so as not to crumble at the first bite.

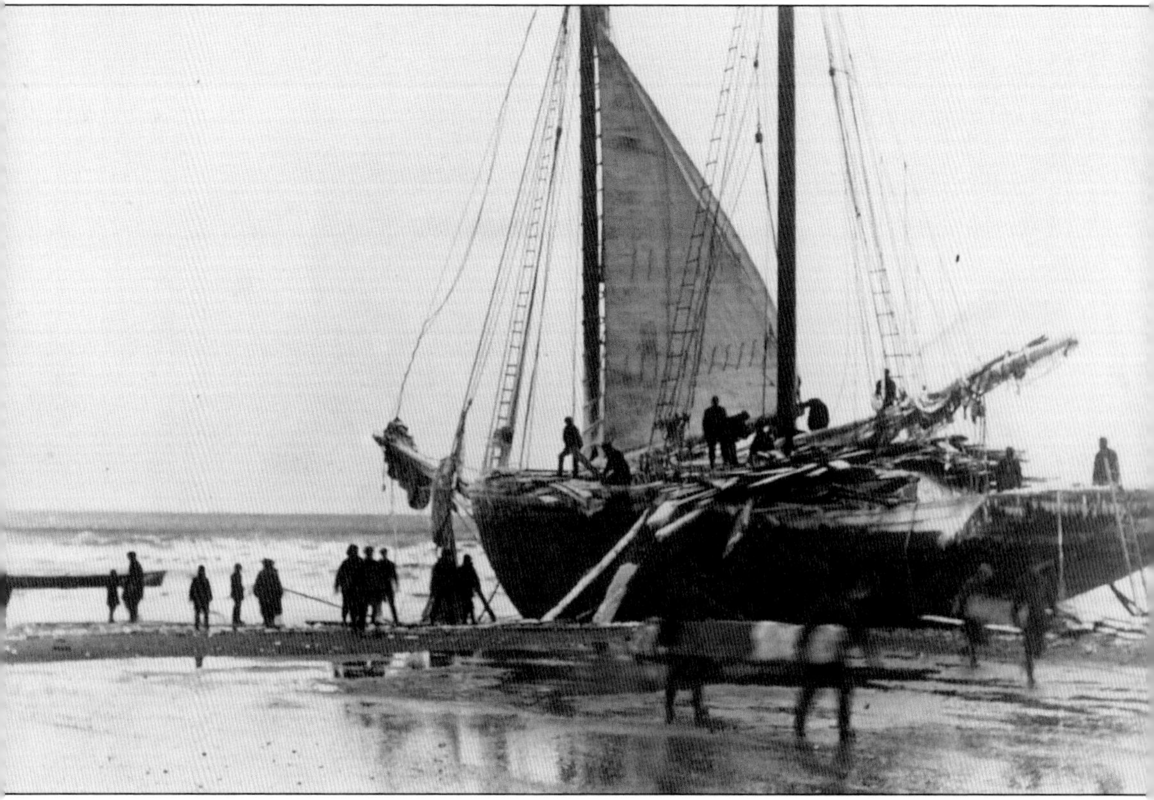

On February 12, 1923, the schooner *Robert W.* went ashore on Long Beach in a blinding snowstorm. The two-man crew was lashed to the rigging for nearly twelve hours before rescuers could reach them.

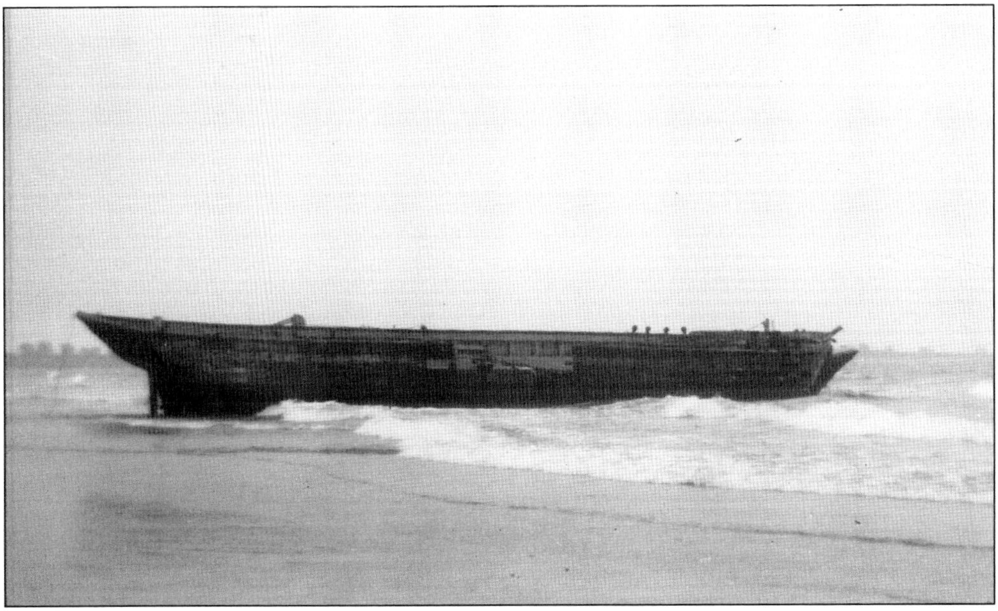

A cargo of lumber kept the *Robert W.* afloat until it settled on the beach as the tide went out. The cargo was removed but the hull remained on the beach for several years.

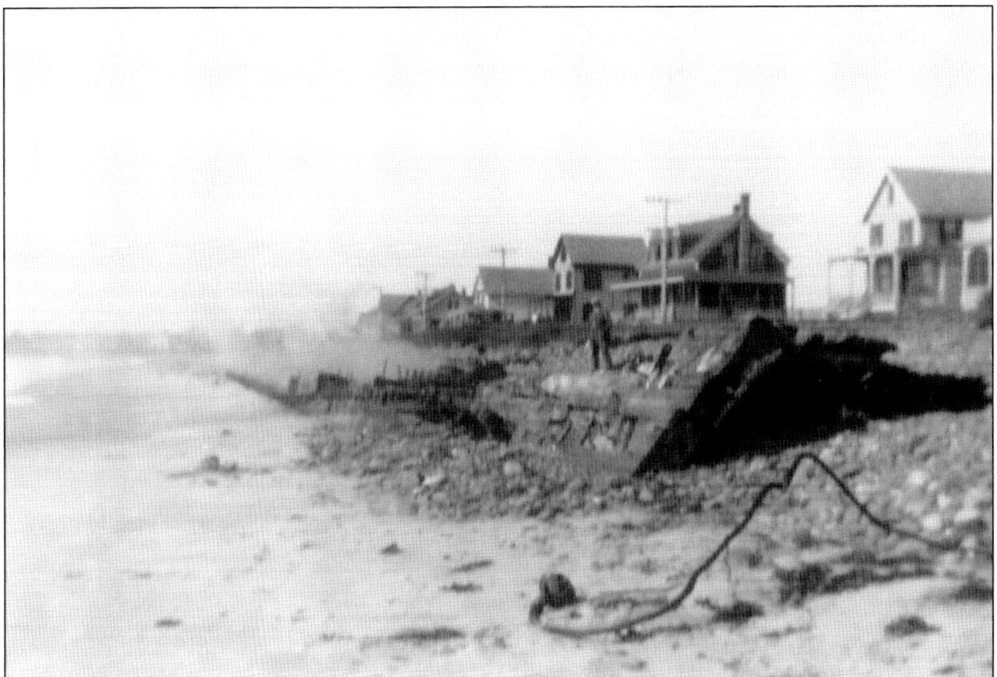

The hull was set afire during several Fourth of July celebrations. It is shown here smoldering after one such incident.

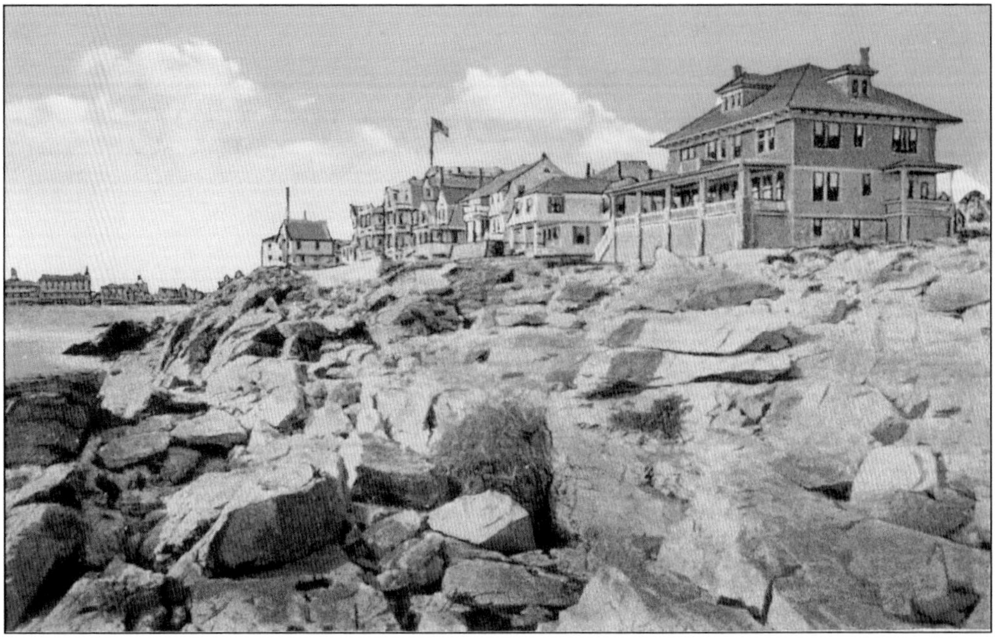

A postcard scene of Union Bluffs when it was lined with hotels and cottages.

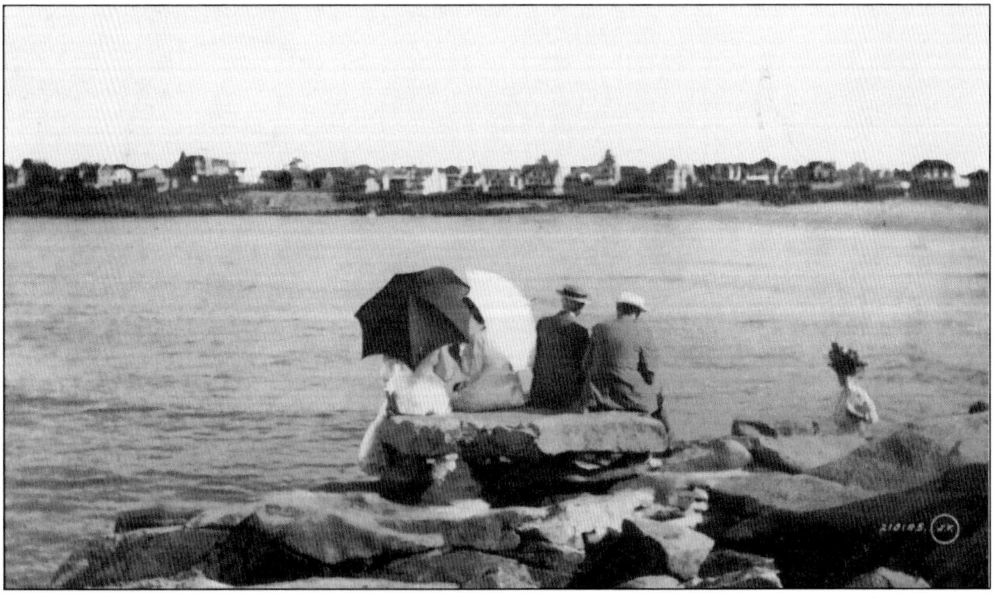

A favorite pastime was sitting on the rocks in front of the Hastings-Lyman Hotel on Union Bluffs. In 1911 a vacationer wrote: "*We are having a very fine time at the beach. Go in bathing every day and can swim fine. This is a very restful place . . .*"

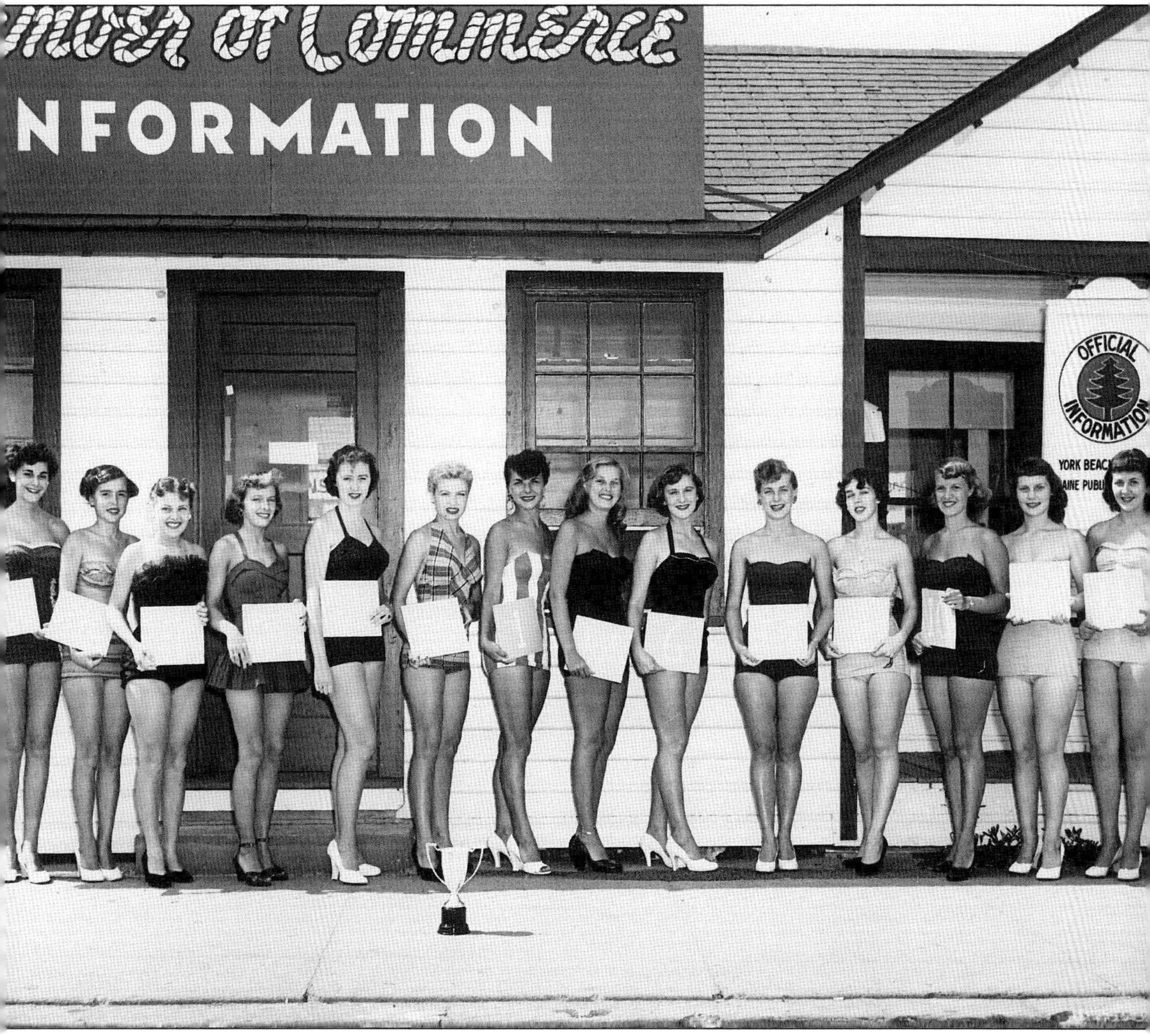


Beauty contest participants competing for the title of "Miss York Beach" are assembled in front of the Chamber of Commerce Information Center.

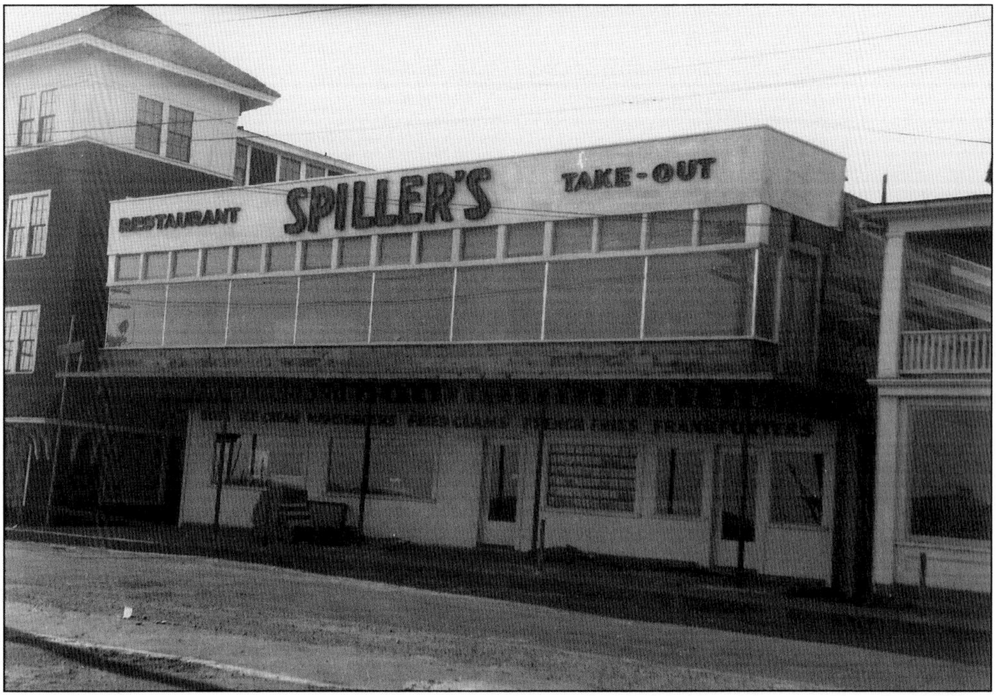


In 1949–50 a second-floor dining room was added to Spiller's Restaurant on Ocean Avenue.

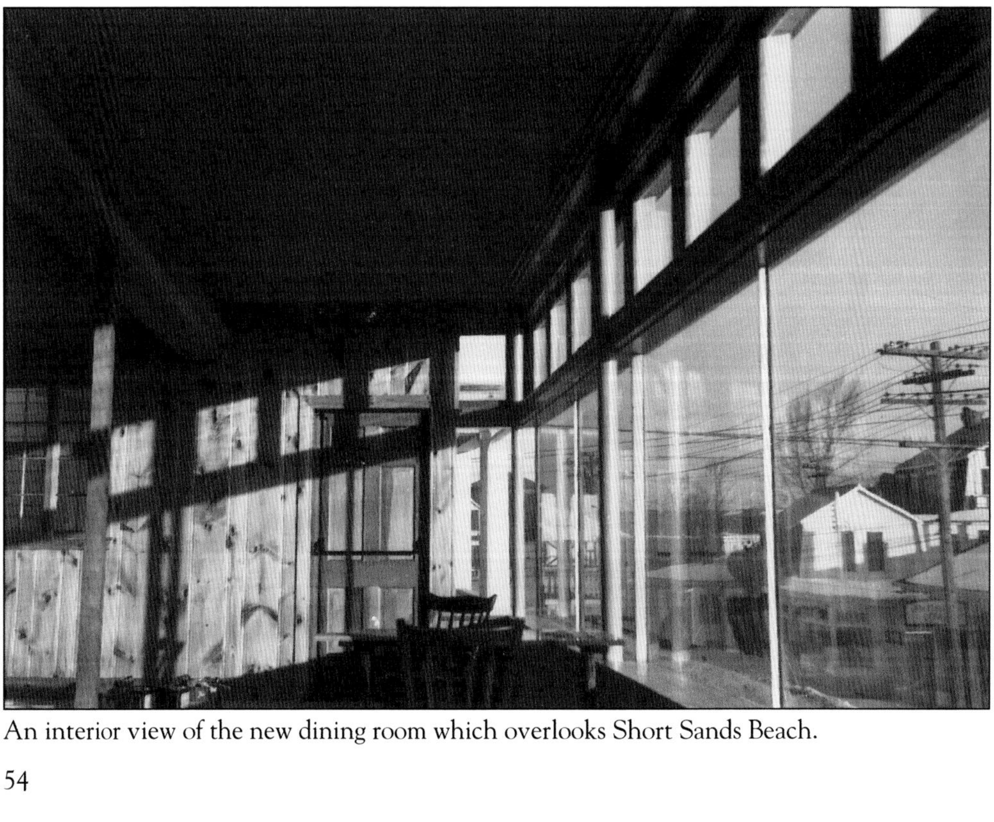

An interior view of the new dining room which overlooks Short Sands Beach.

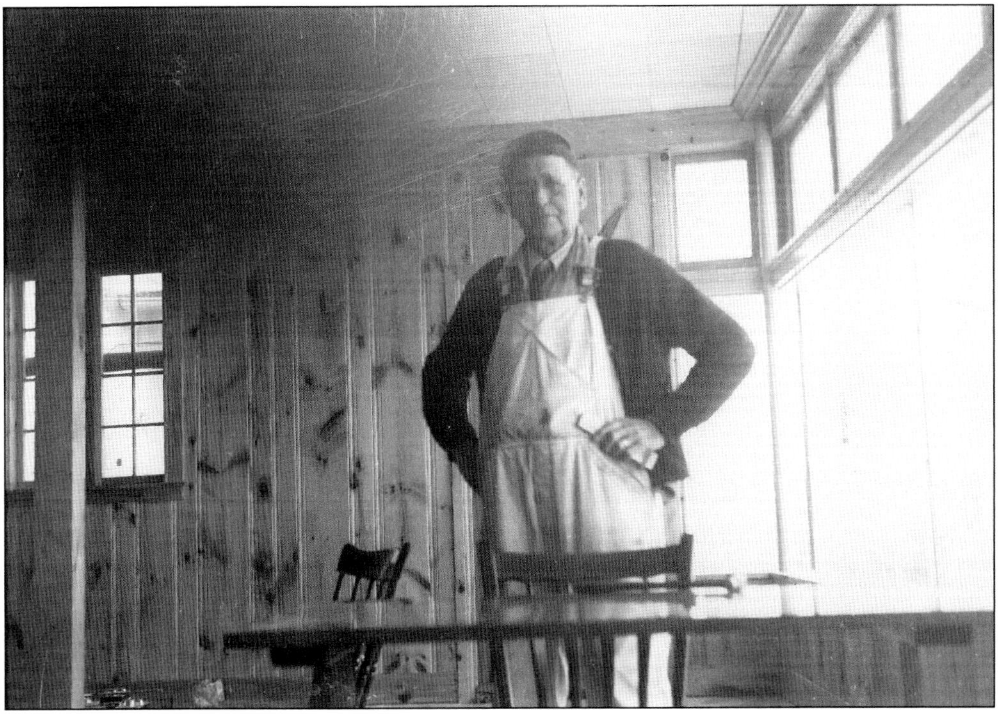

Fred Moore, a carpenter and York Beach building inspector, at work on the expansion of Spiller's Restaurant. He was assisted by Harry and Arthur Moore and Harmon Freeman.

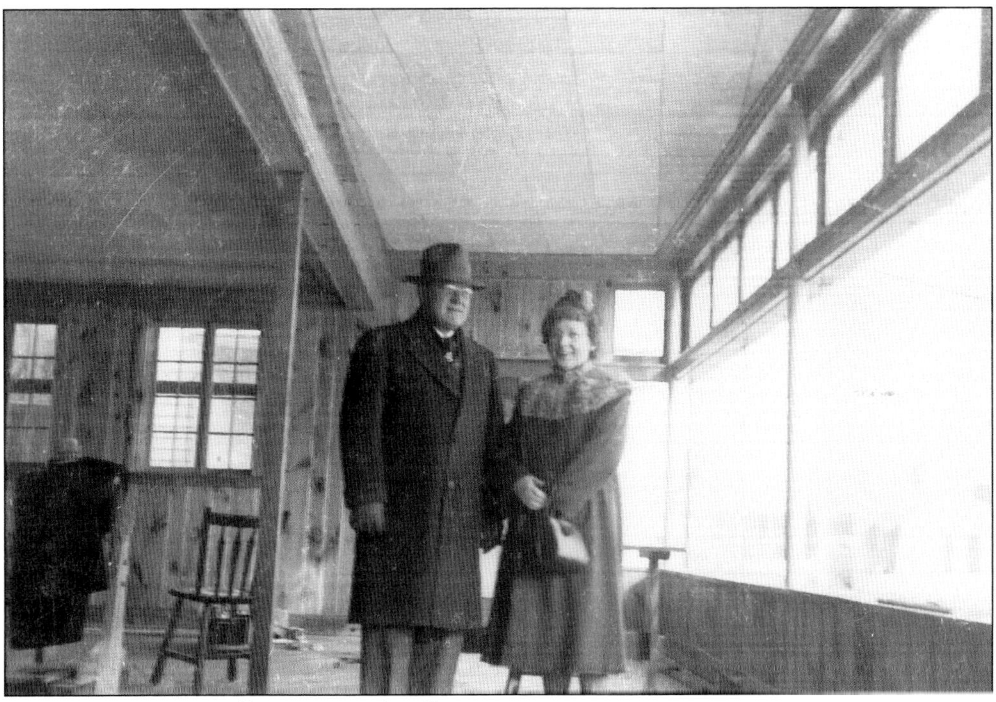

Alpheus and Nina Spiller, owners of Spiller's Restaurant.

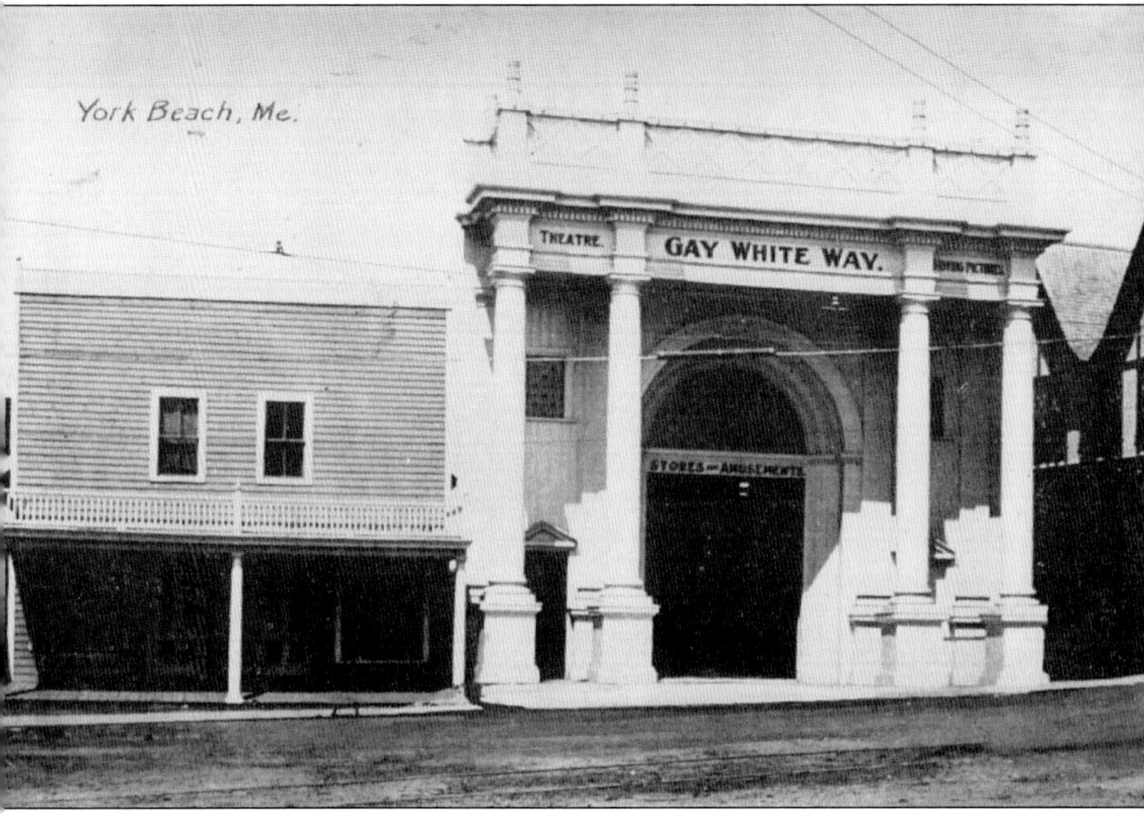


The Gay White Way. Frank Ellis acquired the dance hall at Saint Aspinquid Park in 1908–9 and moved it behind Garfield's Store. He added a theater wing (to the right of the entrance) that extended behind Dr. Hawkes' drug store. The dramatic entrance was eventually moved from Revere Beach and the tall white columns were a York Beach landmark for many years.

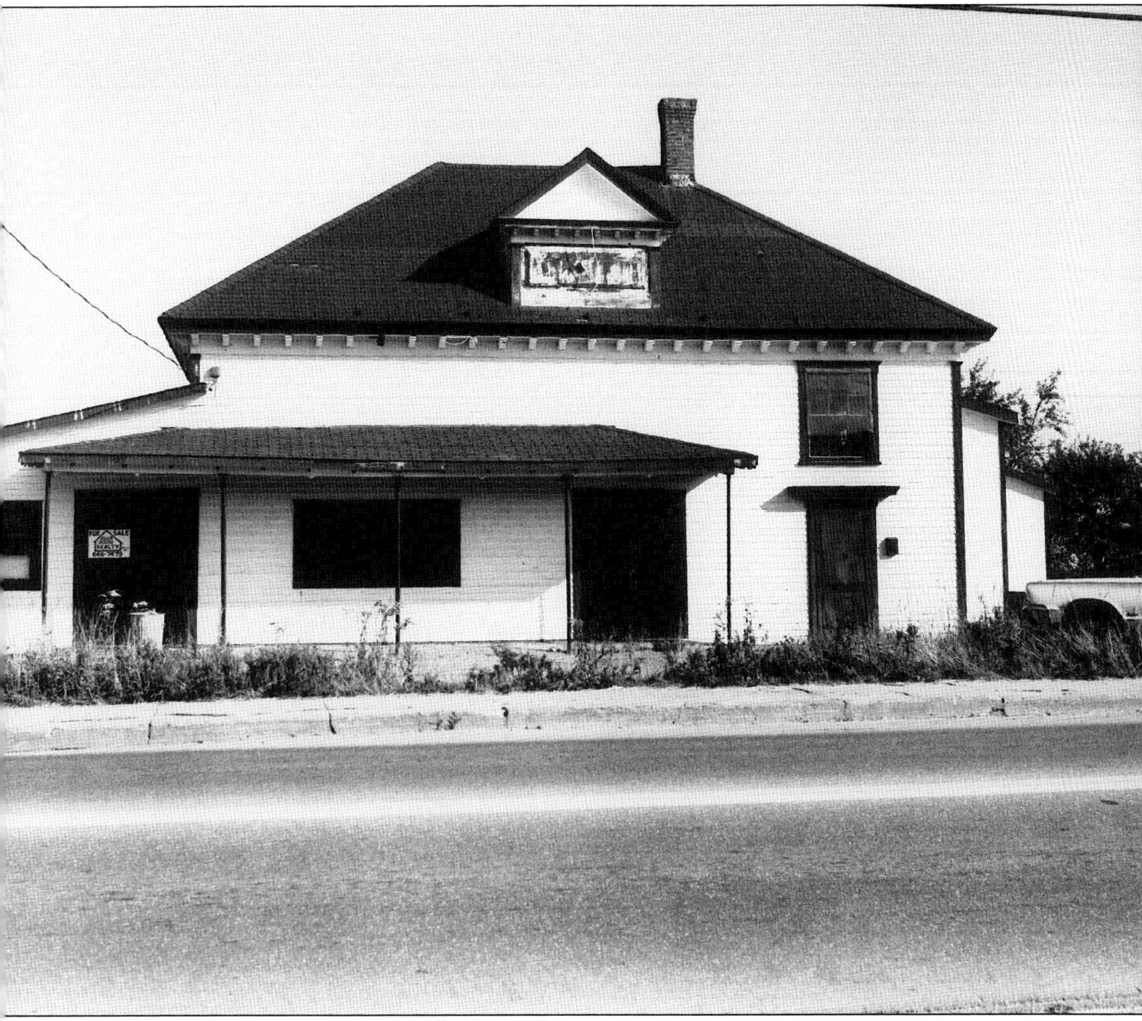

The York Beach Casino was originally a trolley car barn that became a popular dance hall. Located on Long Beach Avenue near Church Street, the building burned on May 6, 1976.

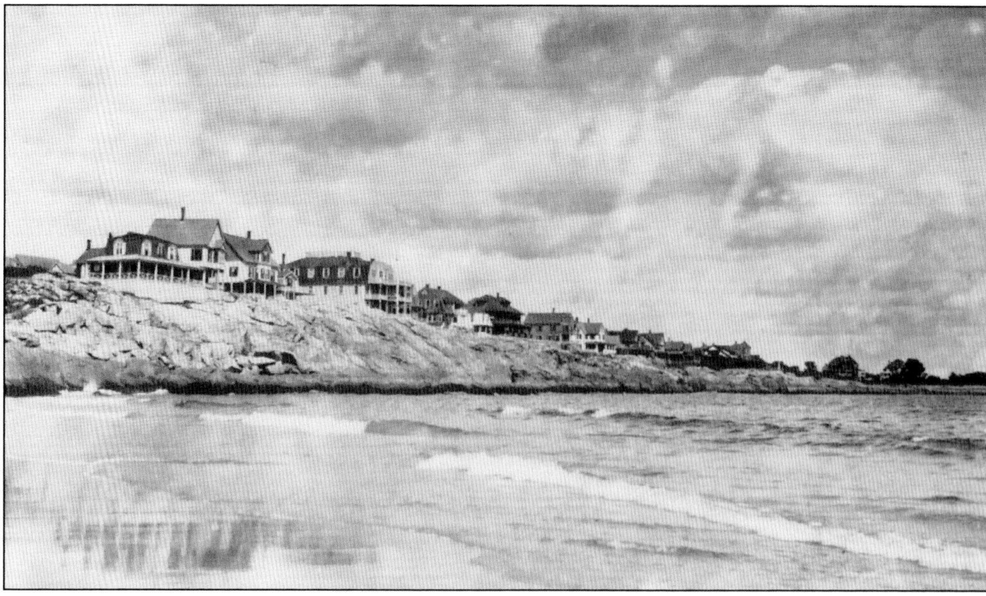

Union Bluffs in 1922. This photograph is from the Wagner Collection and was the type of image that was made into postcards for sale at the Goldenrod.

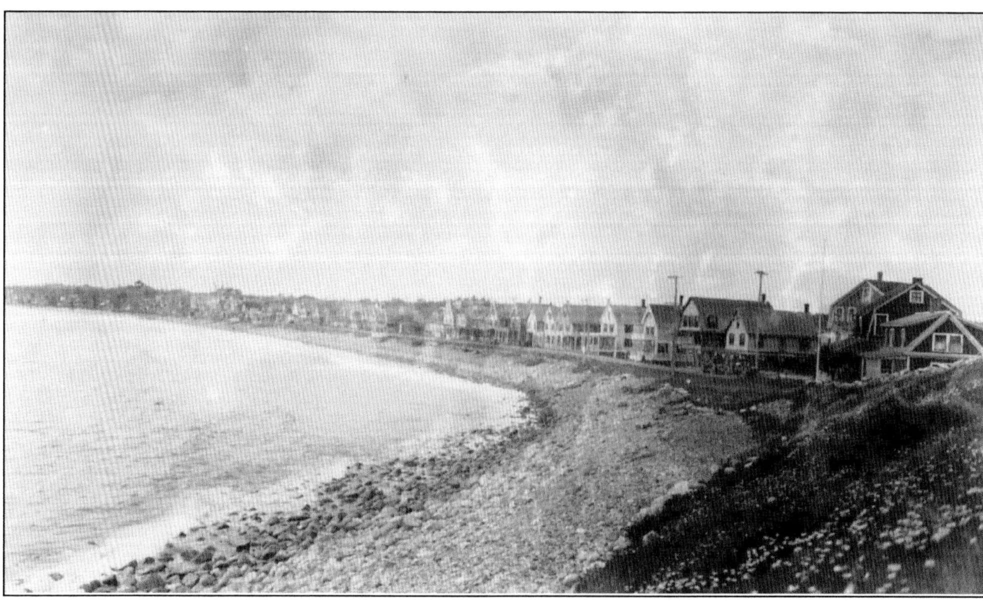

Another potential postcard image of Long Sands Beach in 1922.

## *Three*

# Sun, Surf, and Sand

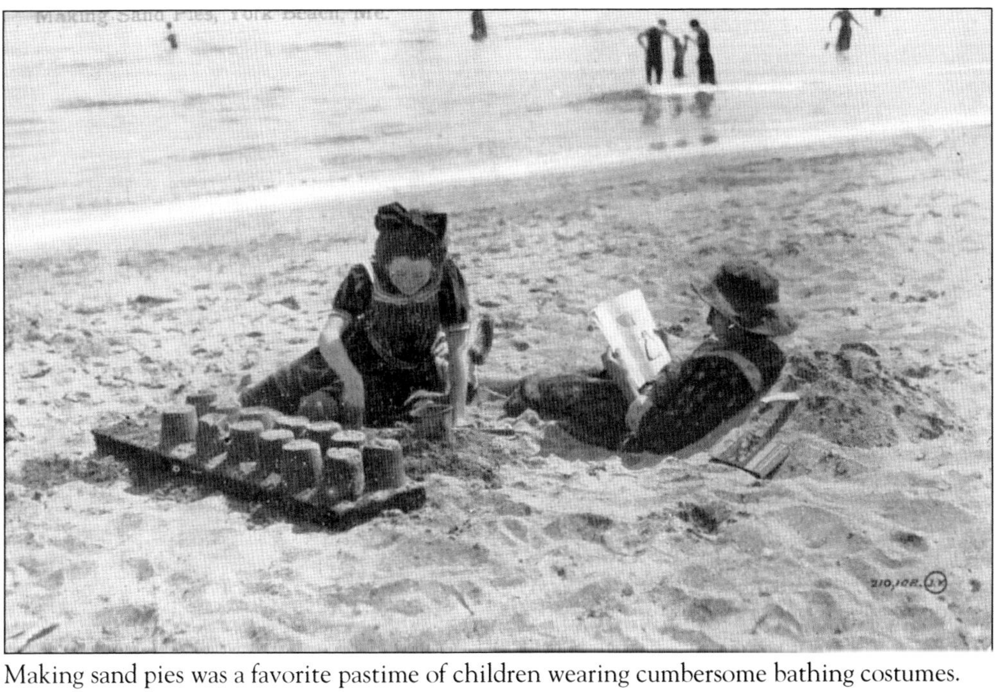

Making sand pies was a favorite pastime of children wearing cumbersome bathing costumes.

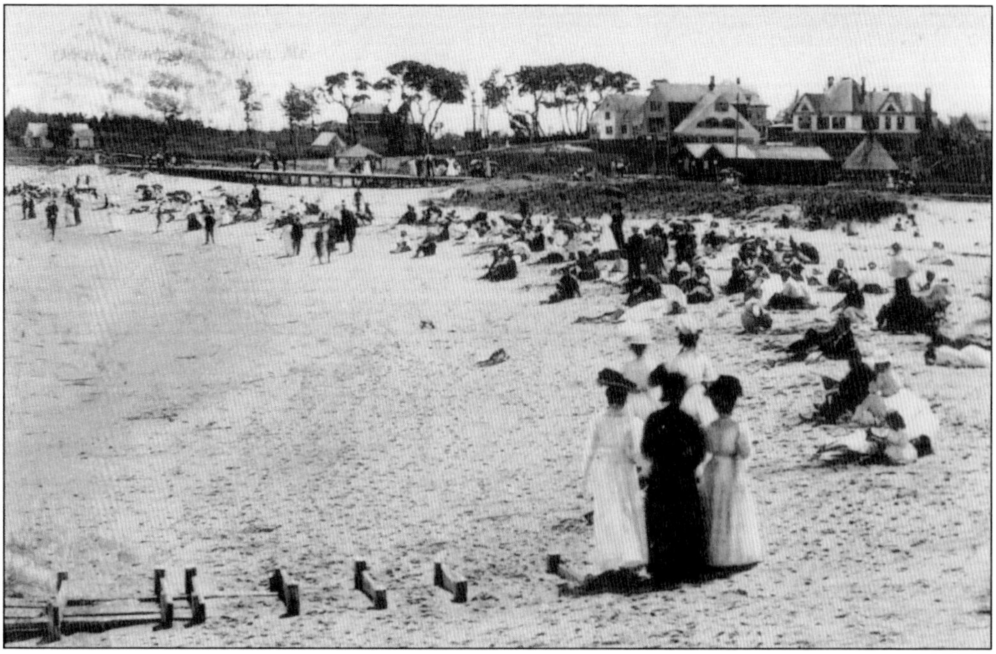

Men and women dressed rather formally for their walks on the beach. Large hats and parasols protected ladies from the sun. Men wore straw hats.

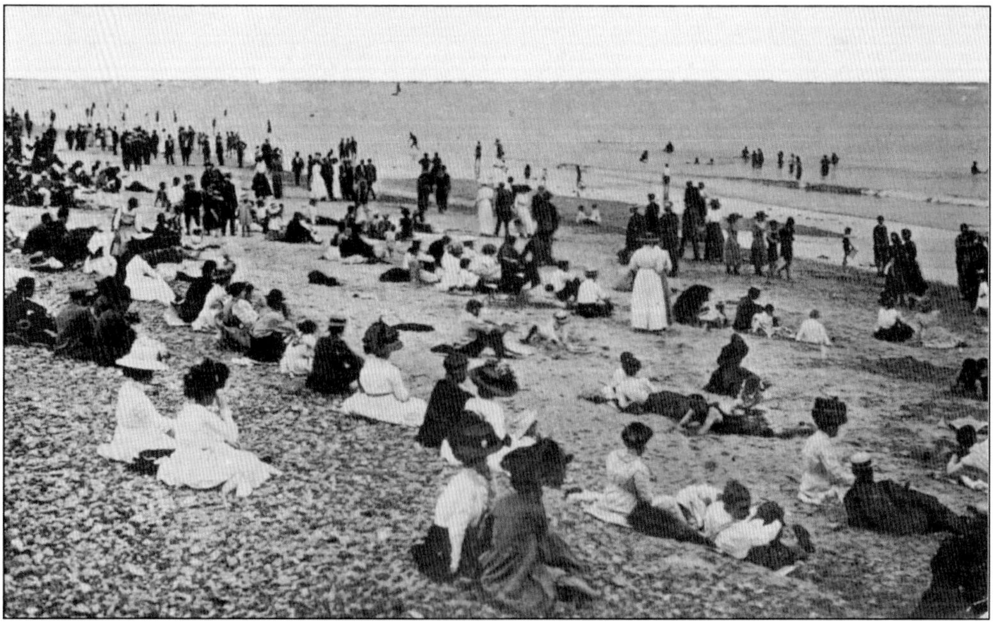

There are few bathers in this picture. Most of the vacationers were content to walk on the beach or sit on the rocks. Perhaps they were enjoying the cool ocean breezes.

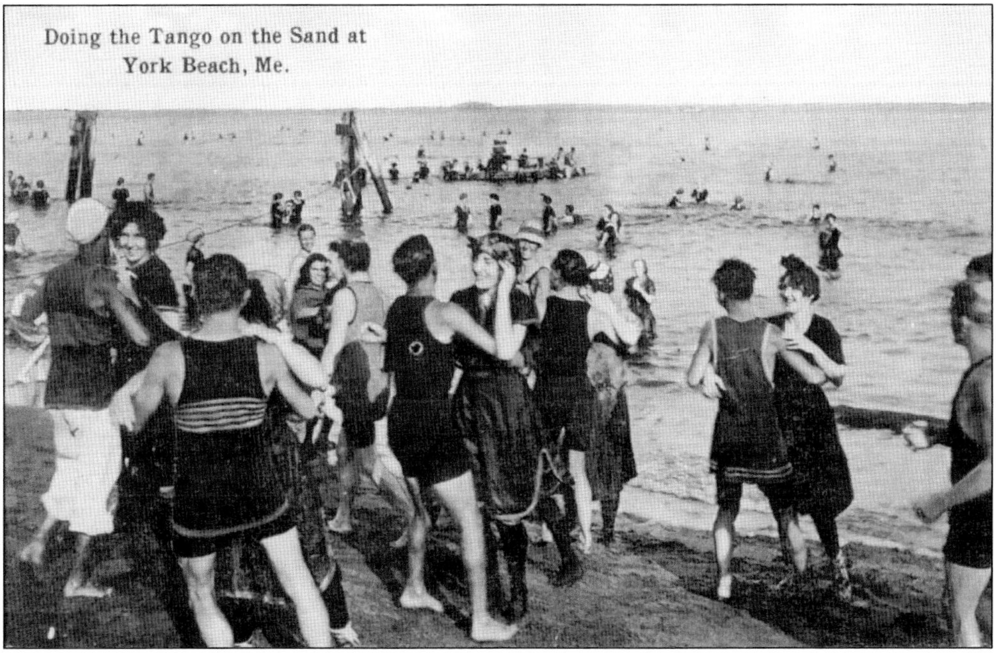


"Doing the tango on the sand" features some of the younger vacationers. A postcard message confirms: "*We are having a fine time here at Grampa Flanders cottage. Good weather and have a fine appetite. Will be home by the end of the week . . .*"

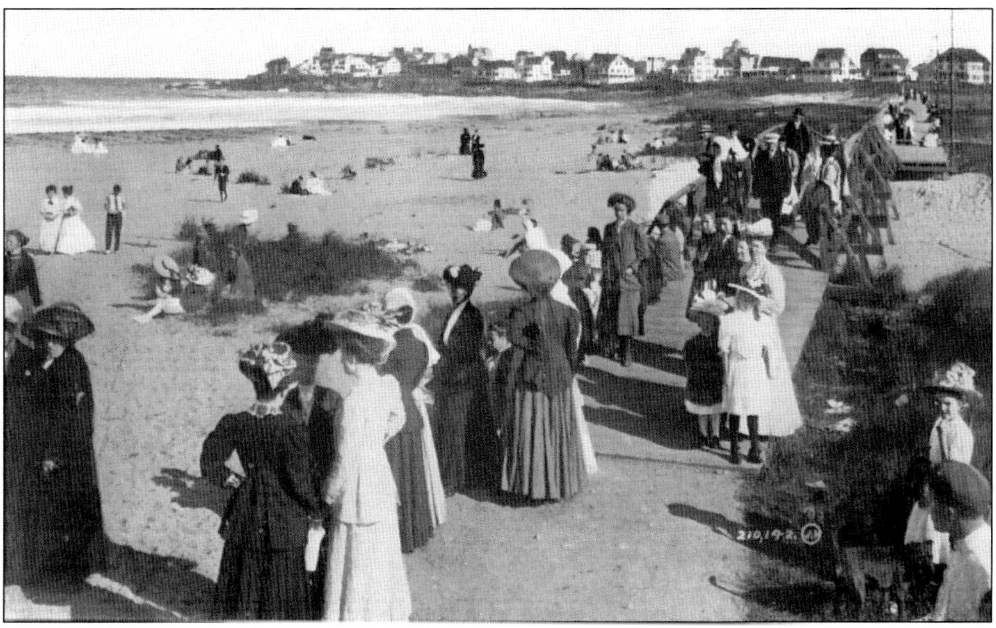

The boardwalk along Short Sands Beach was popular among over-dressed ladies who did not want sand in their shoes.

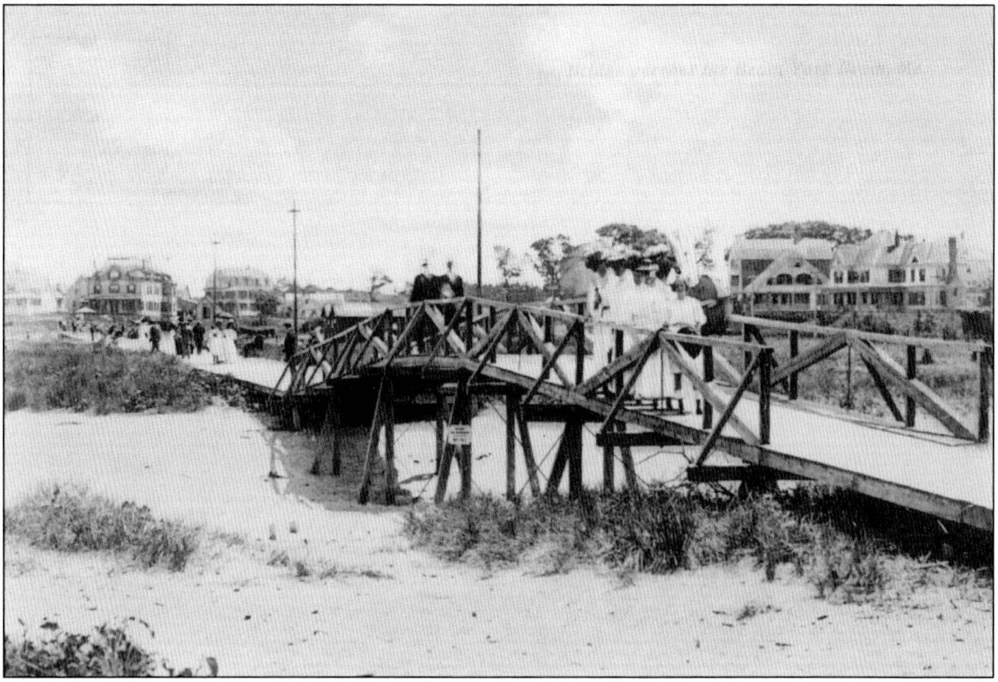

This bridge across a drainage ditch led to the boardwalk. The bridge was removed when a penstock was installed to carry the water directly to the ocean.

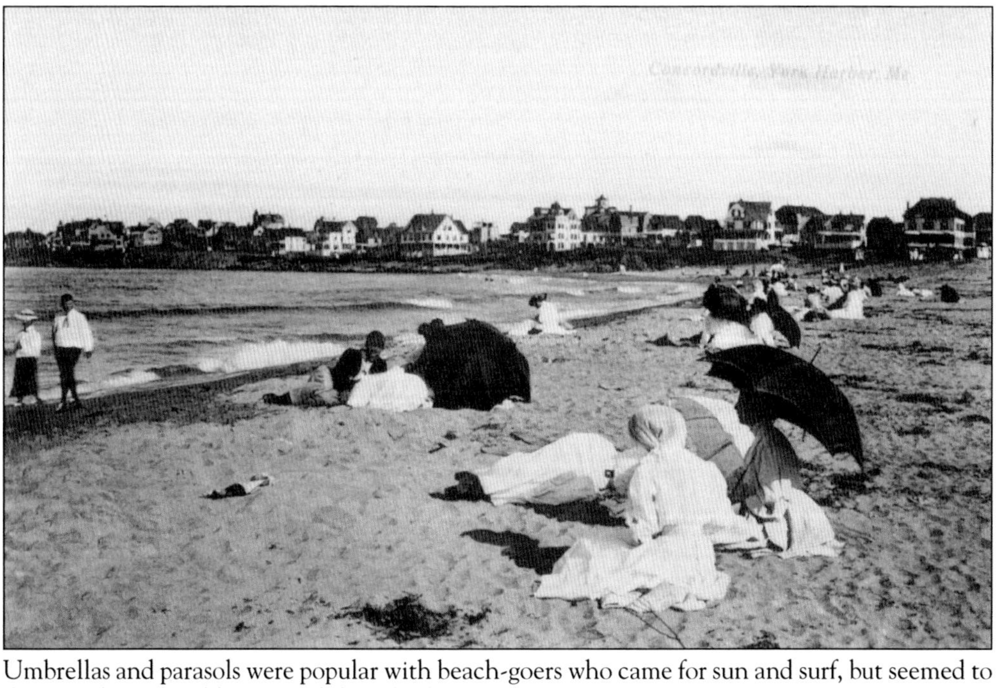

Umbrellas and parasols were popular with beach-goers who came for sun and surf, but seemed to do everything possible to avoid them both.

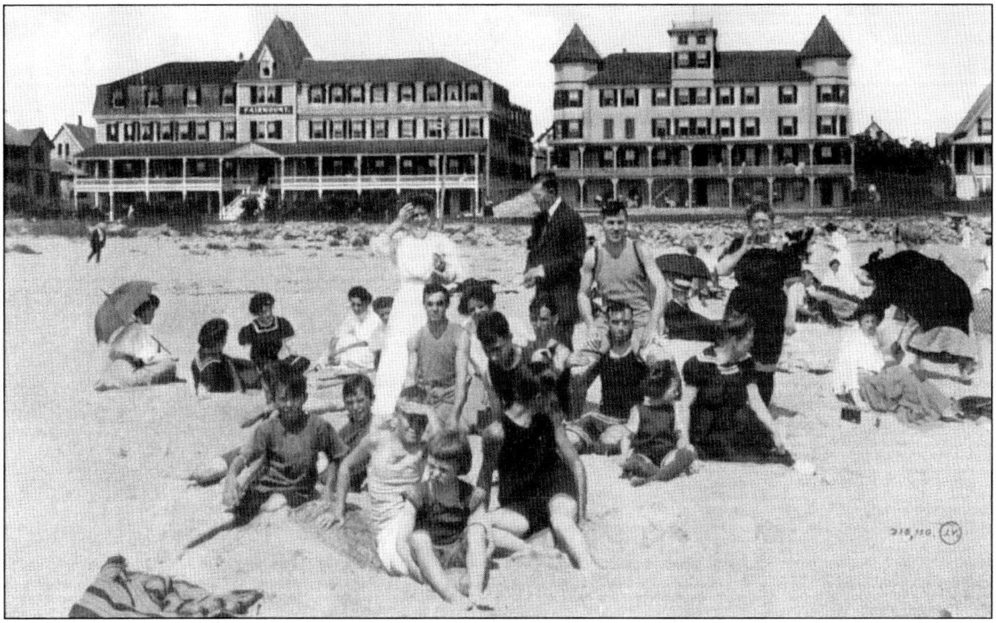

The Fairmont and Wahnita Hotels provide a backdrop for this early beach scene.

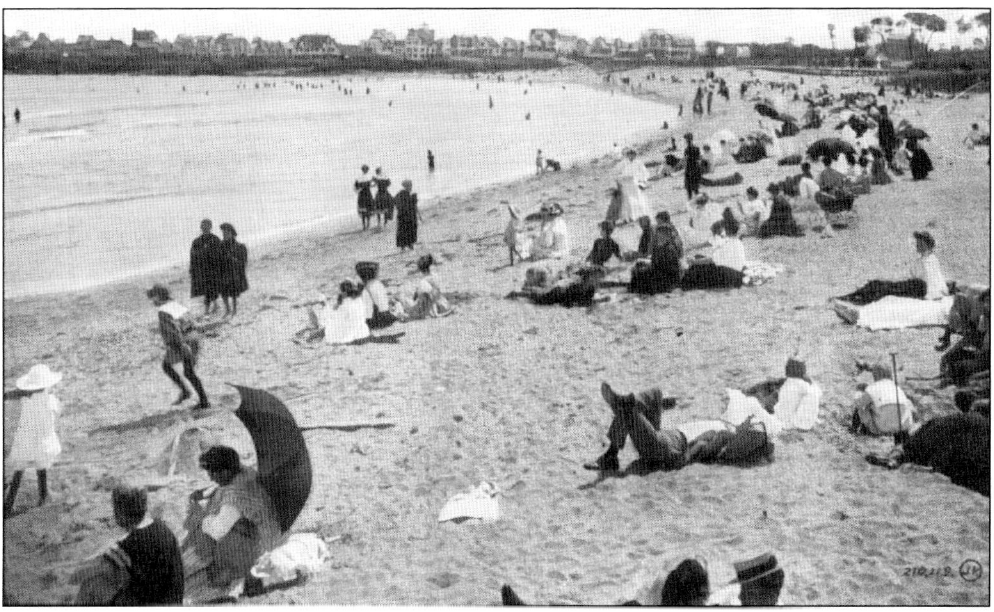

The number of bathers has increased. Perhaps the water was warmer than usual. Concordville is in the background.

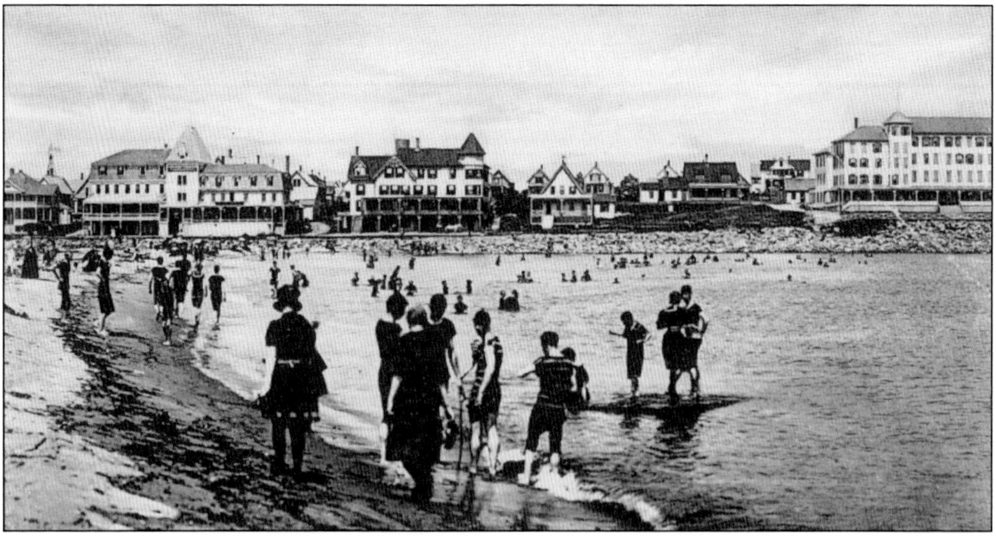

Three major hotels are pictured here. From left to right are: the Fairmont, the Wahnita, and Young's Hotels.

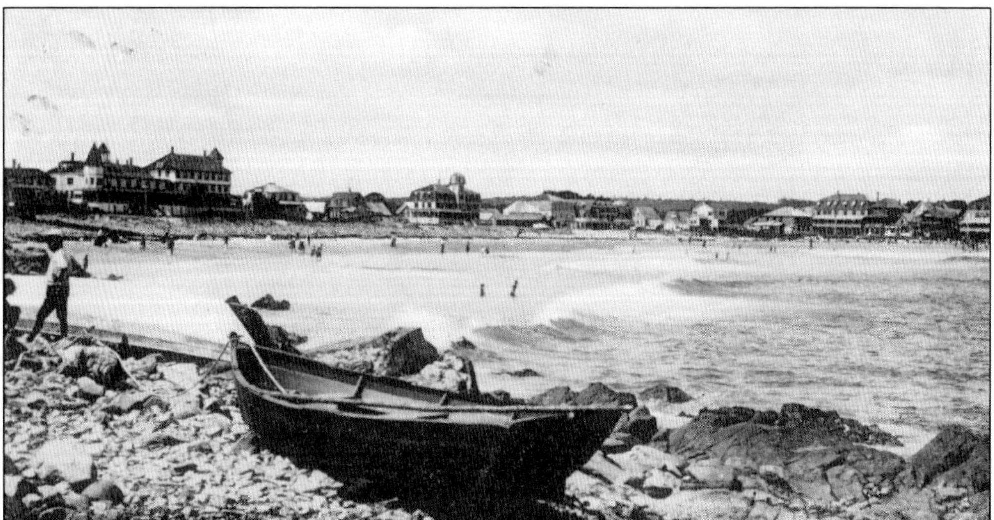

Short Sands from Pebble Beach in 1906. "*Went swimming this morning. Temperature of the water 54 degrees. Just a little cold . . .*"

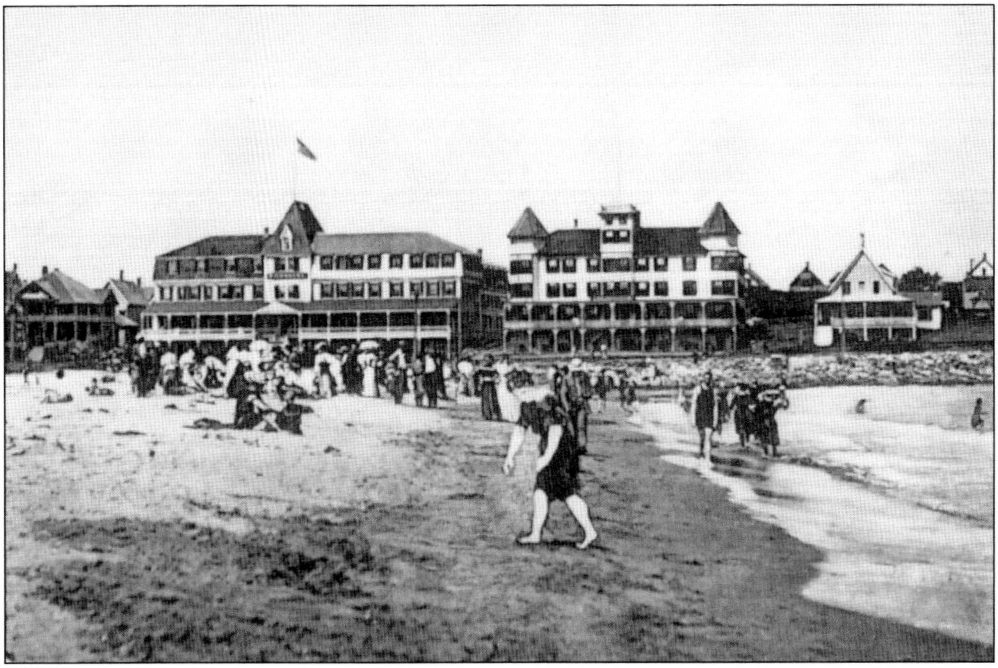

In 1911 a summer employee wrote: "*Am having a fine time. It has been very cool up here but is just lovely today. We are working like sixty . . .*"

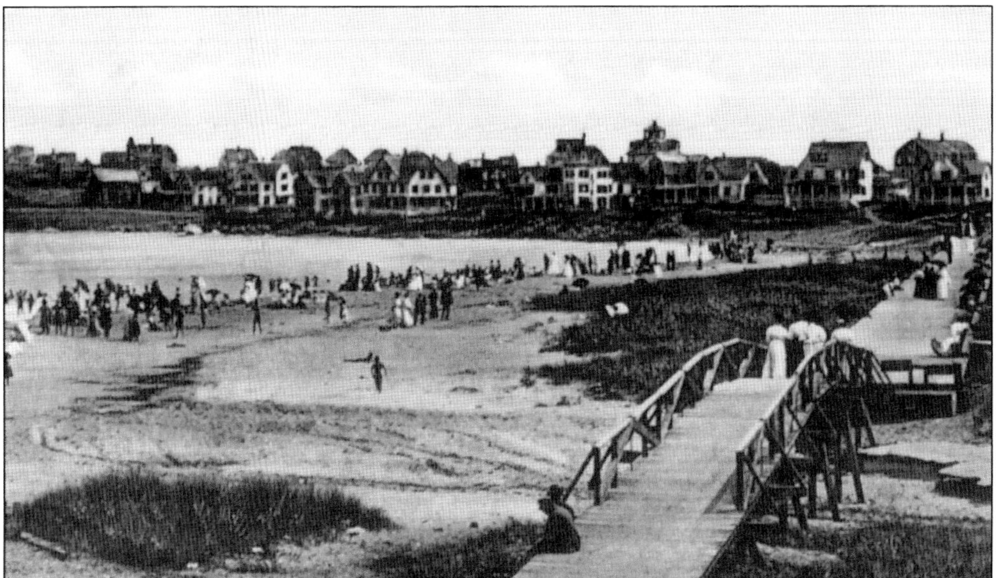

This was also written in 1911: "*You can come down anytime. Get the teams to bring you over. It is too far to walk with a suitcase . . .*"

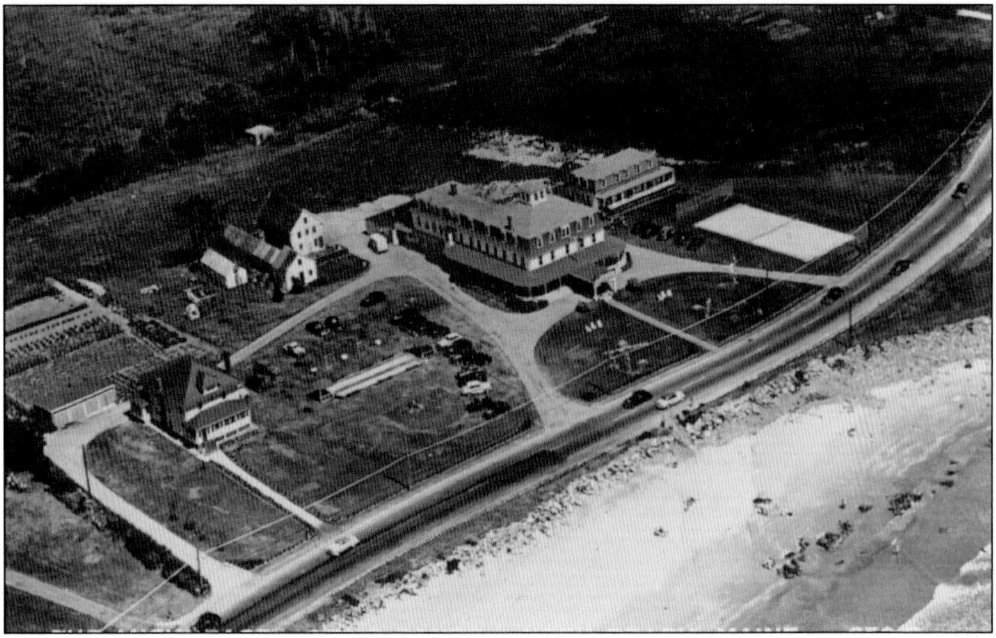

An aerial view of the Anchorage Hotel complex when it was operated by Sears Duarte in 1951.

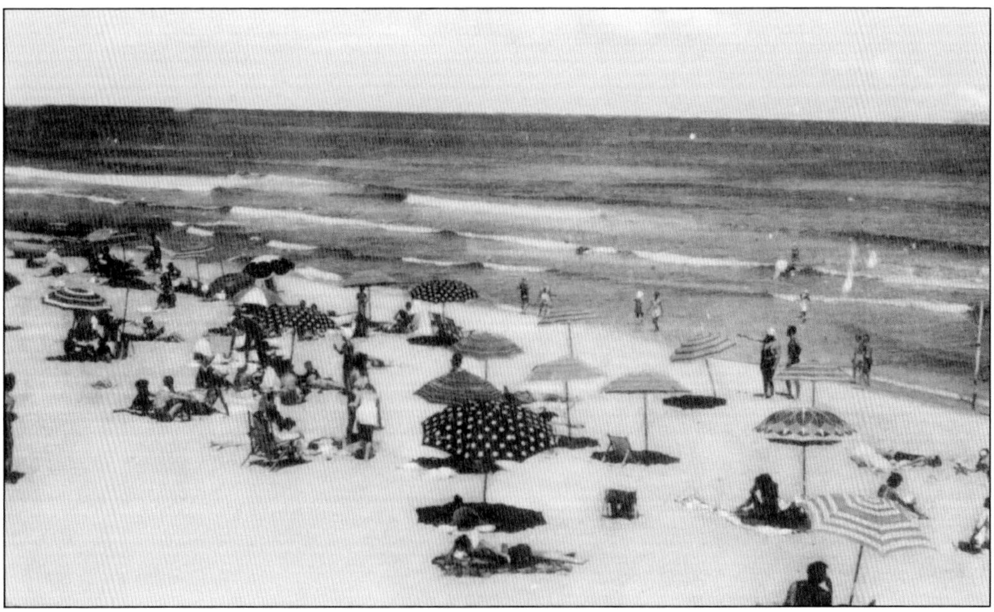

Colorful beach umbrellas gradually replaced the black parasols and became standard equipment for beach-goers. Each party used the umbrella and a blanket to stake out a small piece of real estate until the tide came in.

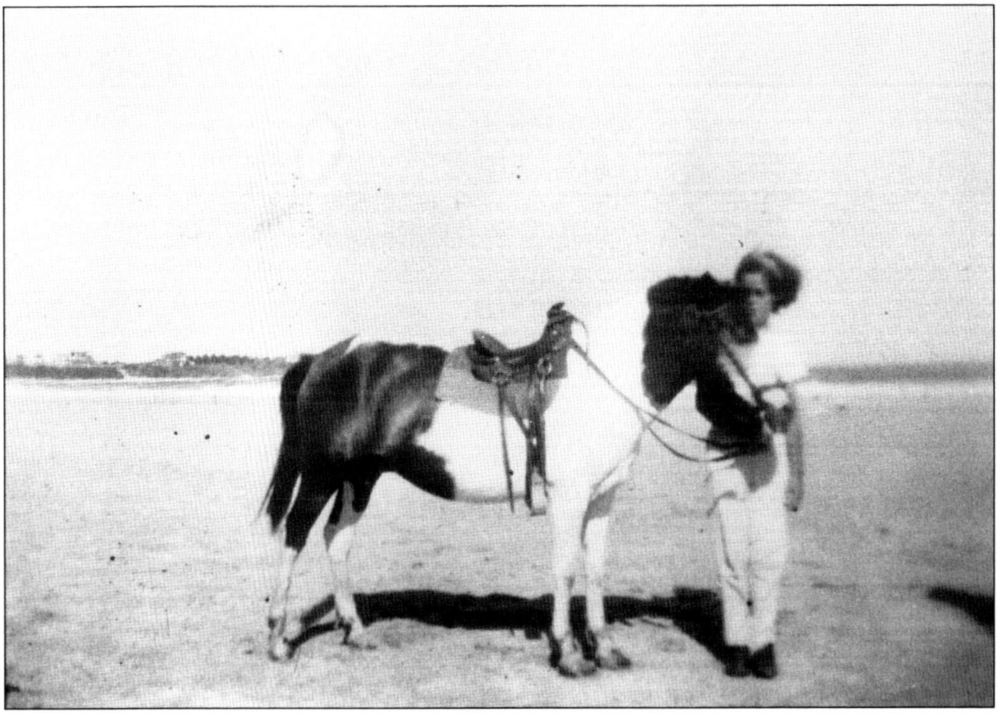

Pony rides on the beach were popular with the younger set. Mike was a pony who could perform twenty-eight tricks including counting, praying, playing dead, and bowling. All tricks were performed under the direction of a youthful master using neither bridle nor halter.

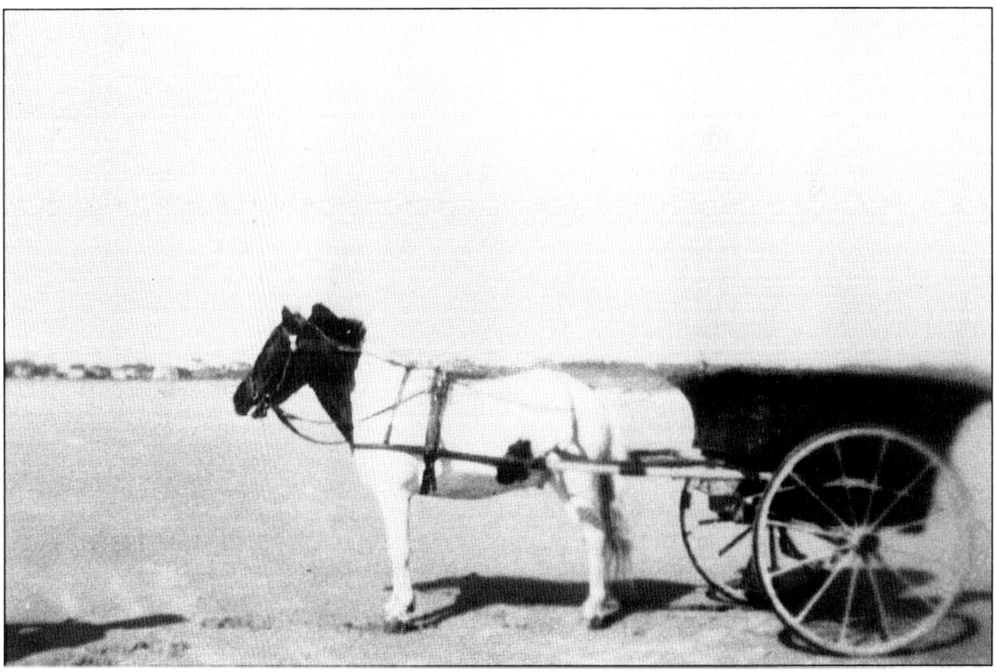

The pony was trained by Joanne and Edmund Butler at the Mibato Stables in Manchester, New Hampshire. He is shown here pulling a wicker cart in 1949.

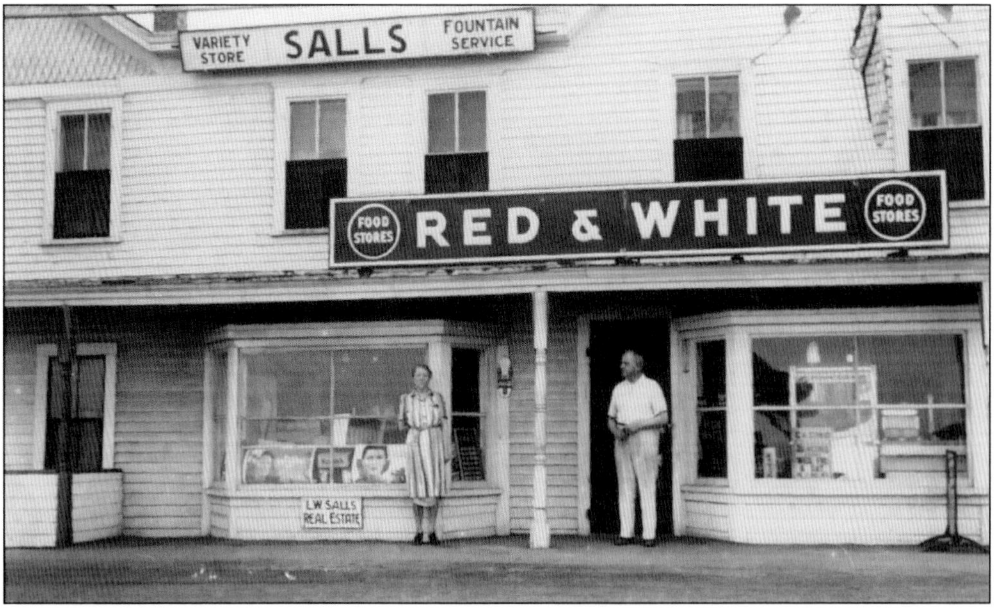


Mr. and Mrs. Salls in front of Salls Variety Store in 1942. A soldier wrote: "*Hello Bella... We finally came up to Maine on beach patrol. It was a relief to get out of Fort Edwards. We all like it very much. Bernie, Co. F 181st Infantry.*"

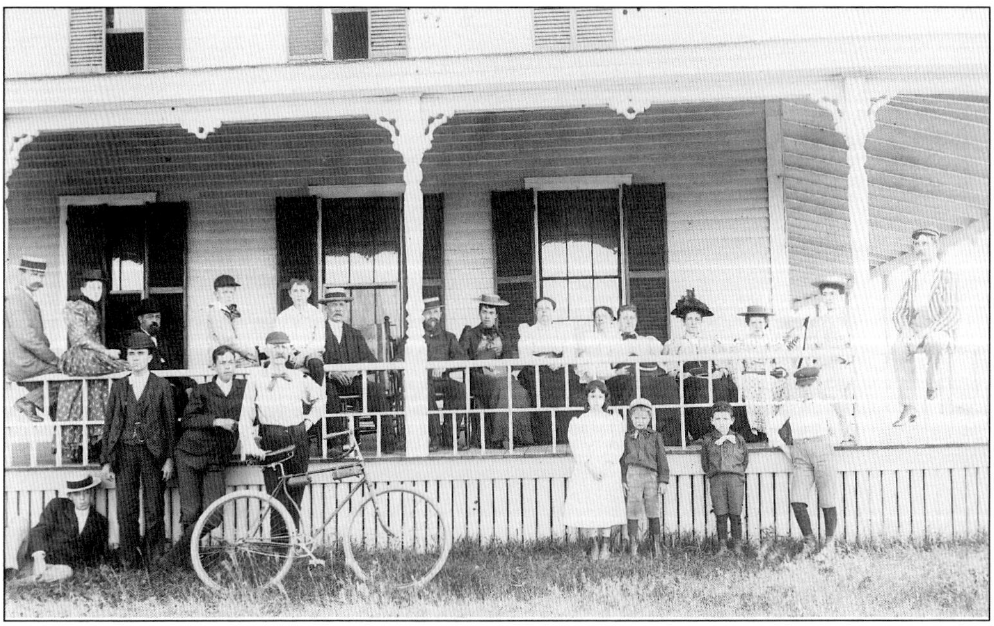

This may be a Freeman family reunion on the porch of the Hotel Mitchell annex. Special groups and over-nighters were usually assigned to the annex, where they would be less apt to disturb the regular guests.

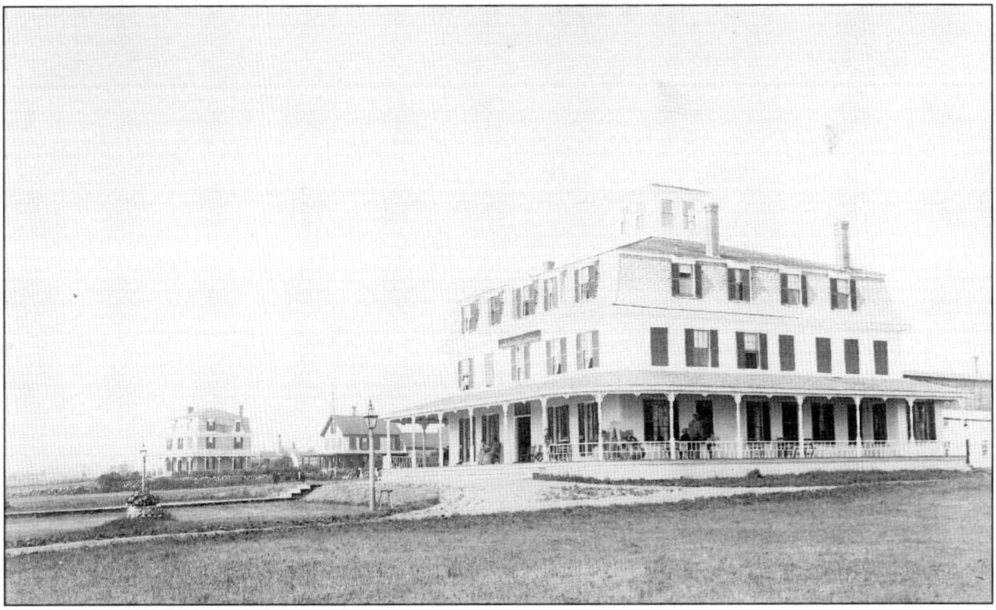

A very early picture of the Sea Cottage, which was also called the Hotel Mitchell and the Anchorage.

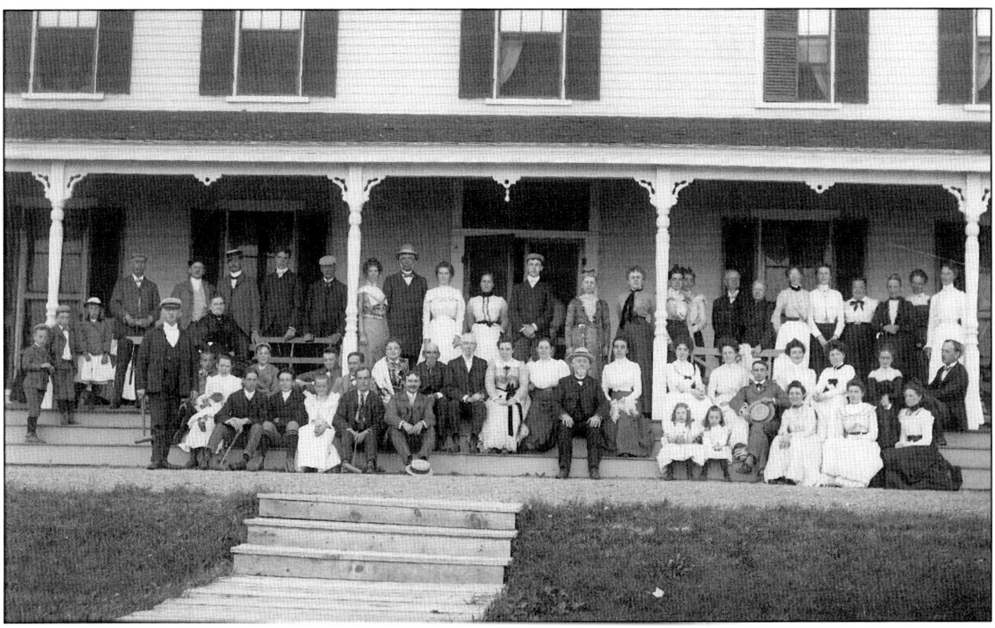

Group pictures of hotel guests were very popular. Hotel proprietor E.E.F. Mitchell, wearing a bow tie, is standing just to the left of the doorway. His wife, Ada Stark Mitchell, is on his left.

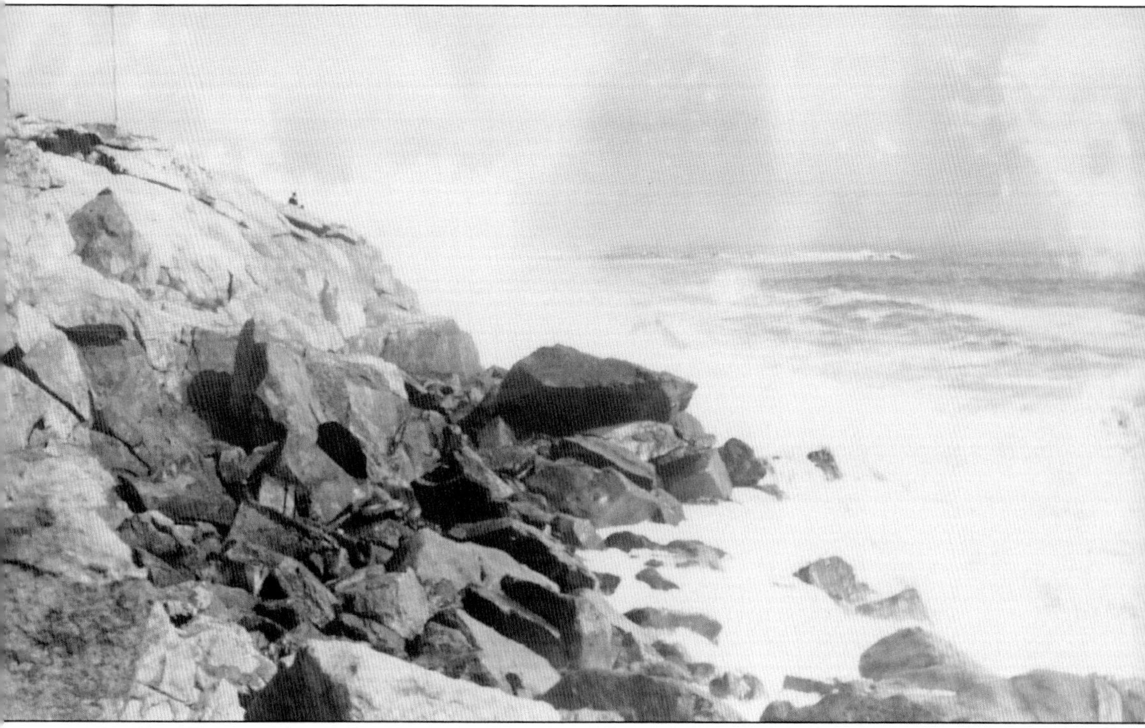
Surf breaking on the rocks in 1922.

*Four*

# The Nubble

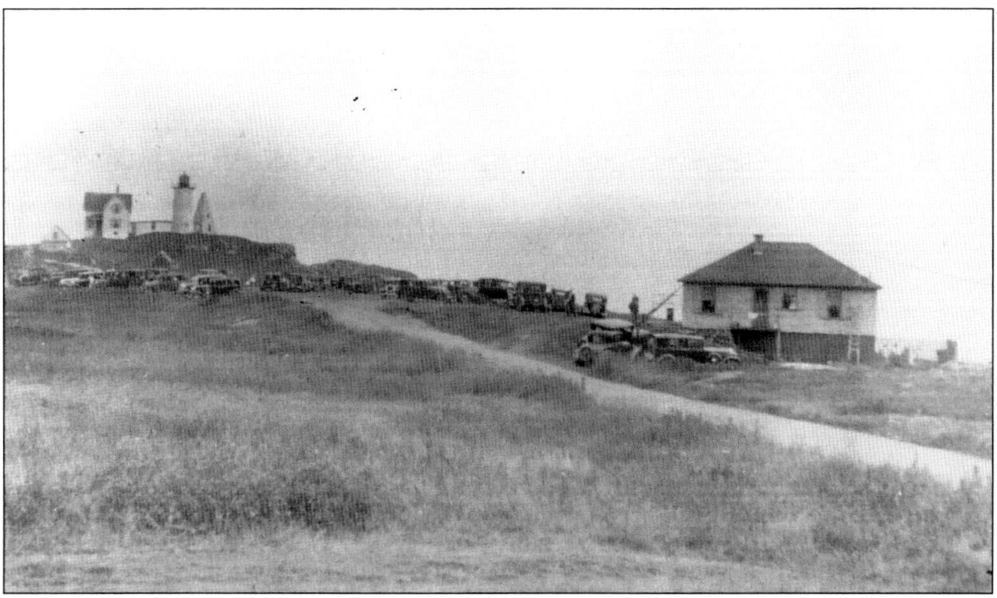

Sohier Park with the Cape Neddick Light Station and the gift shop. In 1929, William Davies Sohier gave about 4 acres of land on the point to the York Beach Corporation to be kept as a public park.

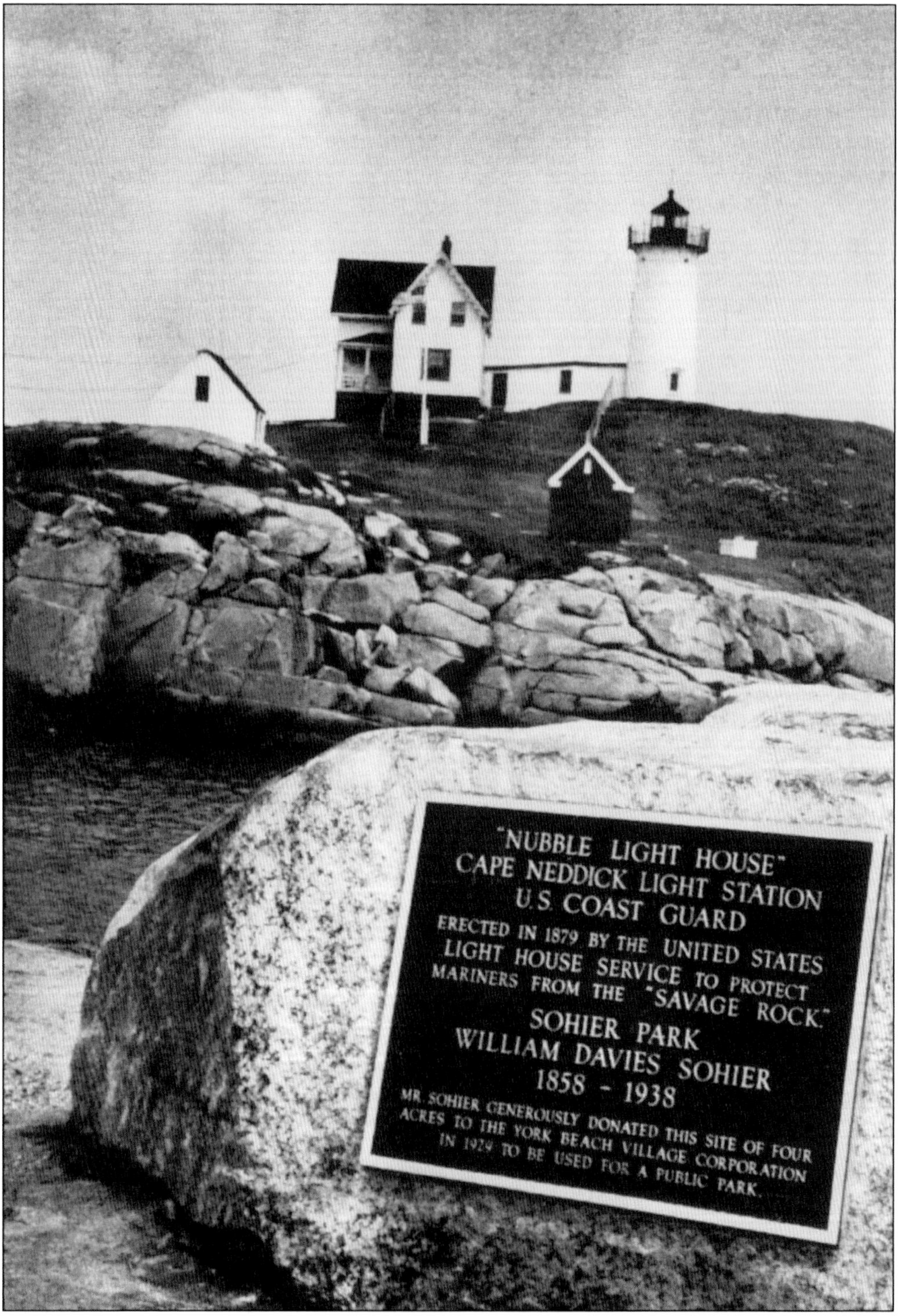
"NUBBLE LIGHT HOUSE"
CAPE NEDDICK LIGHT STATION
U.S. COAST GUARD
ERECTED IN 1879 BY THE UNITED STATES
LIGHT HOUSE SERVICE TO PROTECT
MARINERS FROM THE "SAVAGE ROCK."
SOHIER PARK
WILLIAM DAVIES SOHIER
1858 - 1938
MR. SOHIER GENEROUSLY DONATED THIS SITE OF FOUR
ACRES TO THE YORK BEACH VILLAGE CORPORATION
IN 1929 TO BE USED FOR A PUBLIC PARK.

Captain James Burke served as lighthouse keeper on the Nubble from 1912 until he retired in 1919. He bought land on the peninsula where he built a home and a store. The building that housed the store still exists in good condition.

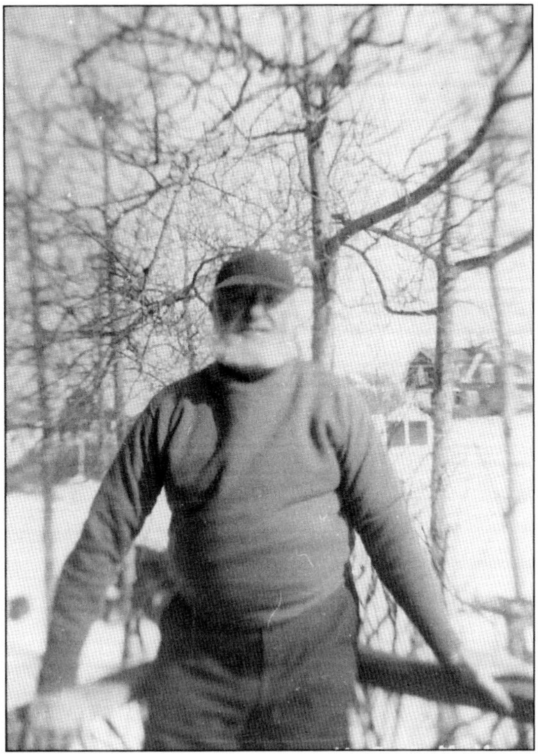

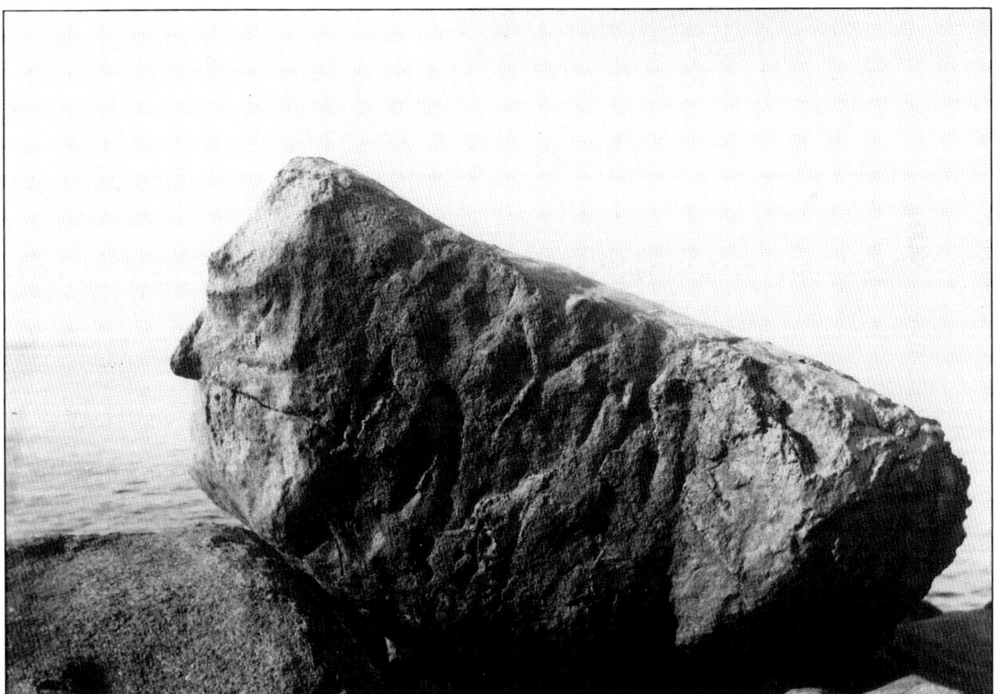

Rock formations stimulated the imagination and were frequent subjects for postcards. This one, called Washington's Profile, is on the east side of the island and not generally seen by tourists.

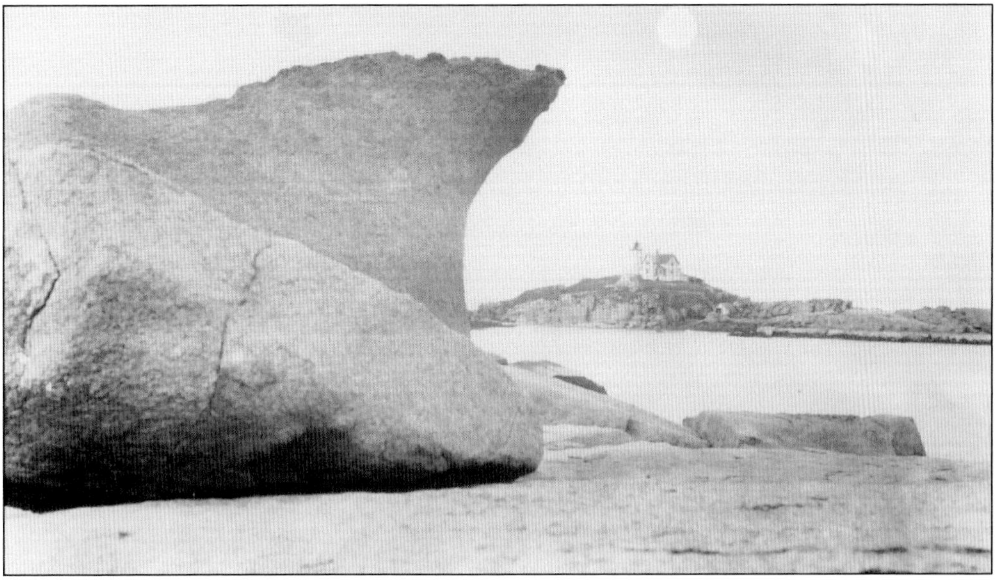

A 1922 photograph of Anvil Rock with the lighthouse in the background. This image later became a postcard.

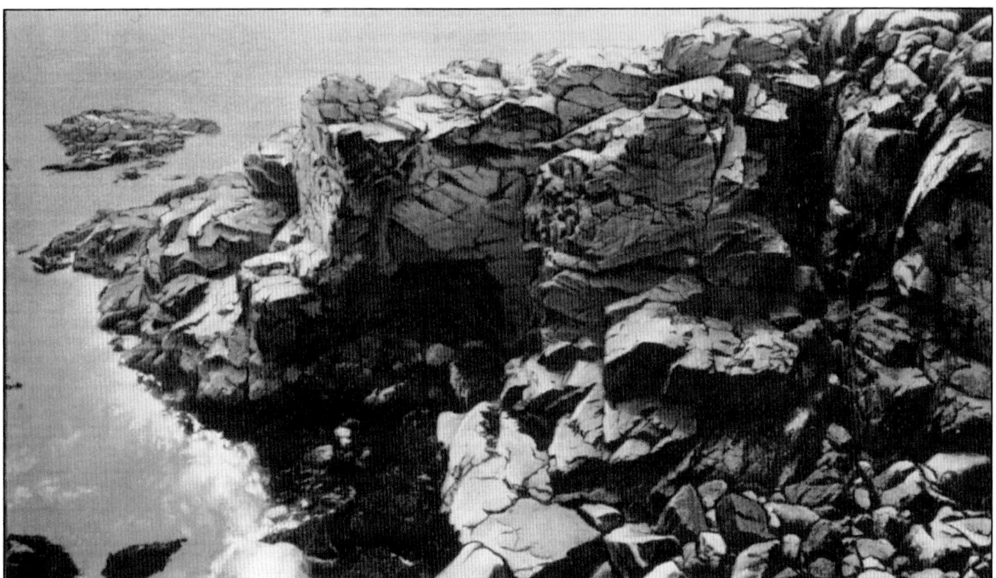

A rocky area on the point was called The Devil's Kitchen.

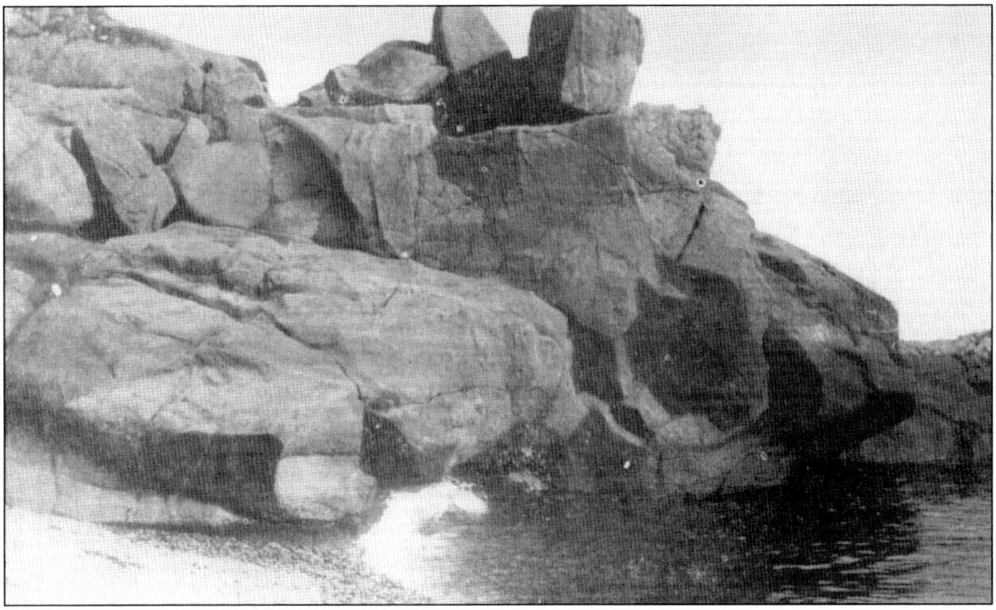

The Devil's Pulpit was another interesting rock formation. Apparently the devil became involved in the names of areas where heavy surf resulted in spectacular breakers.

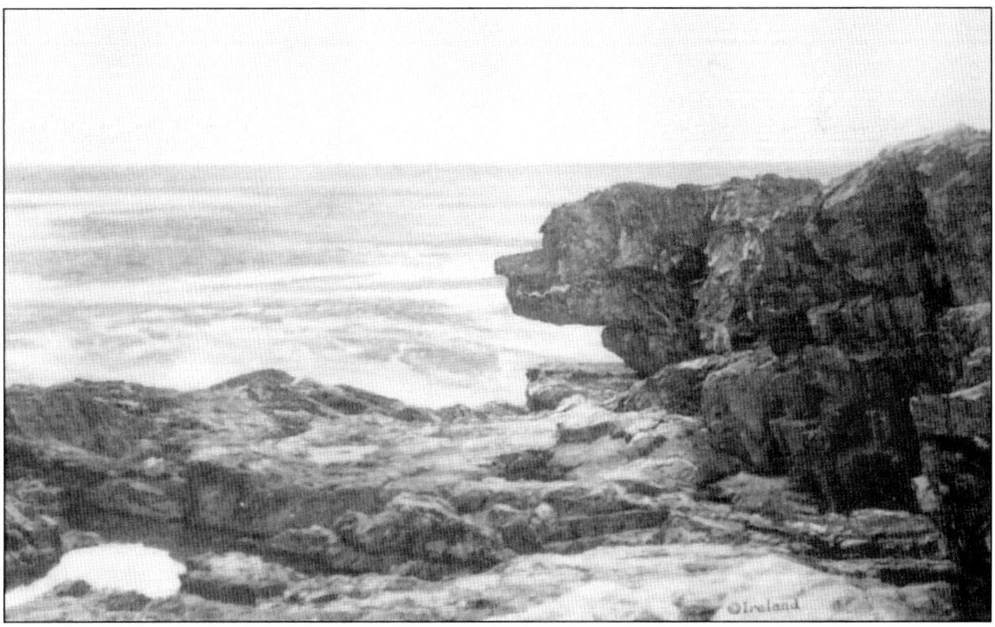


Perhaps you can identify a dog's head in this rock formation that was featured on a postcard.

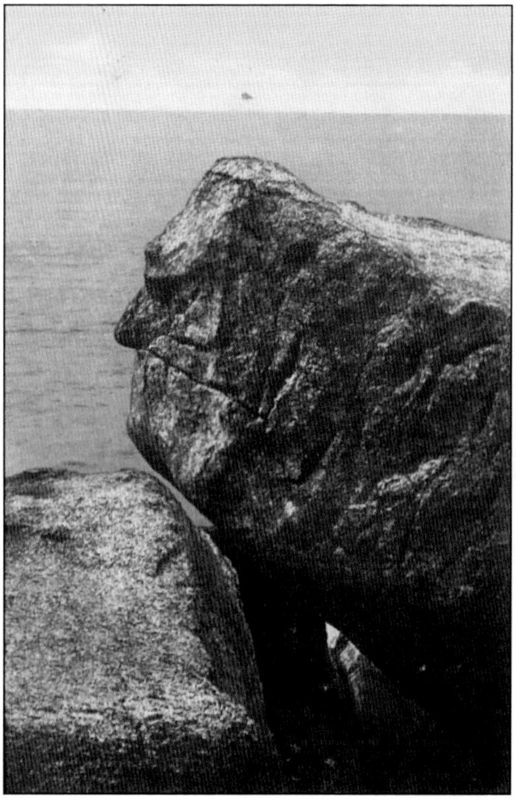

Another view of Washington's Profile that is rarely seen because of its remote location.

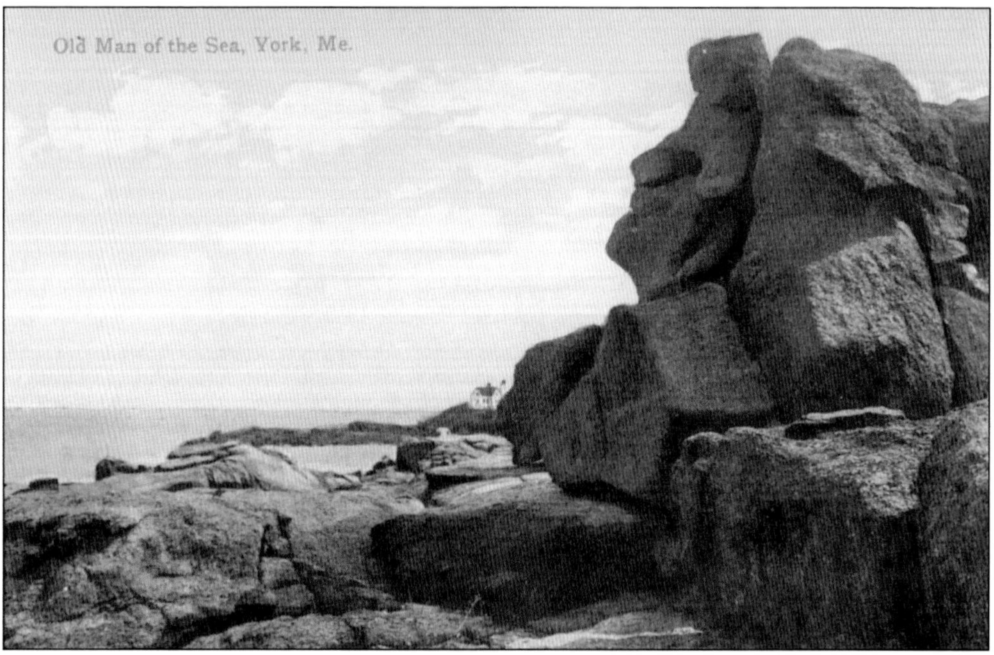


The Old Man of the Sea requires little imagination and was a popular subject for photographers.

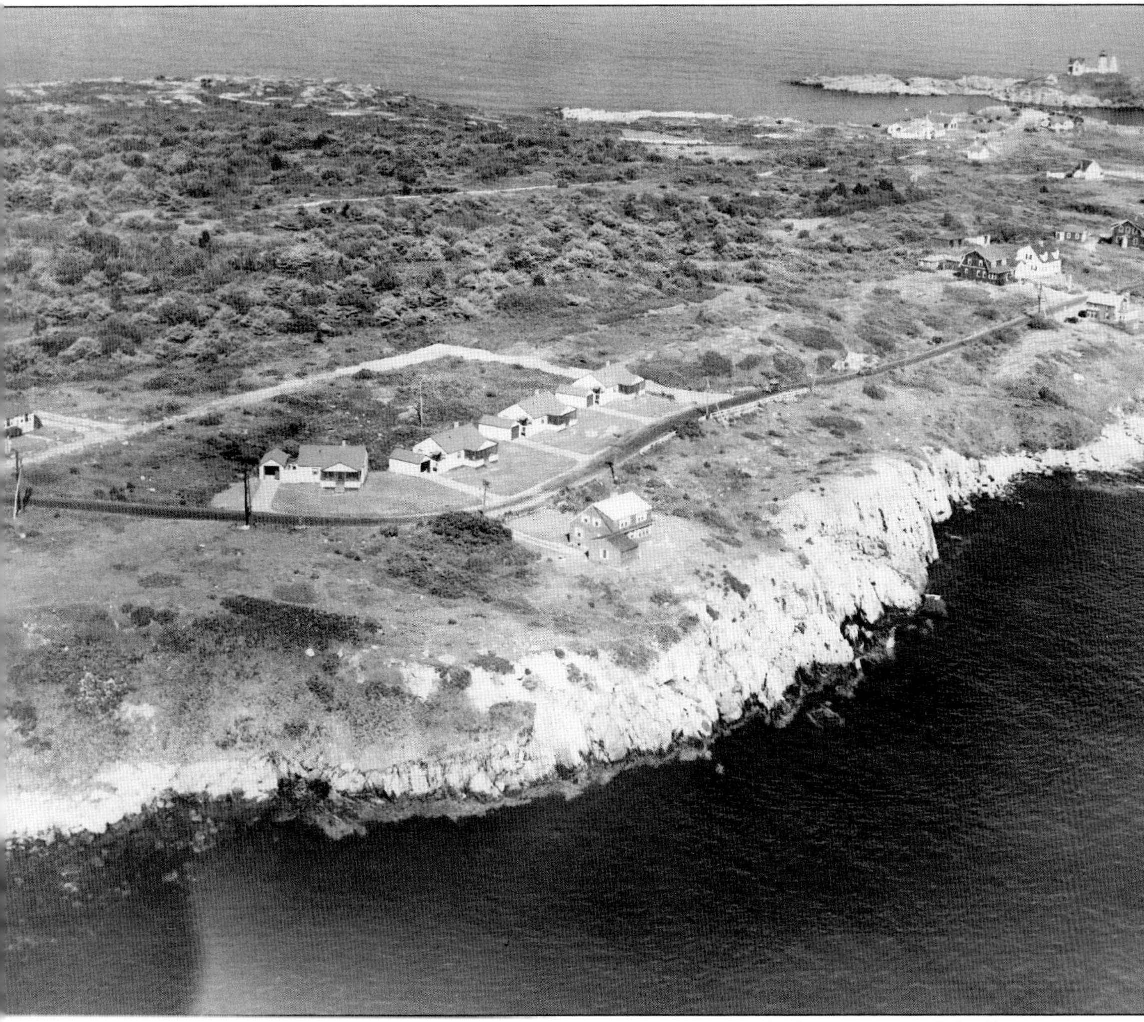

The Cape Neddick peninsula in 1941. Frank Coupe's cottages were built in 1938 and the house on the corner was built in 1941. There are few other structures on Dover Bluff.

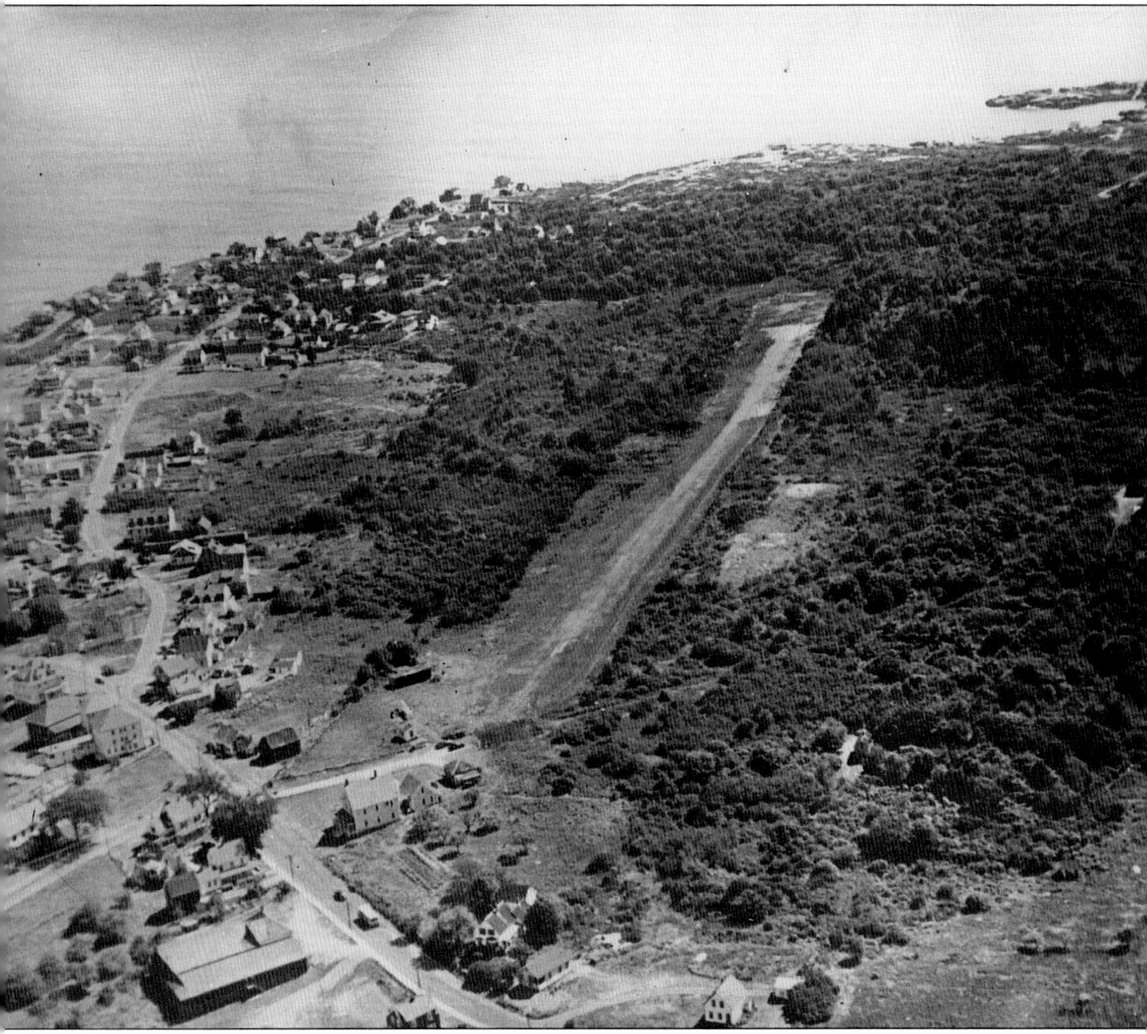

The 1,300-foot runway of the York Beach Aviation Company that was operated by Bob and Gerry Turner from 1946 to 1952. The unobstructed landing strip had a grass surface and extended along the peninsula as far back as Cycad Avenue. Bob Turner operated a flying school for veterans, made unscheduled passenger flights, and flew cargo, including lobsters, to cities on the east coast and in Canada.

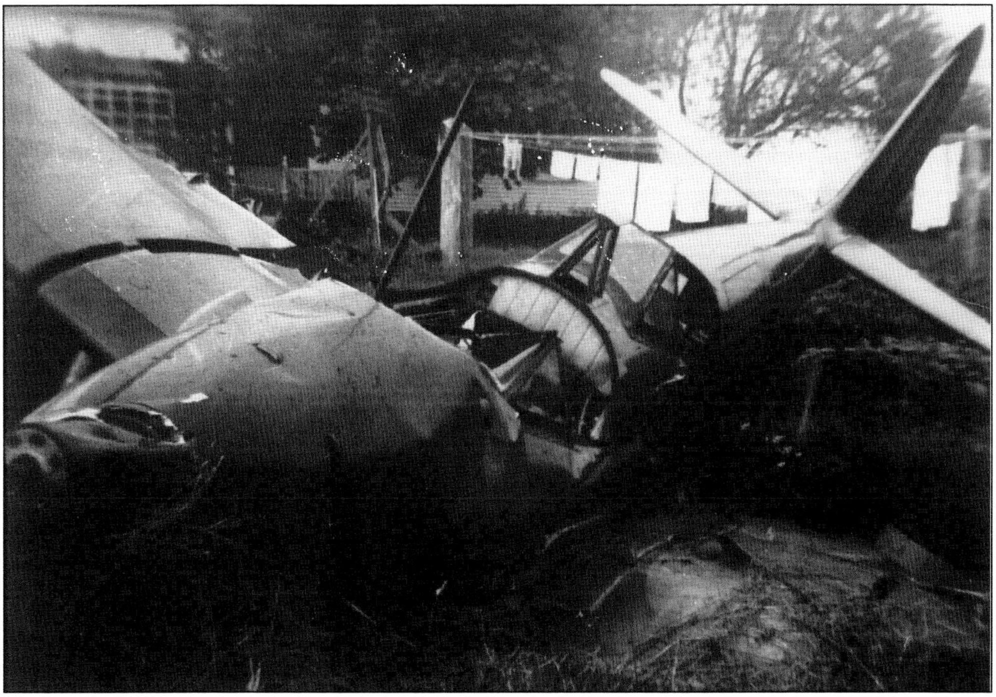

In August 1951 this Ryan PT19 Army Trainer crash-landed in Charlie Burnham's backyard garden and was badly damaged. Fortunately, the two occupants were only slightly injured. The clothes are still drying on the clothesline, but the vegetables have been plowed under.

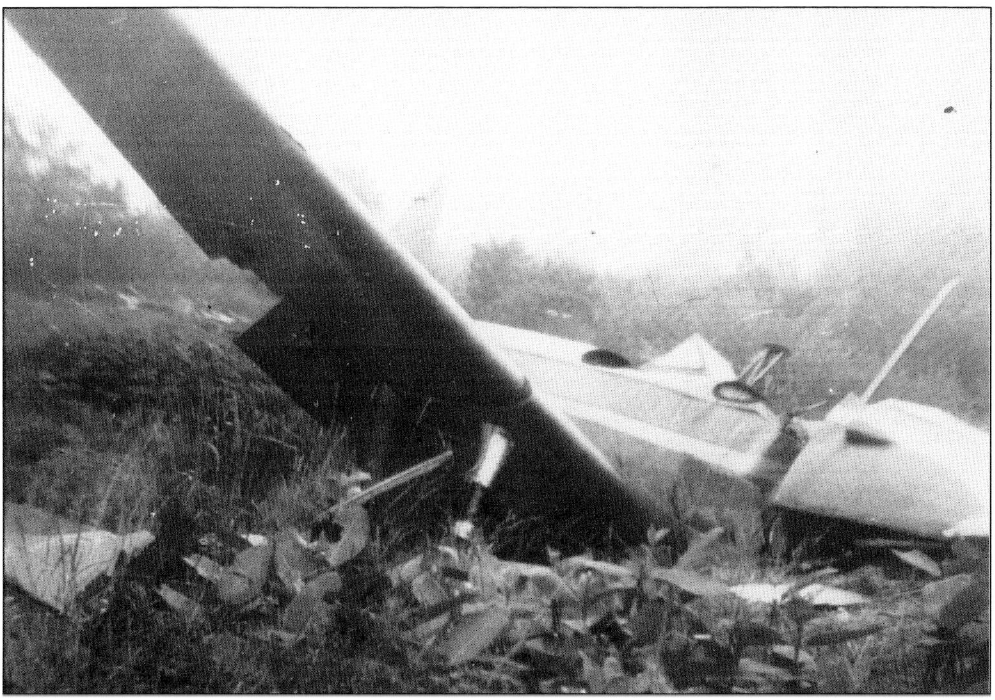

Another view of the small plane that crashed in Charlie Burnham's garden. It came in too low, stalled, and crashed.

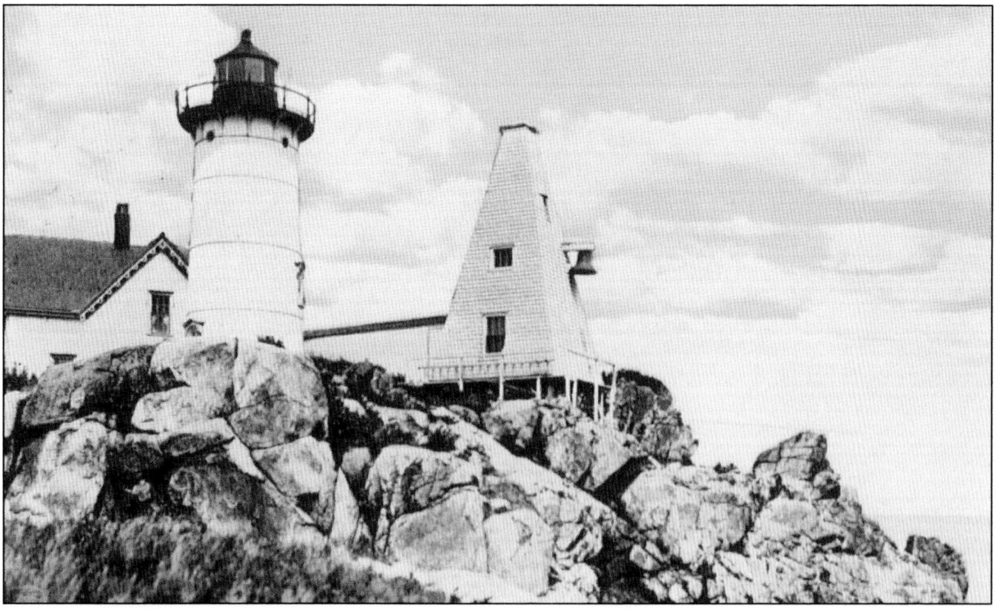

The Cape Neddick Light Station in 1920. In the center of the picture is the covered bell tower with the bell hanging on the outside.

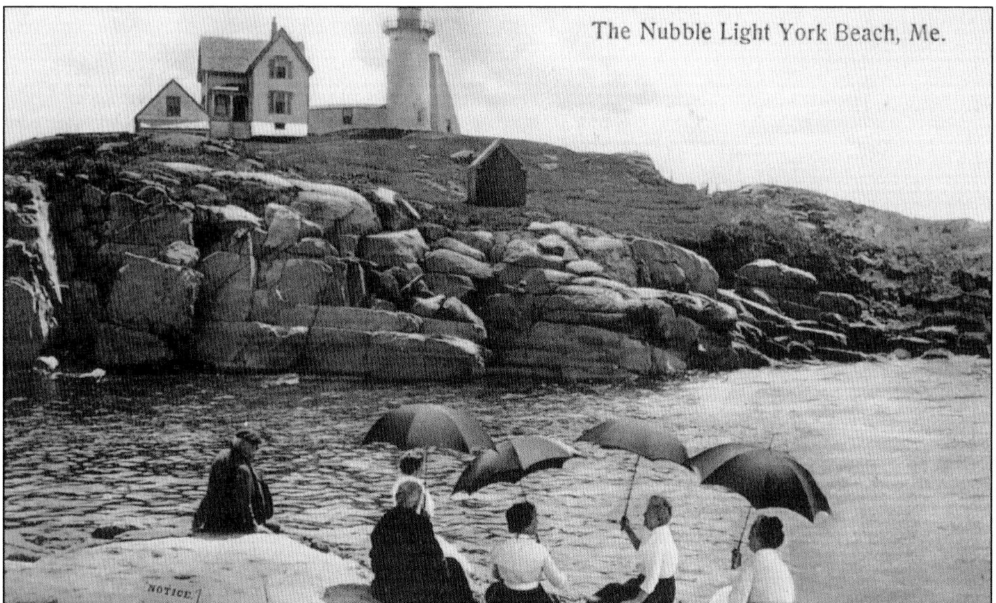


This 1912 postcard features ladies on the rocks with their black parasols. The lighthouse has always been a major tourist attraction.

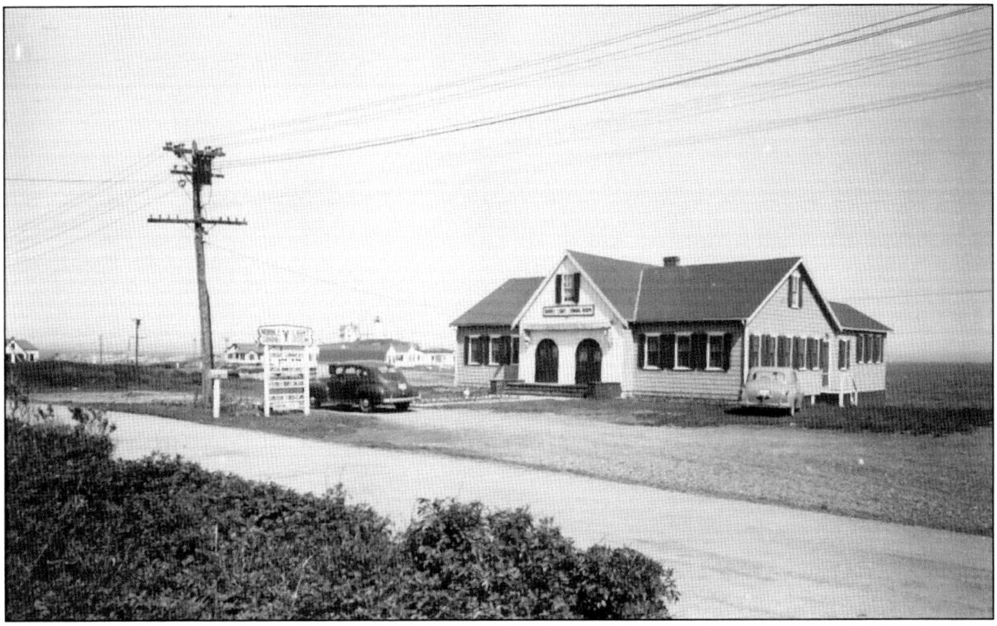

The Nubble Light Dining Room made it possible for tourists to dine at one of Maine's most scenic locations.

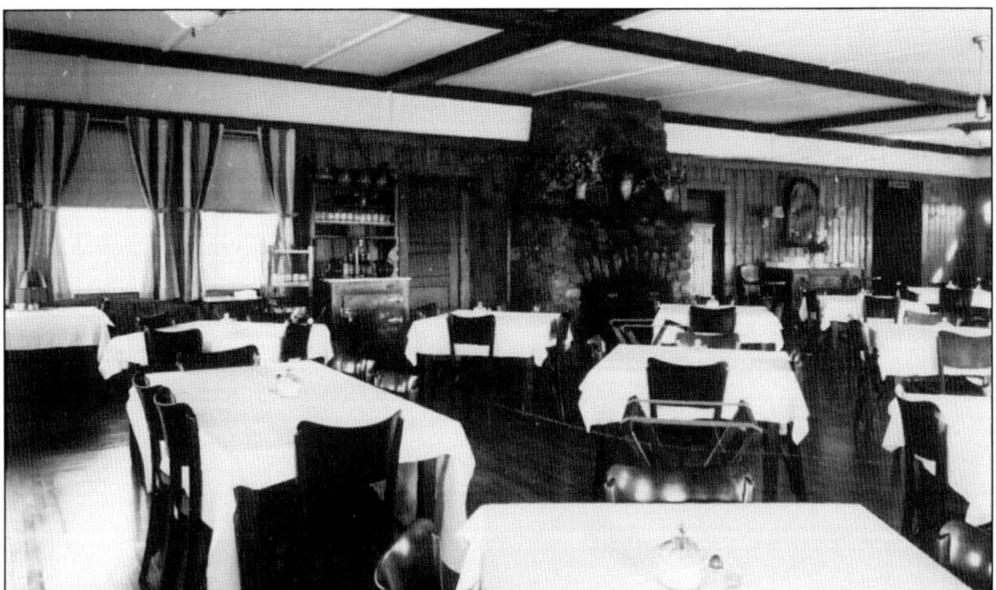

An interior view of the Nubble Light Dining Room on Dover Bluff with a spectacular view of the ocean, the beach, and the lighthouse.

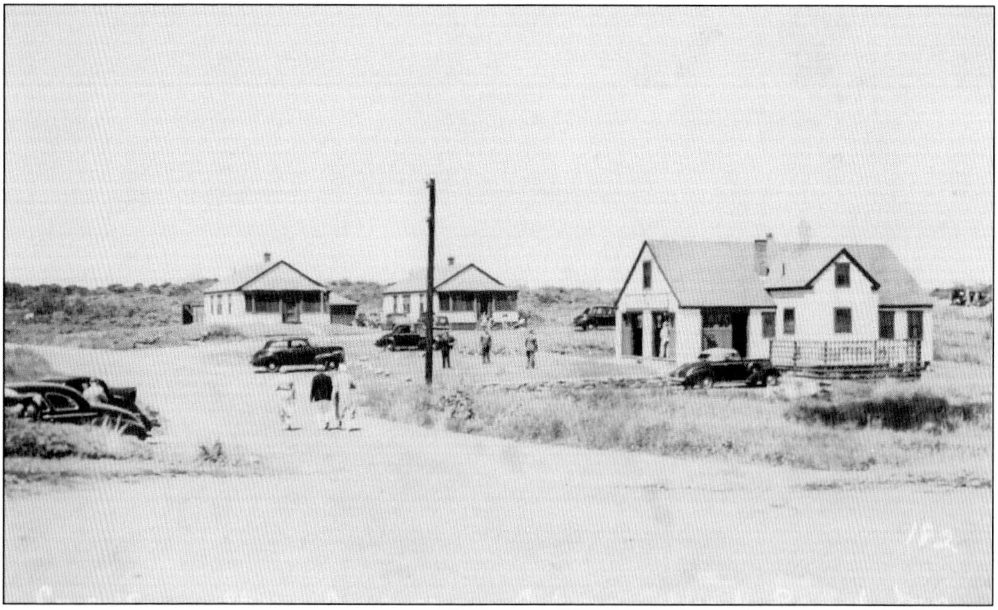

Coupe's Dining Room and Lobster Pound on the edge of Sohier Park. Frank Coupe also built cabins at this scenic location near the Nubble.

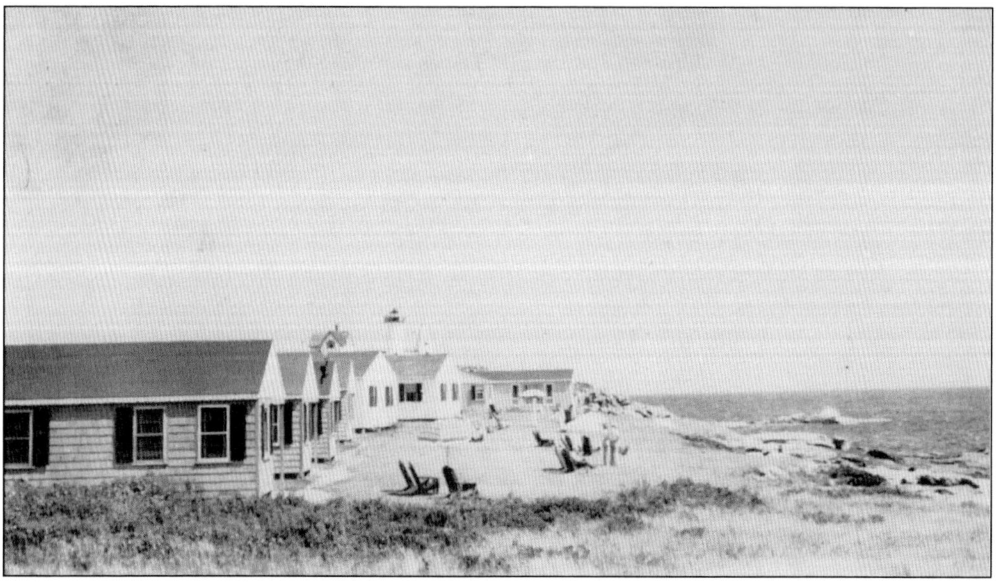

In later years the Lighthouse Village Cottages were built on the Bluff with the light station in the background.

# *Five*

# Winter Scenes

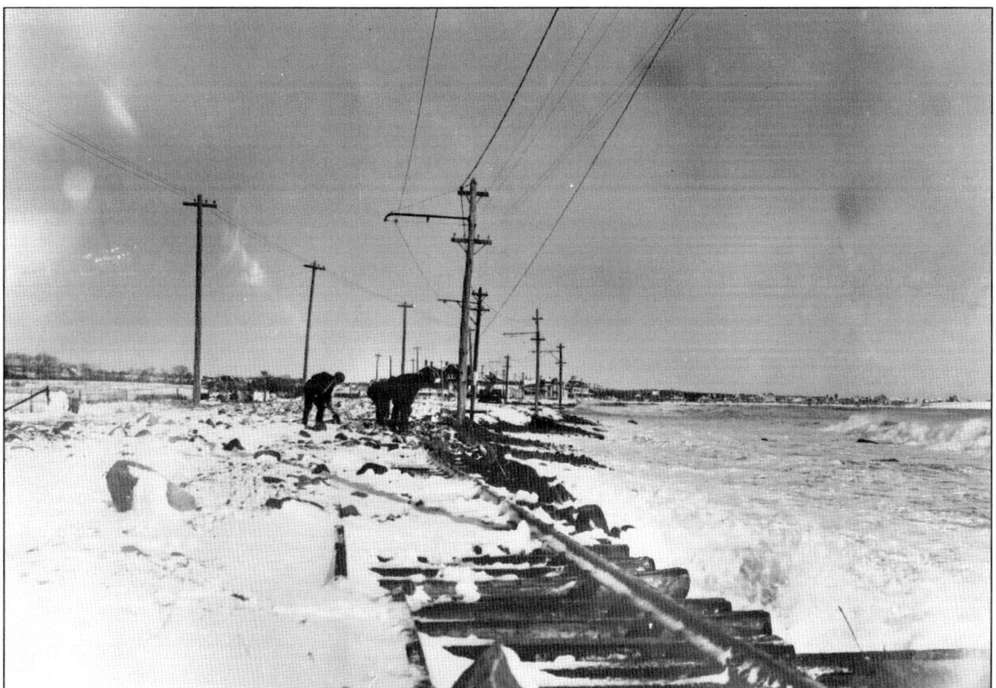

A coastal storm tore up the tracks of the Portsmouth, Kittery and York Electric Street Railway blocking trolley car traffic to York Beach and beyond. Here, repair crews remove debris and repair the tracks so that service can be restored.

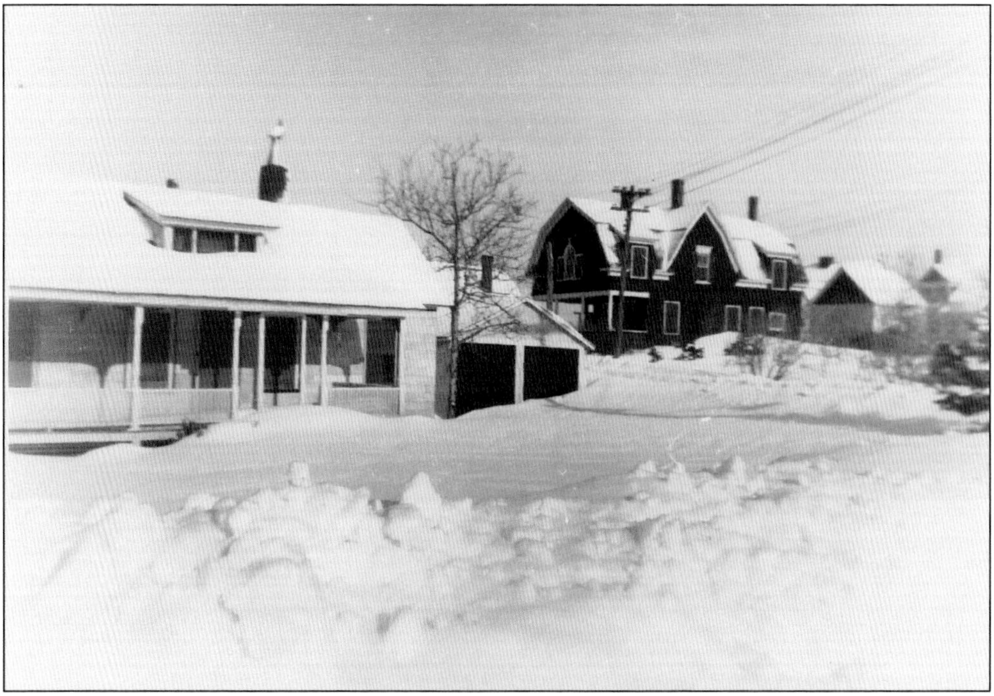

York Beach has an entirely different personality during the winter months. Snow blankets the homes of year-round residents as well as the summer cottages.

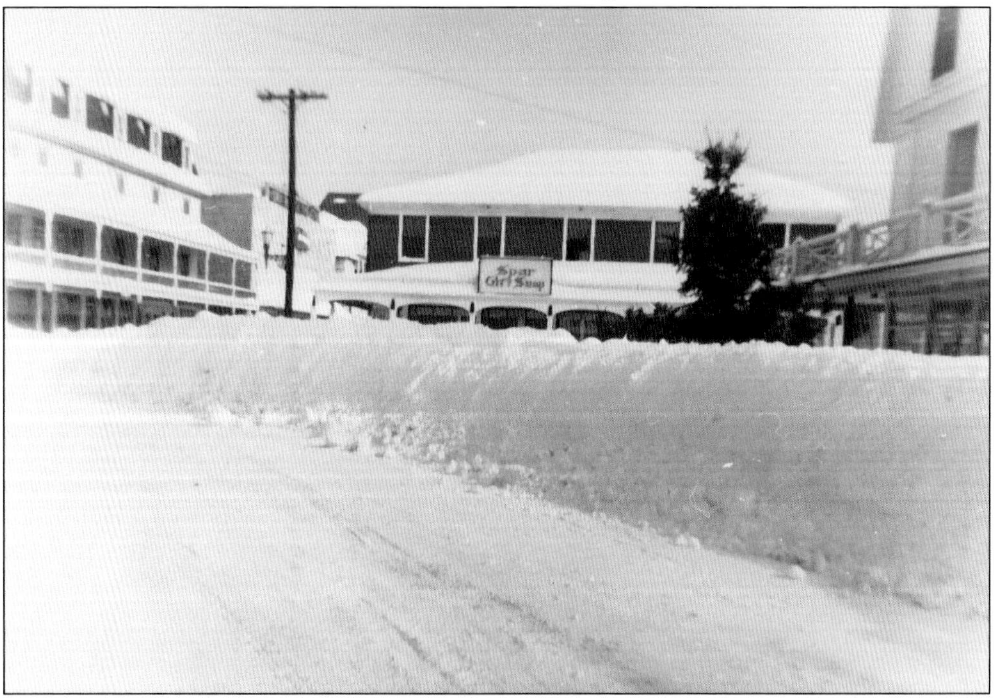

The square, once filled with colorful vacationers and day-trippers, is now filled with snow. The roads are kept open but there is no reason to remove the tons of snow that blanket the sidewalks and parking lots.

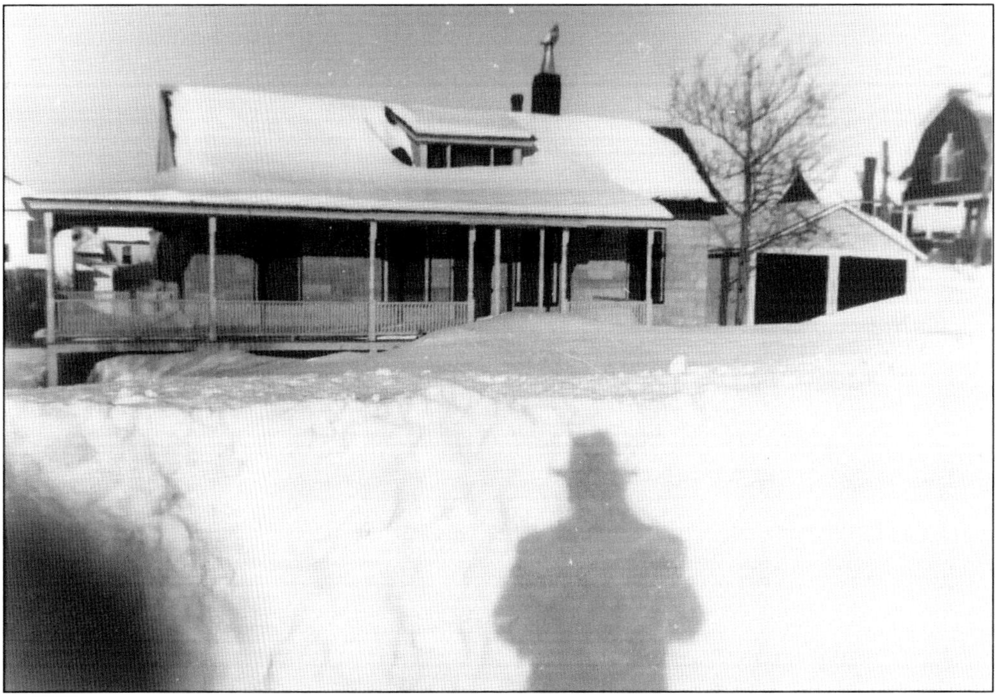

We can see the shadow of a warmly-dressed photographer who is snapping another picture of the house on the left.

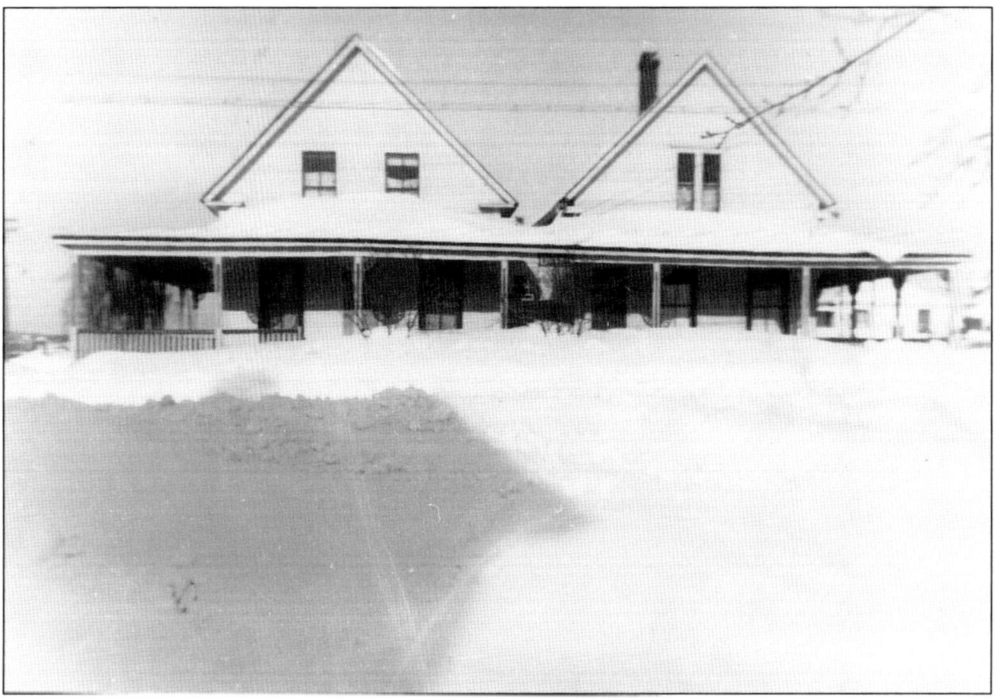

Snow banks as high as the porch rails obscure the cottages and slow the pace of living for those who winter here.

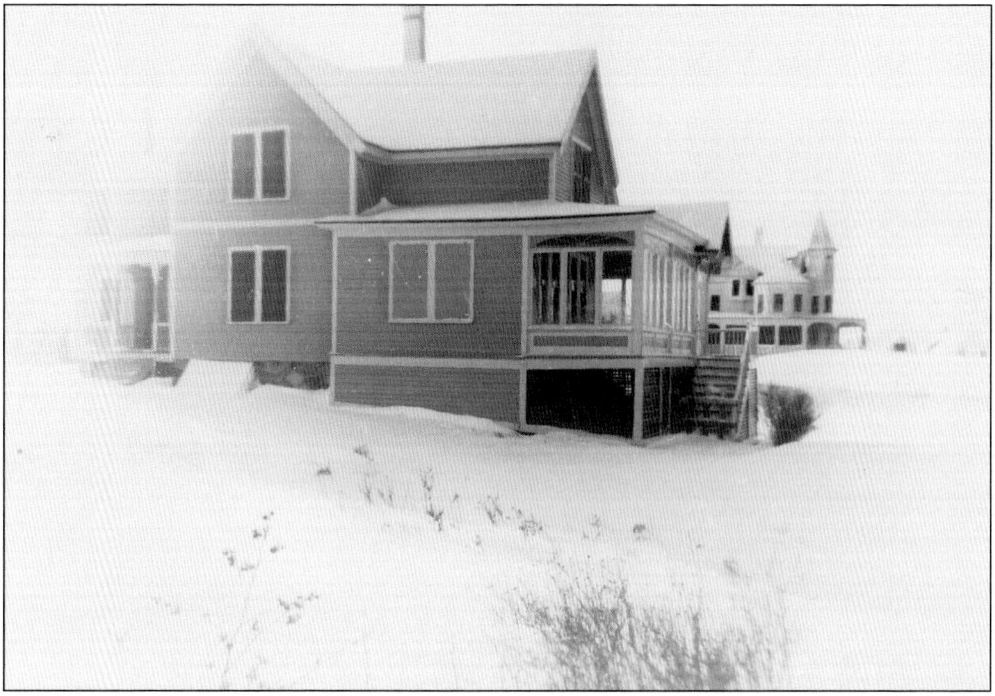

Owners arrive on the weekends to check their cottages and take photographs to show the folks back home.

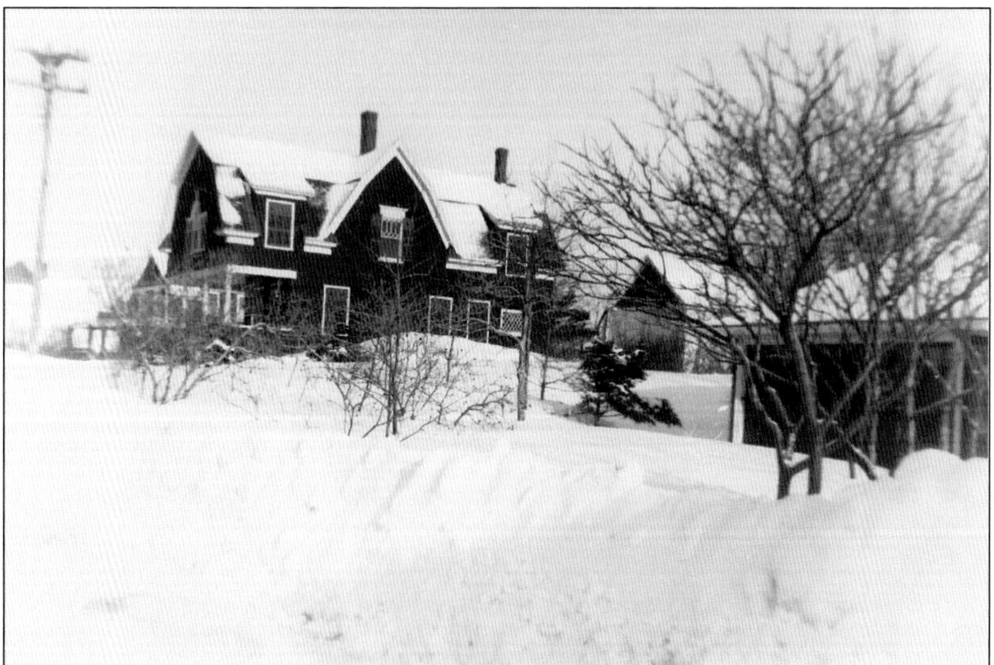

It is a silent, white world that they find when they arrive.

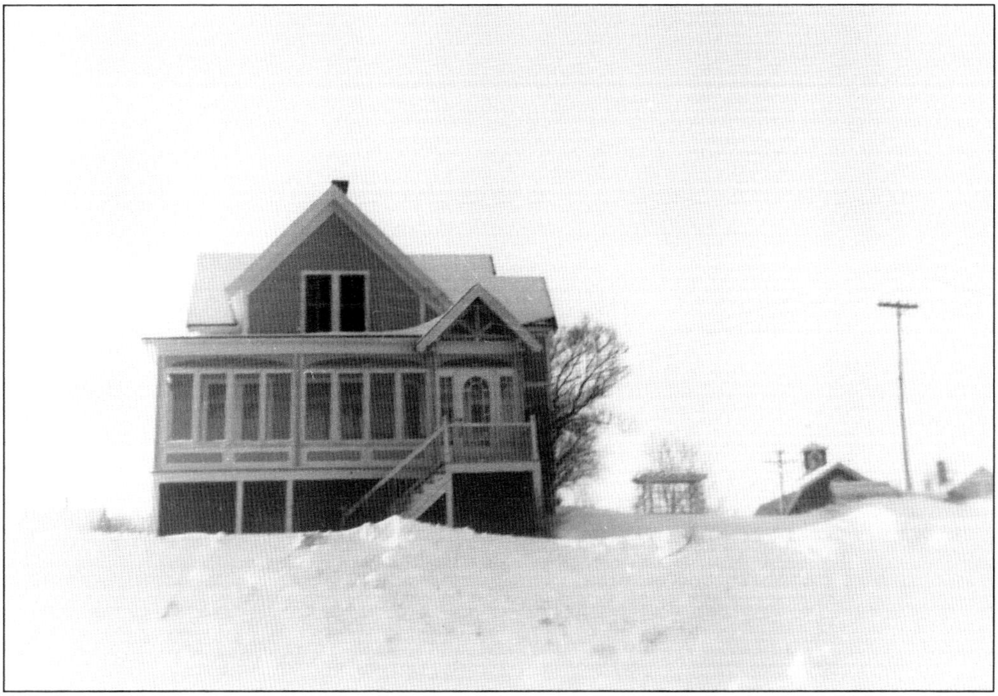

A front view of the house on the left.

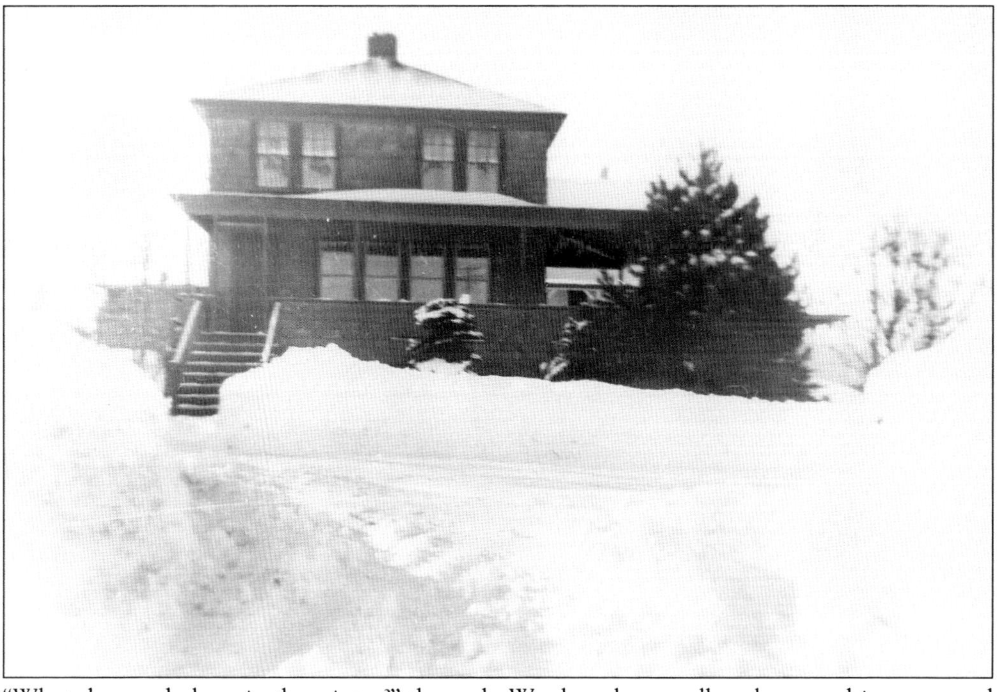

"What do you do here in the winter?" they ask. We shovel our walks, plow our driveways, and enjoy the company of our friends. Our young people play basketball and hockey, our churches become social centers, and we talk about the weather.

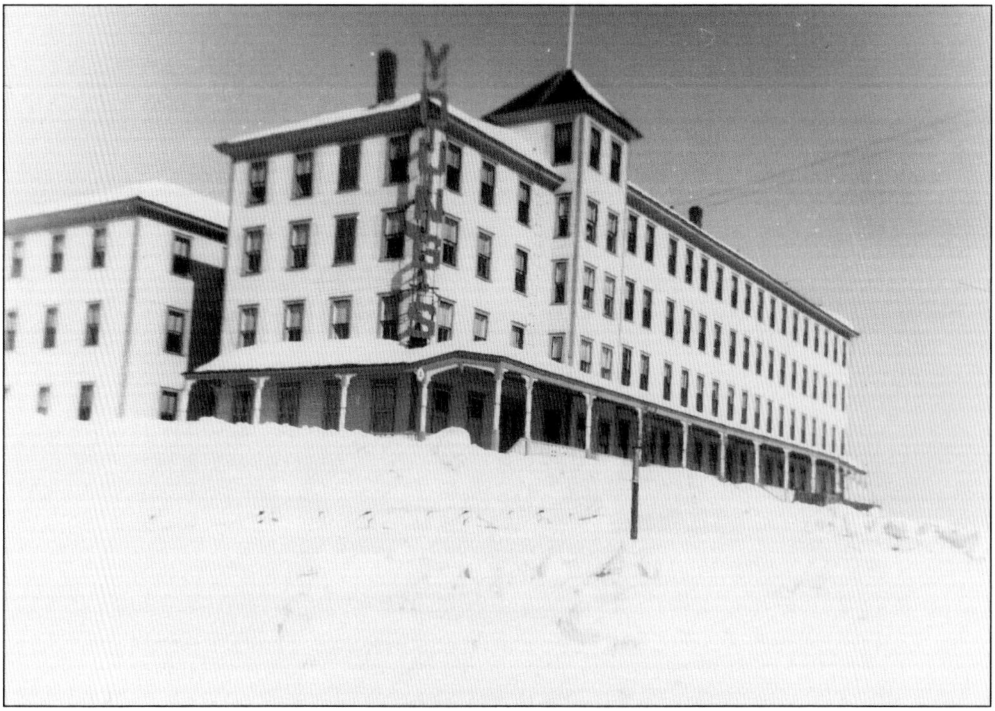

Young's Hotel on Union Bluff. The porches were empty and the building was quiet. There were no visitors to sit on the rocks and watch the surf, which is spectacular during a winter blizzard.

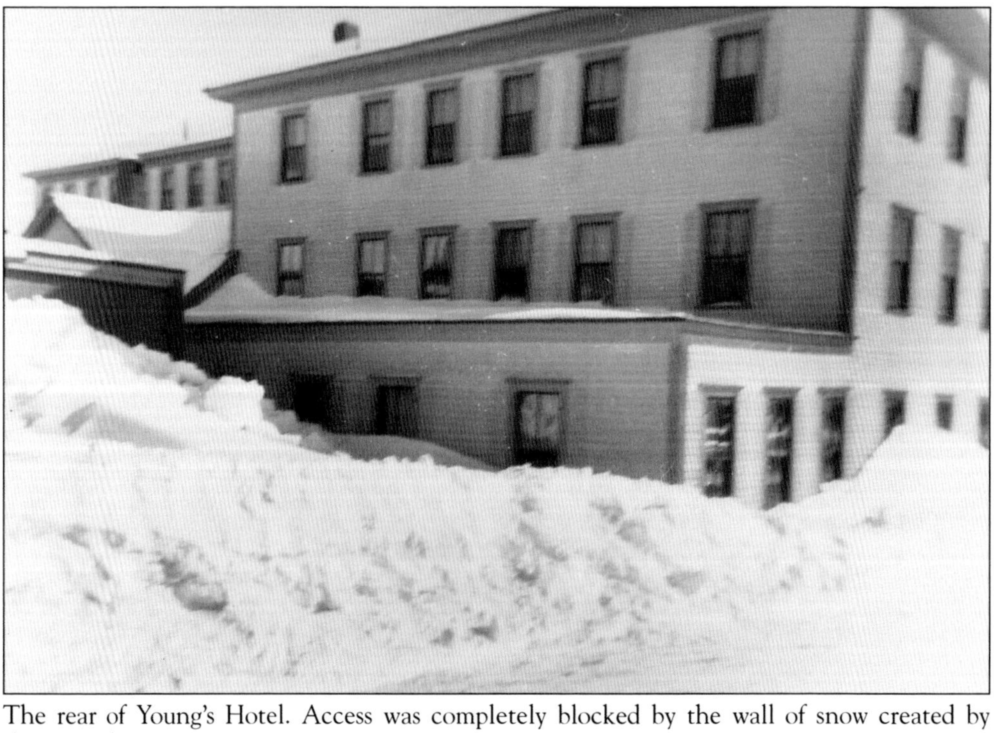

The rear of Young's Hotel. Access was completely blocked by the wall of snow created by the snowplows.

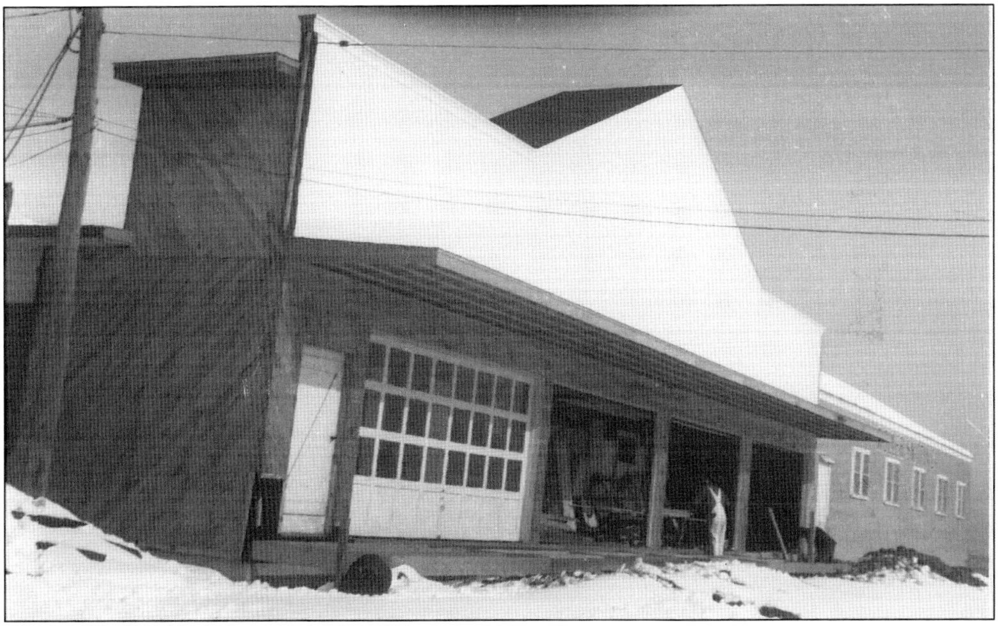

The bowling alley was also silent. Owned by Tom Ford, the entrance to the building originally faced Beach Street. When the building was renovated, the entrance was changed to face Short Sands Beach. It was heavily damaged by a winter storm.

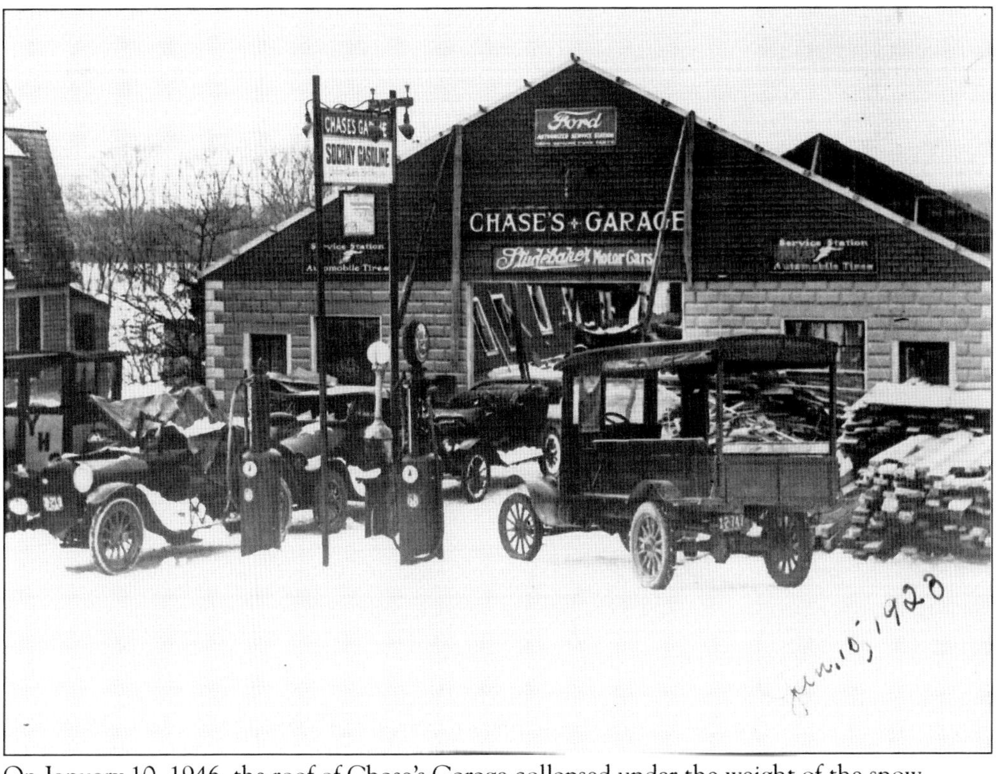


On January 10, 1946, the roof of Chase's Garage collapsed under the weight of the snow.

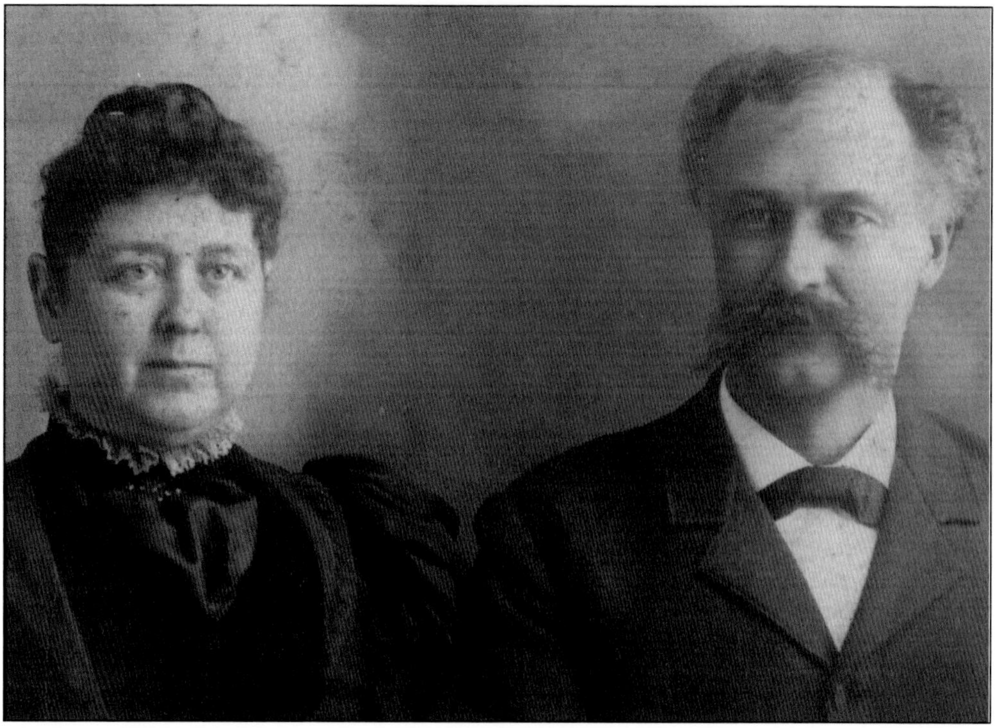

Charles and Susie Worthen, owners of the Worthen House on Broadway Avenue. Worthen was a contractor who built the hotel and operated it with his wife. He also built many of the houses on Ocean Avenue.

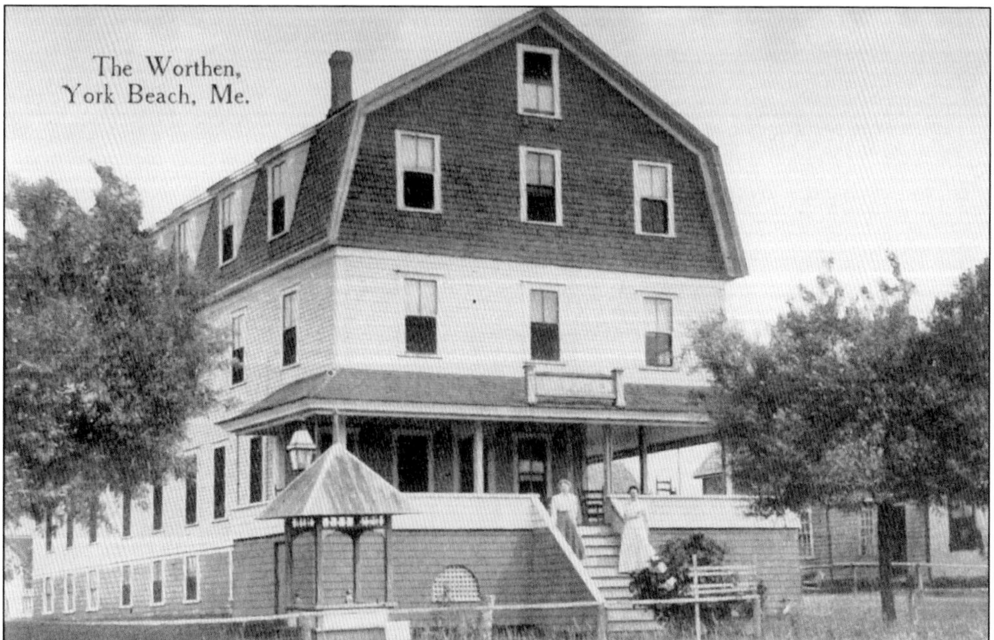


The Hotel Worthen (or Worthen House) is now known as the Massachusetts and has been converted to condominiums.

# Six

# Hotels and Boarding Houses

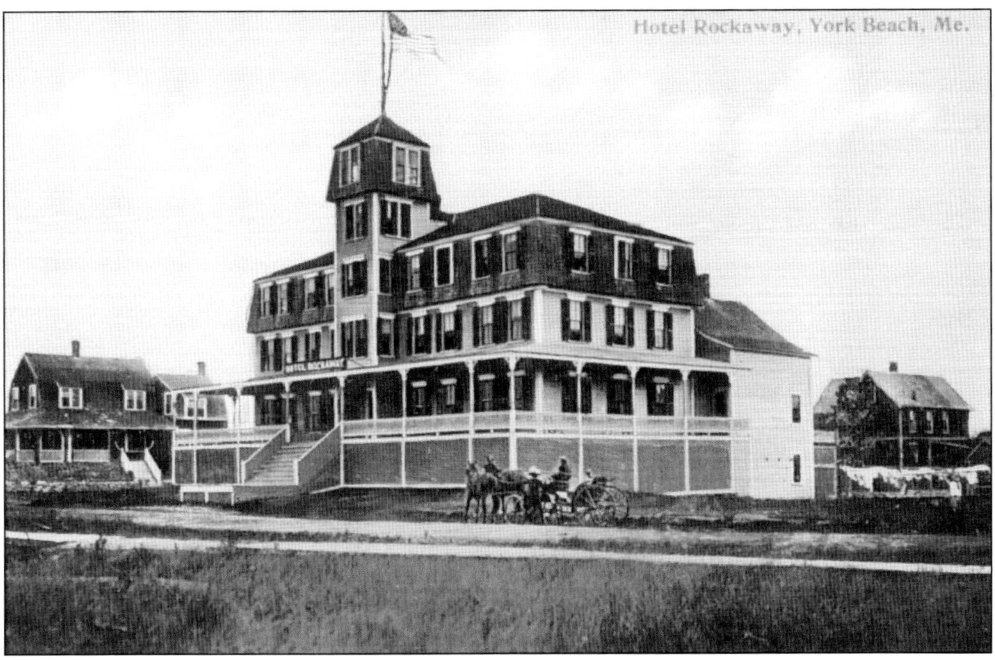


The Hotel Rockaway was one of the oldest hotels on Short Sands Beach. It was incorporated as part of the LaFayette Hotel, later called the Breakers, on the site now occupied by the Sands Motel.

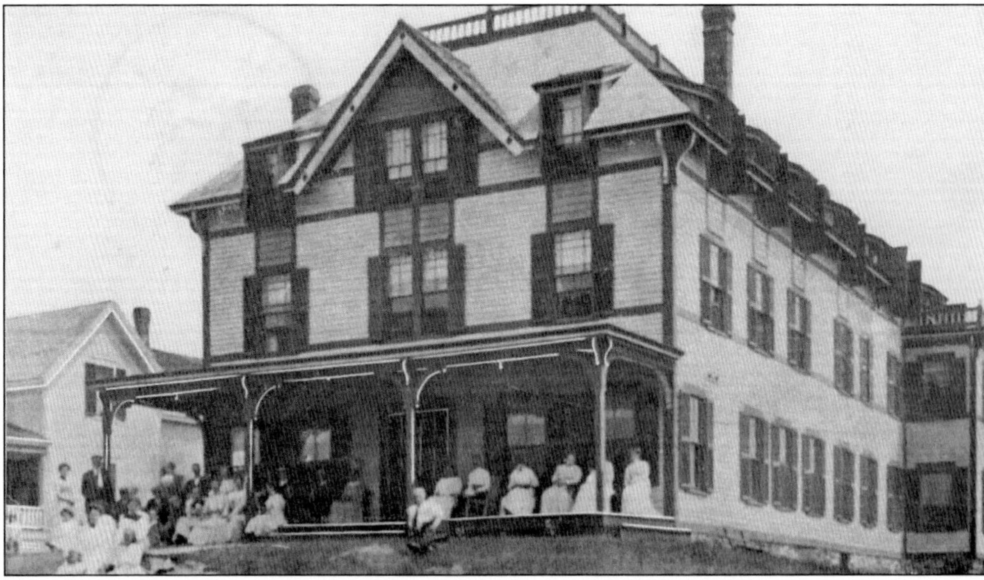

The Fairview Hotel was built in 1887 by Angeline Gordon (a Civil War widow) and her son, George Gordon. It was a three-story building with twelve sleeping rooms and a bath on each floor. Each room was furnished with a washbowl, commode, bed, and chamber pot. The Gordons also operated a livery and boarding stable.

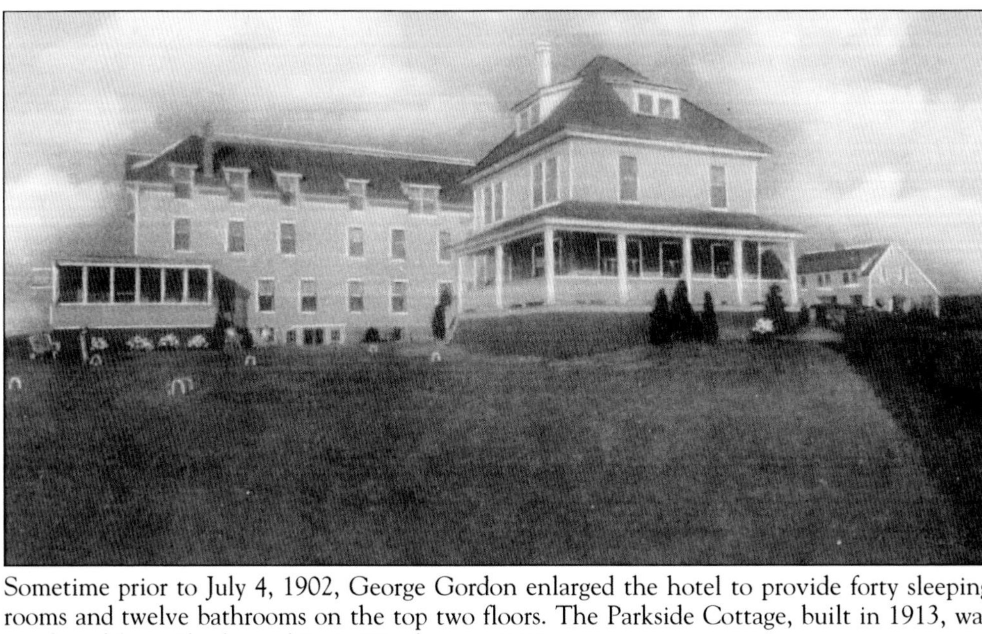

Sometime prior to July 4, 1902, George Gordon enlarged the hotel to provide forty sleeping rooms and twelve bathrooms on the top two floors. The Parkside Cottage, built in 1913, was purchased from Charles and Susie Worthen in 1945.

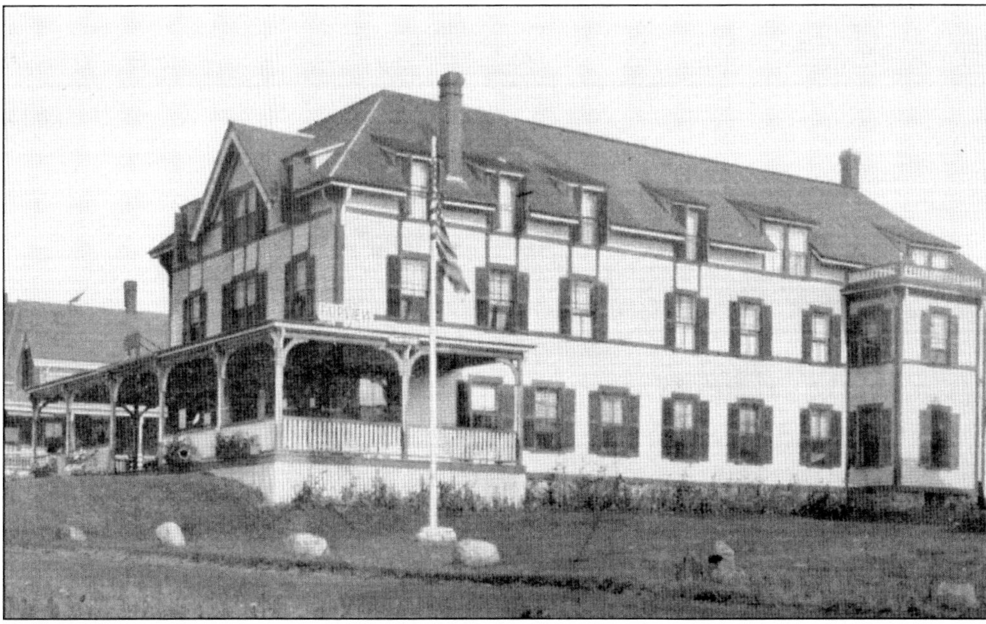

The first floor of the enlarged Fairview had a kitchen, a dining room, two living rooms, a breakfast room, a pantry, and a laundry room.

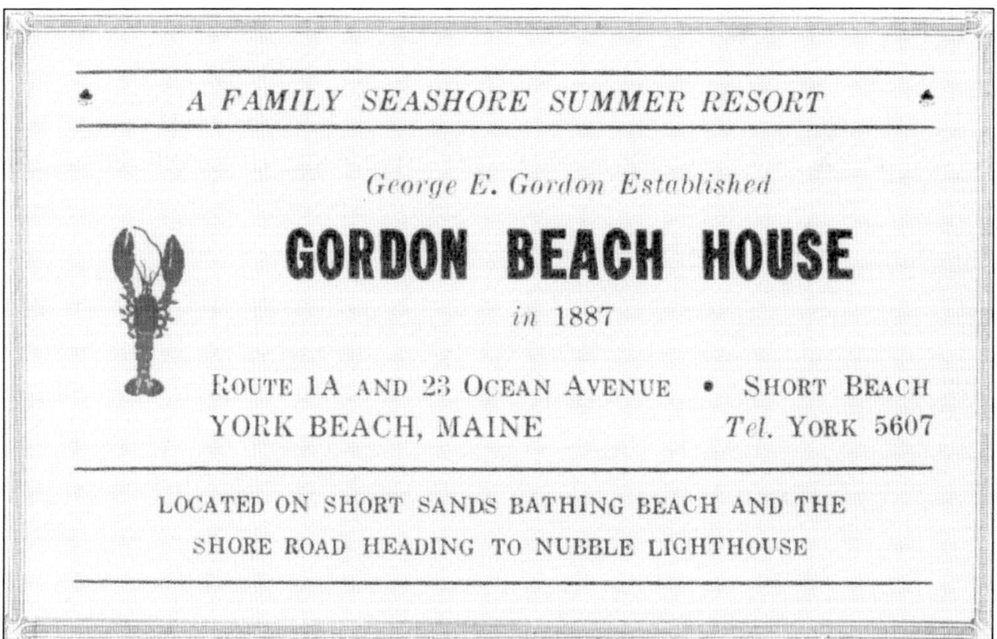


The name of the hotel was changed to Gordon's Beach House in 1961.

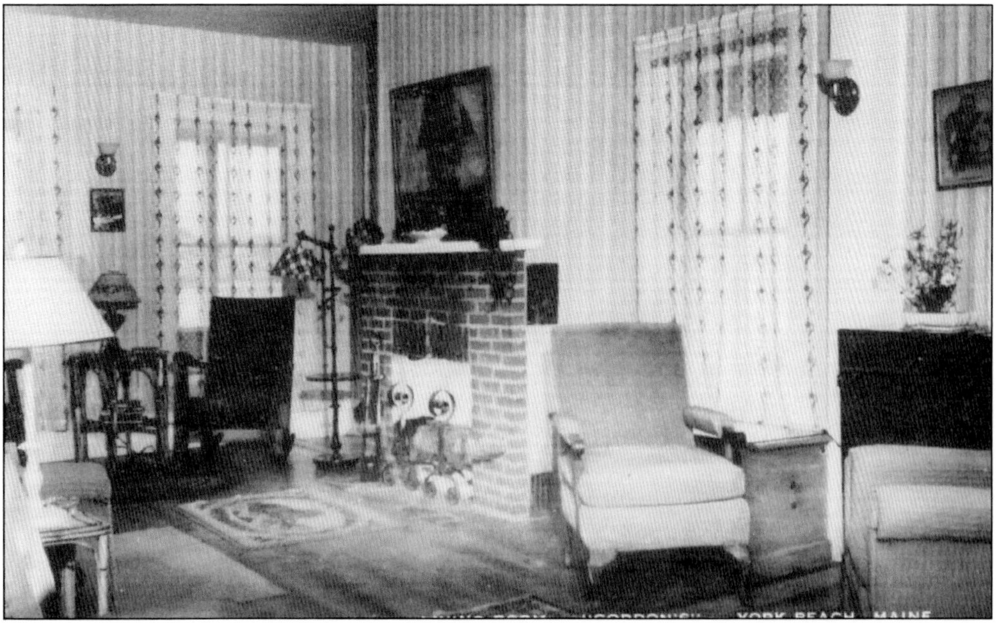

The hotel did not reopen after the season of 1962. It was occupied by the Gordon family until 1964, when the building was torn down.

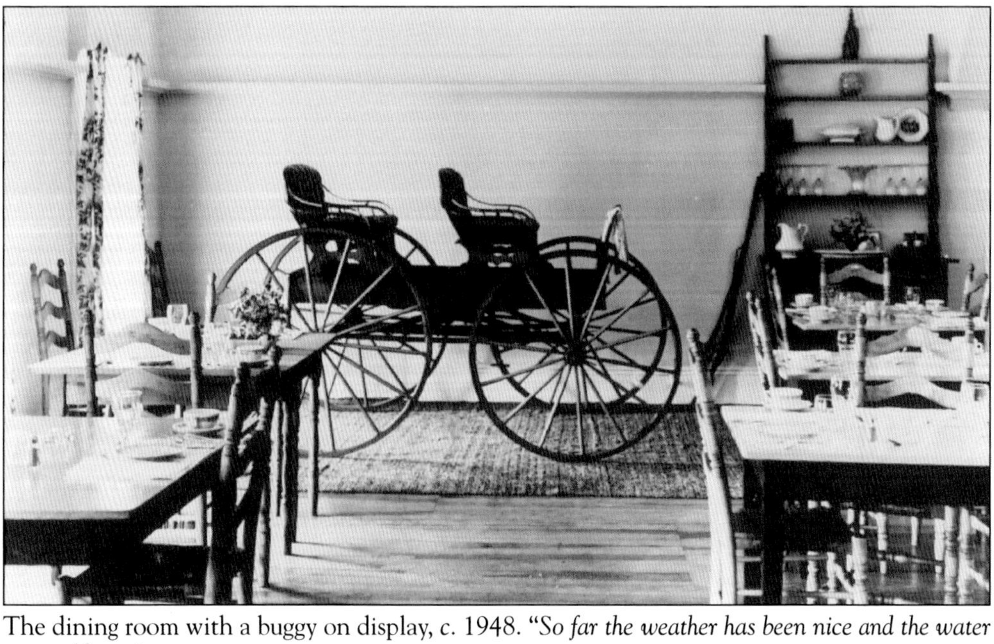

The dining room with a buggy on display, c. 1948. "*So far the weather has been nice and the water very cold . . .*"

| *Room Prices* | *Daily* | *Weekly* |
|---|---|---|
| DOUBLE and SINGLE—PRIVATE BATH FOR 3 | $10.00 | $60.00 |
| TWIN—PRIVATE BATH FOR 2 | $8.00 FOR 2 | $48.00 |
| TWIN | $6.50 FOR 2 | $39.00 |
| SINGLE | $5.00 FOR 1 | $30.00 |
| DOUBLE | $6.00 FOR 2 | $36.00 |

*Daily Rate Applies to Fractions of a Week*

Efficiency Apartments Accommodating 4 — $80.00 Weekly (Additional occupancy $10 weekly per person). Parkside Cottage: Rates on request. A 25 percent Deposit required for Reservations. Maine 3% Tax additional.

*Winter Address:*

CHARLES GORDON, 922 ELM ST., *Tel.* NATIONAL 5-9725, MANCHESTER, N. H.
*Tel.* NATIONAL 5-6834

TABLE OF DISTANCES IN MILES

| | | | | | | | |
|---|---|---|---|---|---|---|---|
| York Harbor | 3 | Albany | 190 | Quebec | 300 | Ogunquit | 6 |
| Portsmouth | 9 | Sea Level | 25′ | Manchester | 59 | Portland | 39 |
| Boston | 60 | Montreal | 200 | Concord | 57 | New York | 276 |

A rate schedule for Gordon's Beach House in 1961–62.

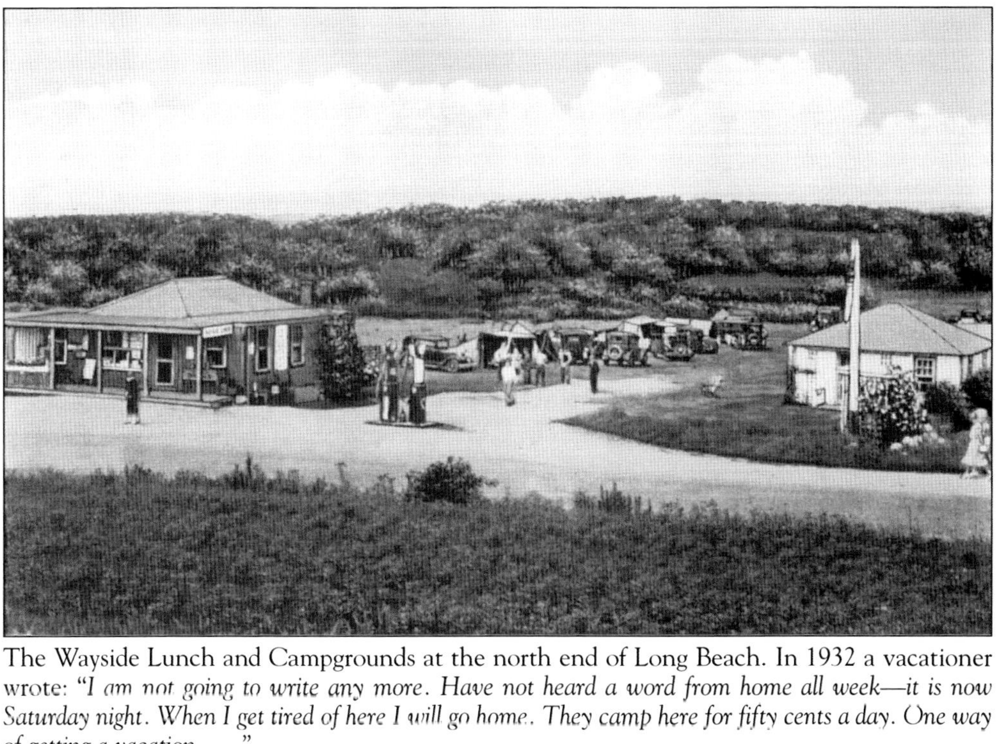

The Wayside Lunch and Campgrounds at the north end of Long Beach. In 1932 a vacationer wrote: "*I am not going to write any more. Have not heard a word from home all week—it is now Saturday night. When I get tired of here I will go home. They camp here for fifty cents a day. One way of getting a vacation . . .*"

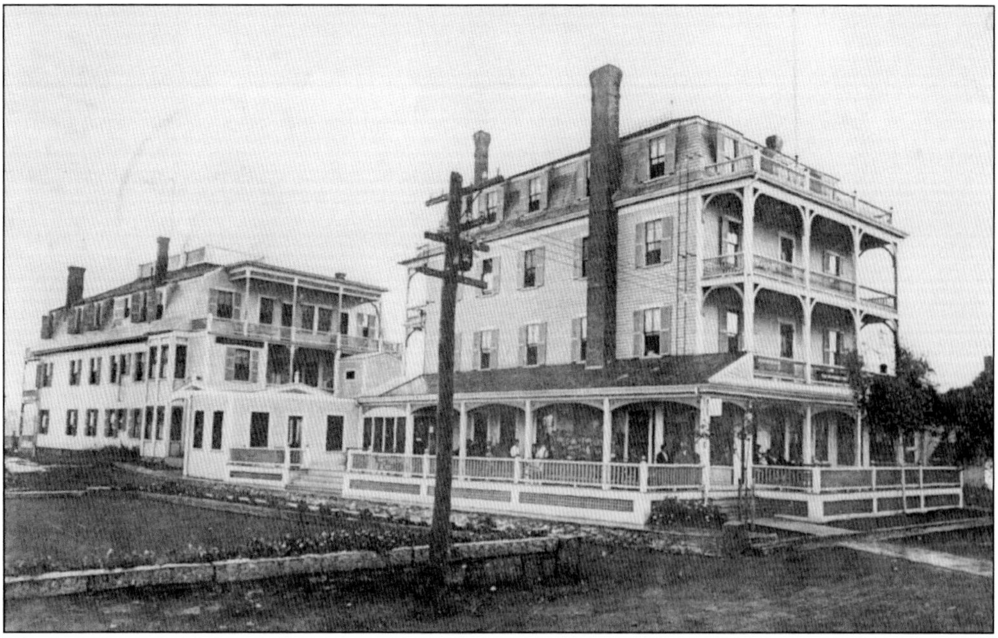

The Hastings-Lyman Hotel on Union Bluff as it looked in 1909.

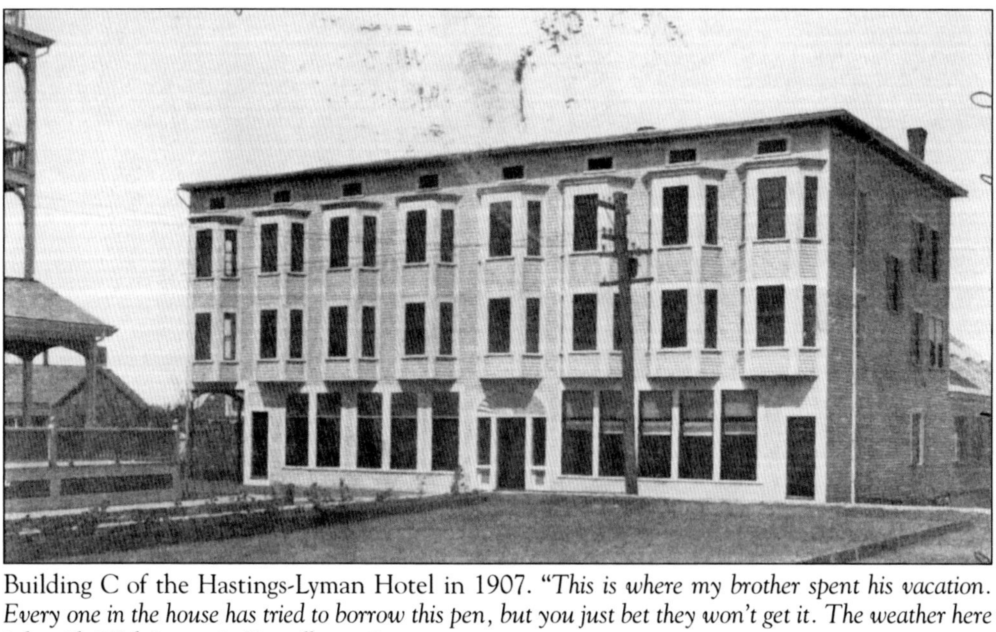

Building C of the Hastings-Lyman Hotel in 1907. "*This is where my brother spent his vacation. Every one in the house has tried to borrow this pen, but you just bet they won't get it. The weather here is horrid. Wish I were in Danville . . .*"

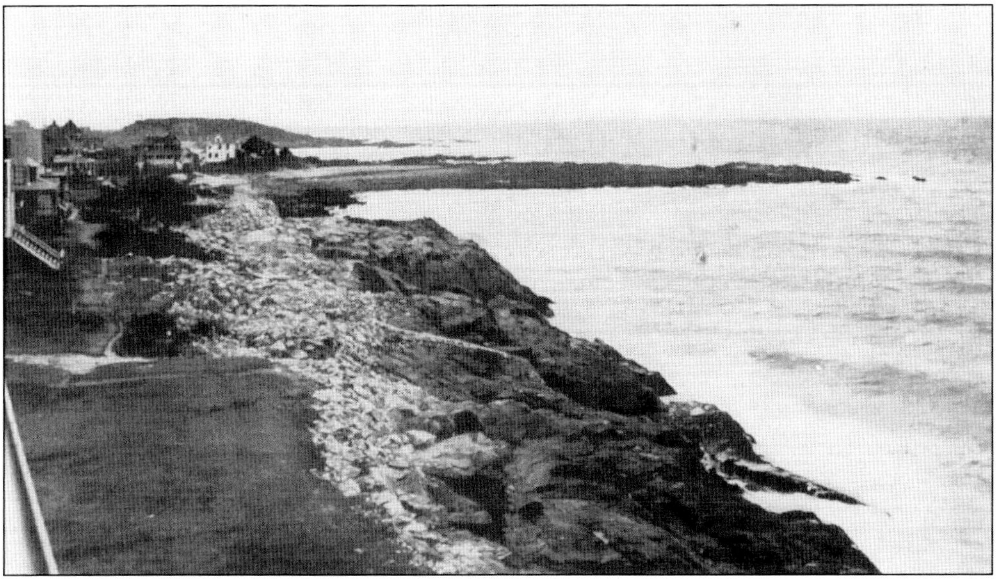

View from the porch of the Hastings-Lyman Hotel.

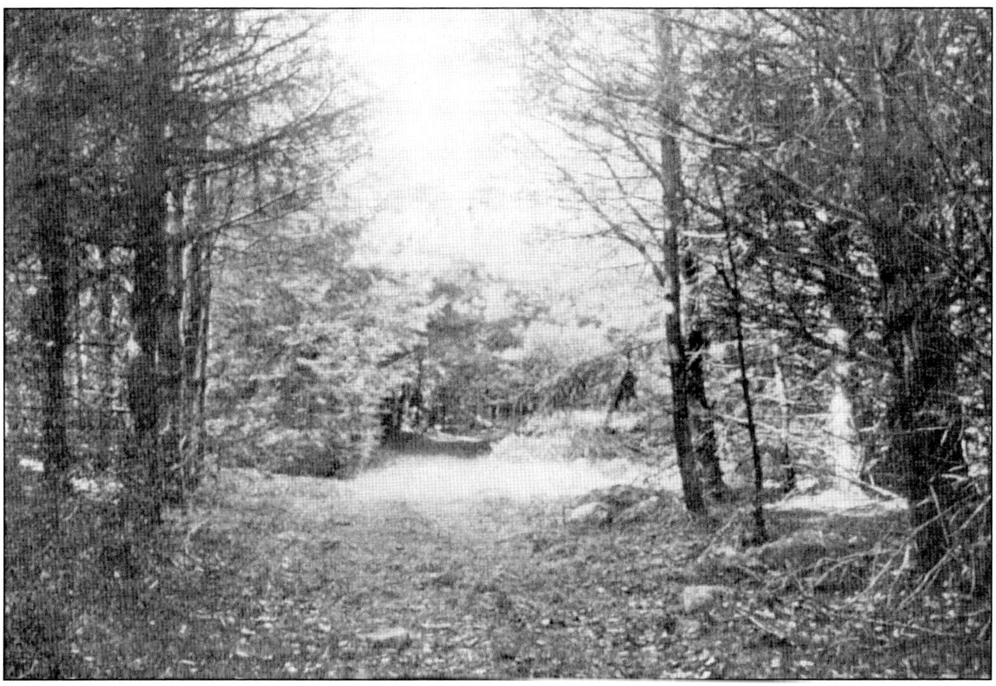

The fields and woods near the Hastings-Lyman.

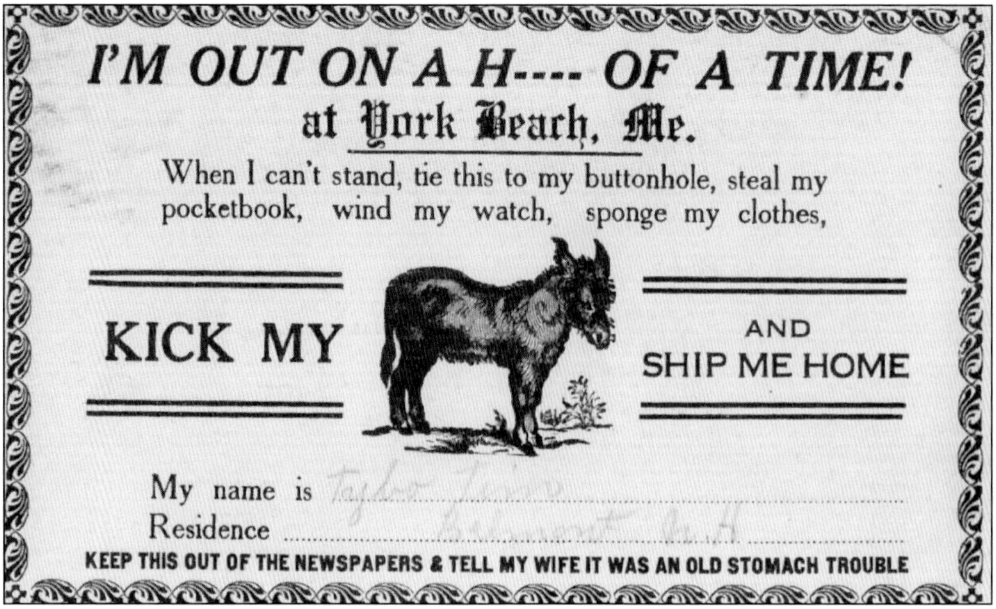

A slightly rowdy 1926 postcard.

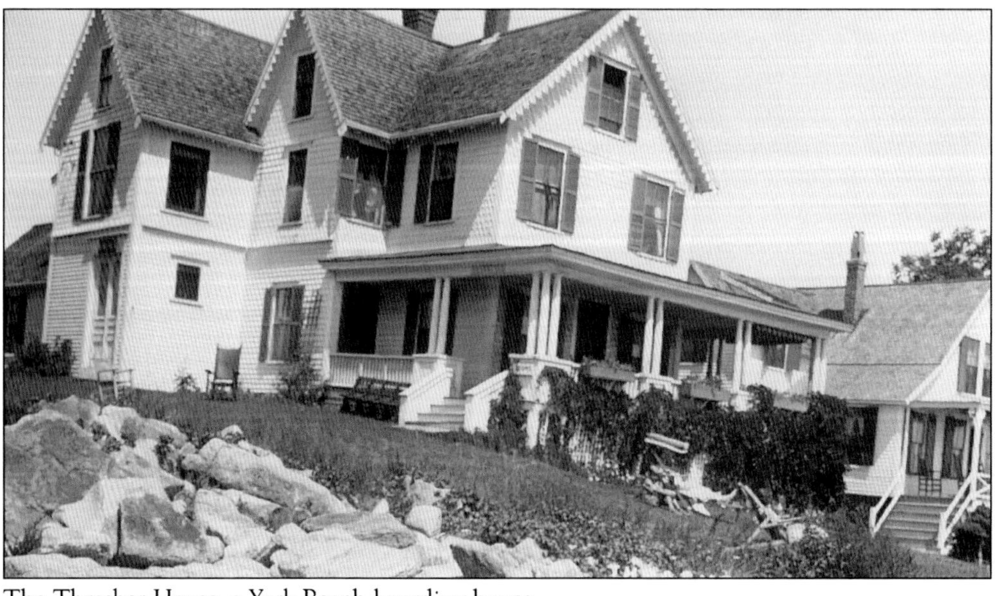
The Thrasher House, a York Beach boarding house.

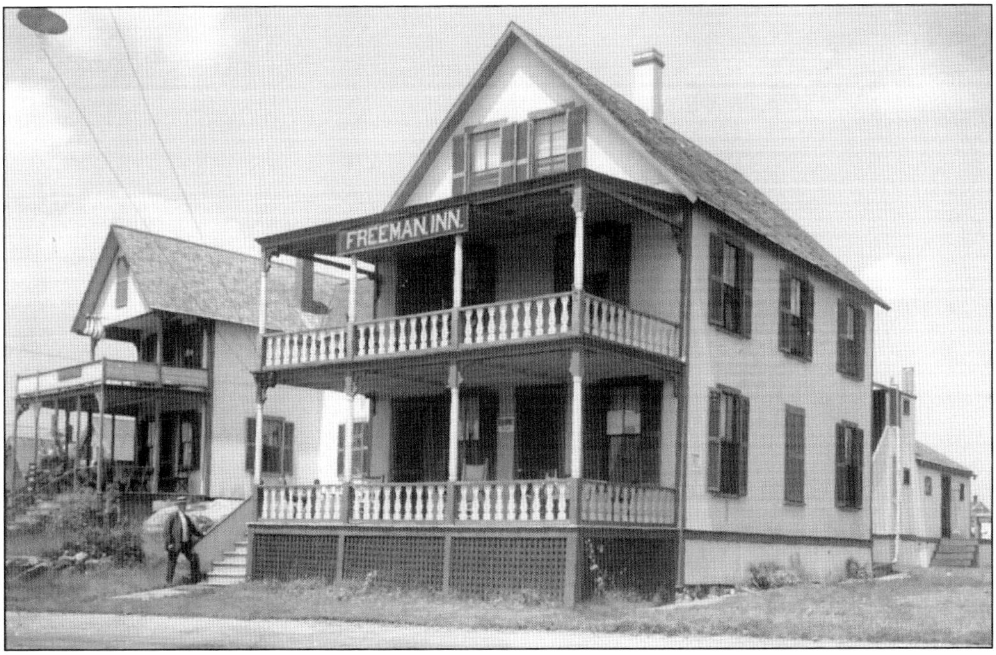


The Freeman Inn.

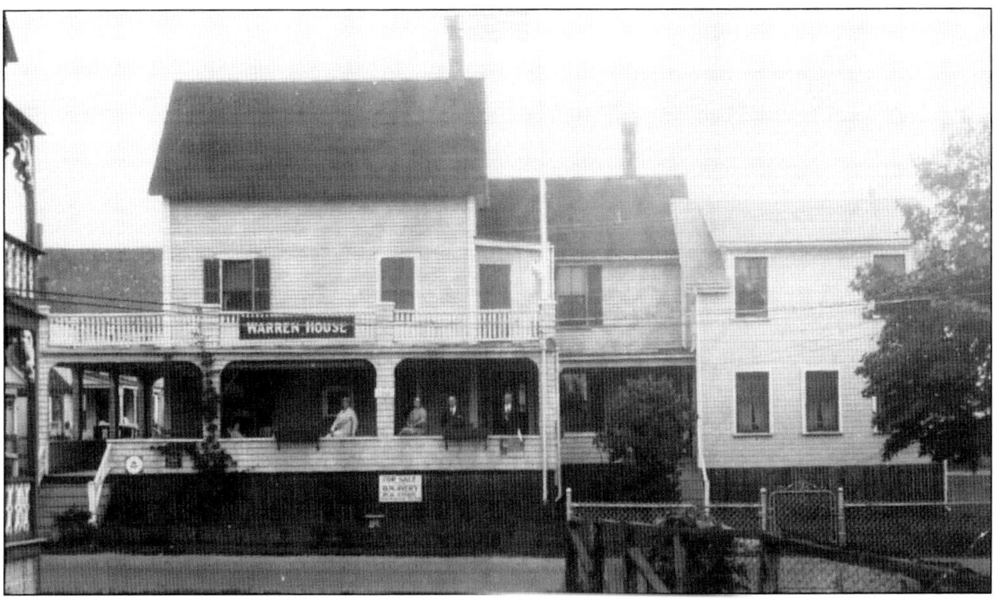


The Warren House.

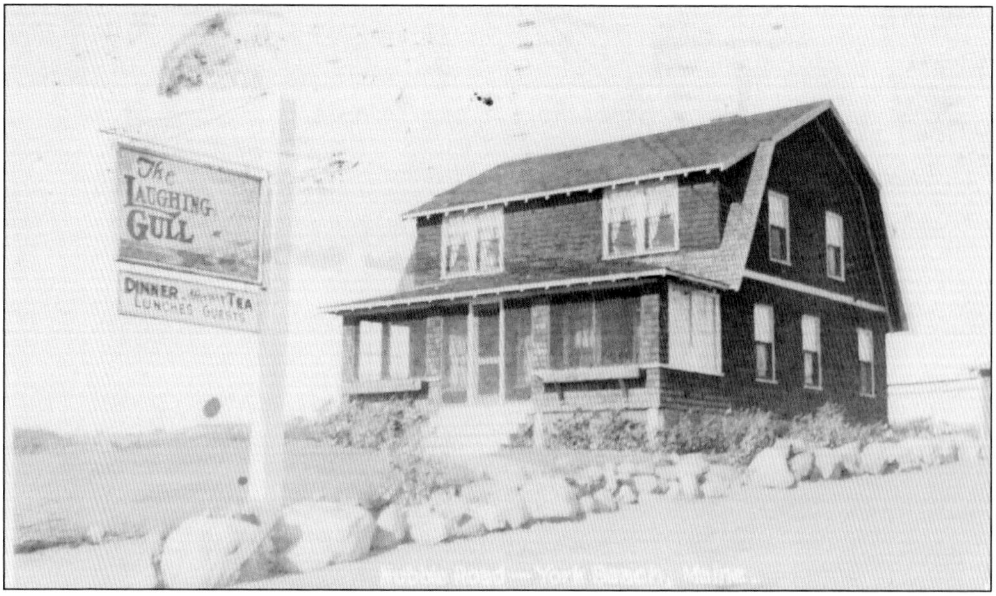


The Laughing Gull Guest House.

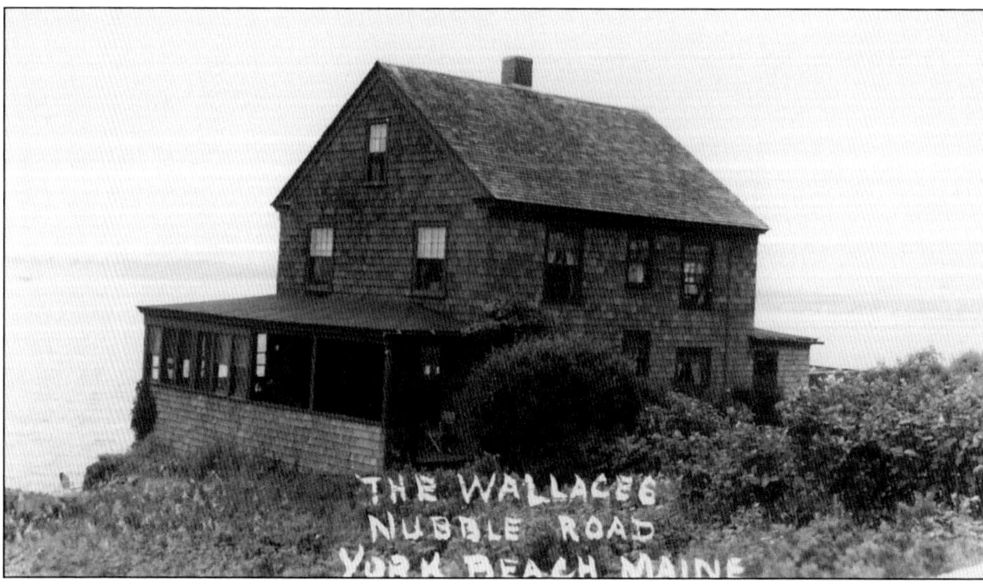


*"Open July 1st. G.I. Wallace. c. 1932."*

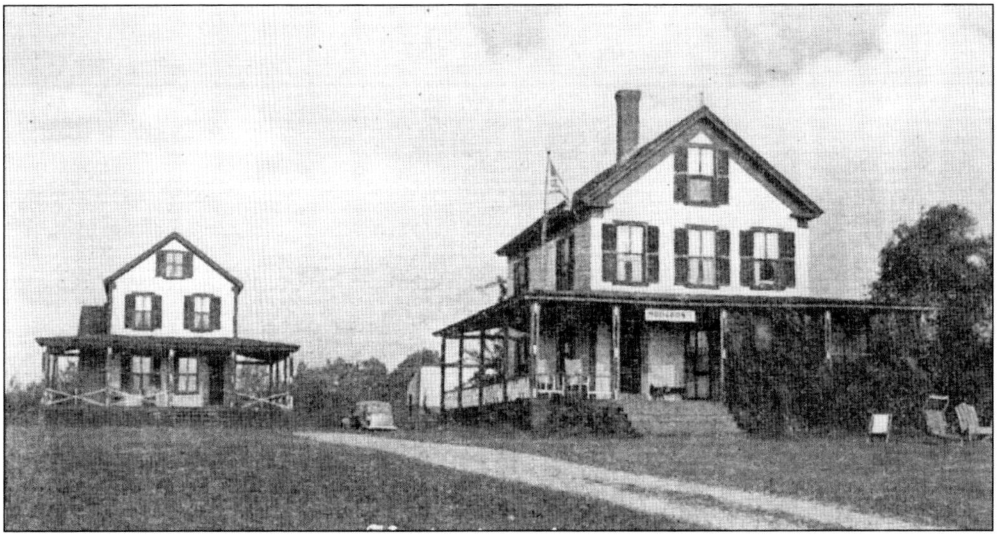

Hodgdon's Guest Houses on Long Beach.

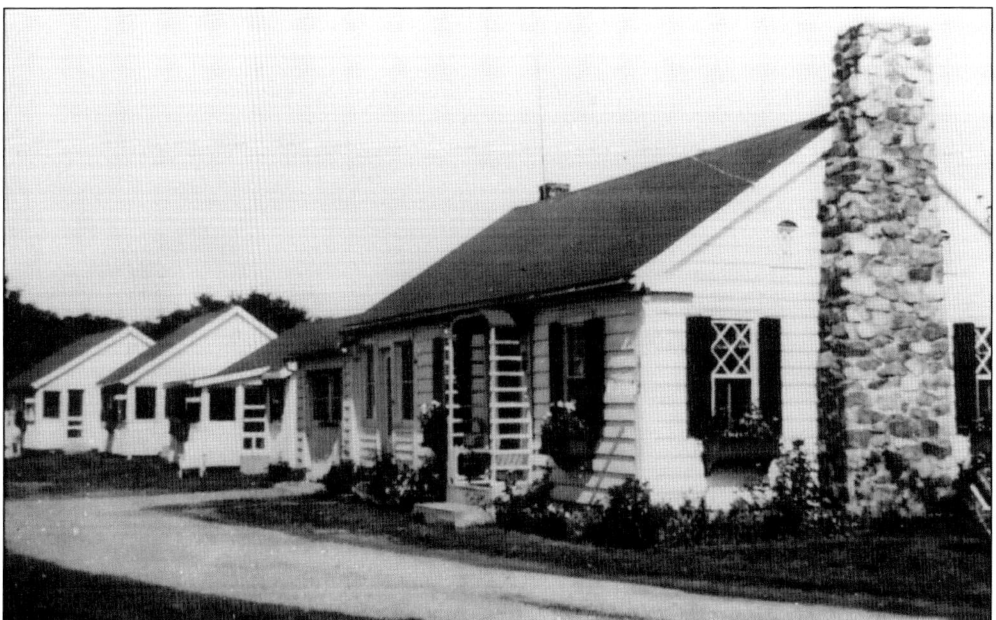

Whitten Cottages on Long Beach.

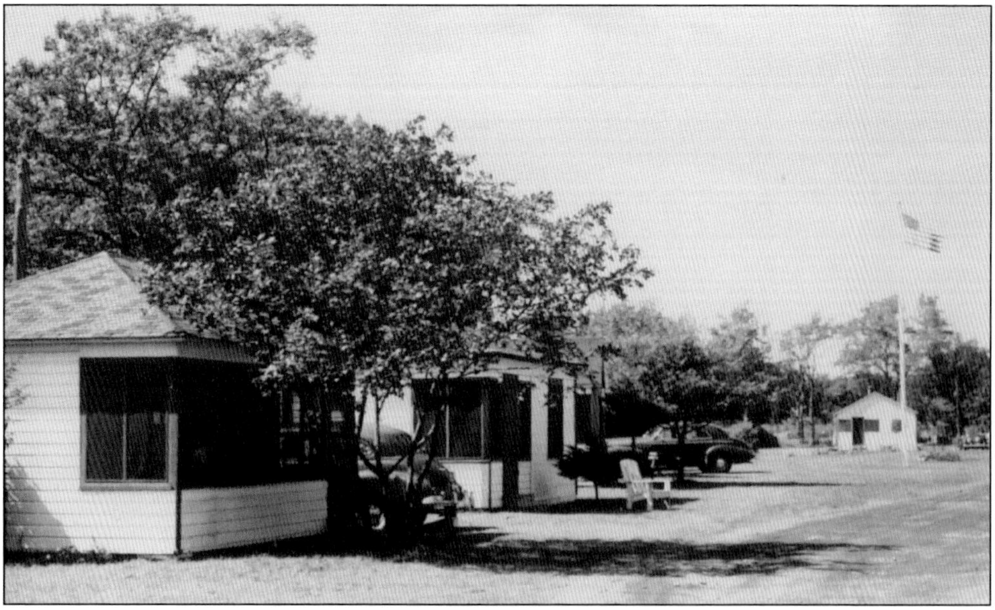

Burnett's Housekeeping Camp and Trailer Court in York Beach.

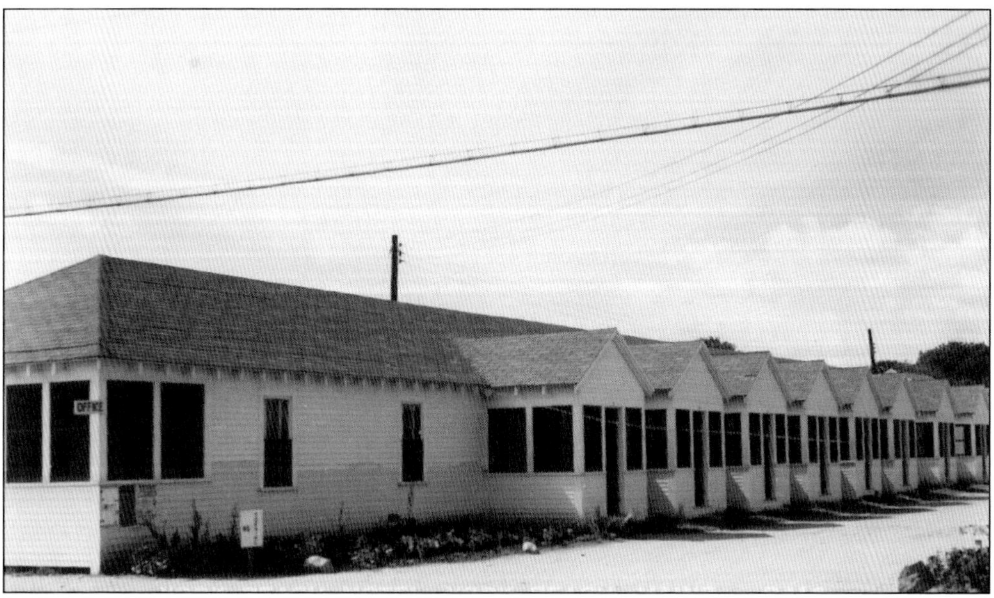

This tourist facility demonstrates the gradual evolution from cabins to motel units on York Beach.

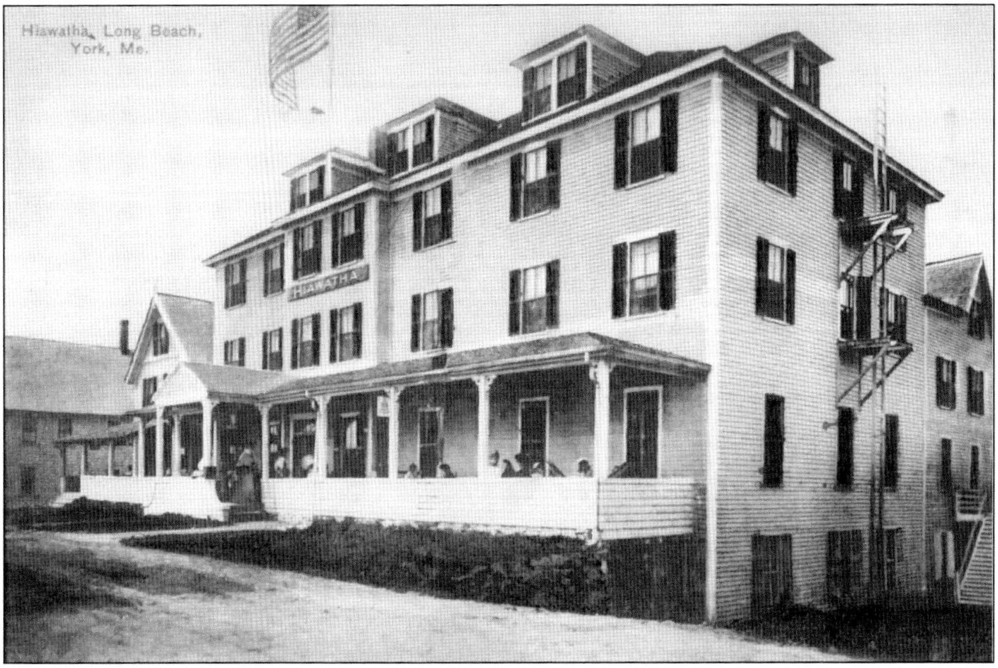

The Hiawatha Hotel on Long Beach. Located near the Oceanside railroad station, it was one of the oldest hotels on the beach.

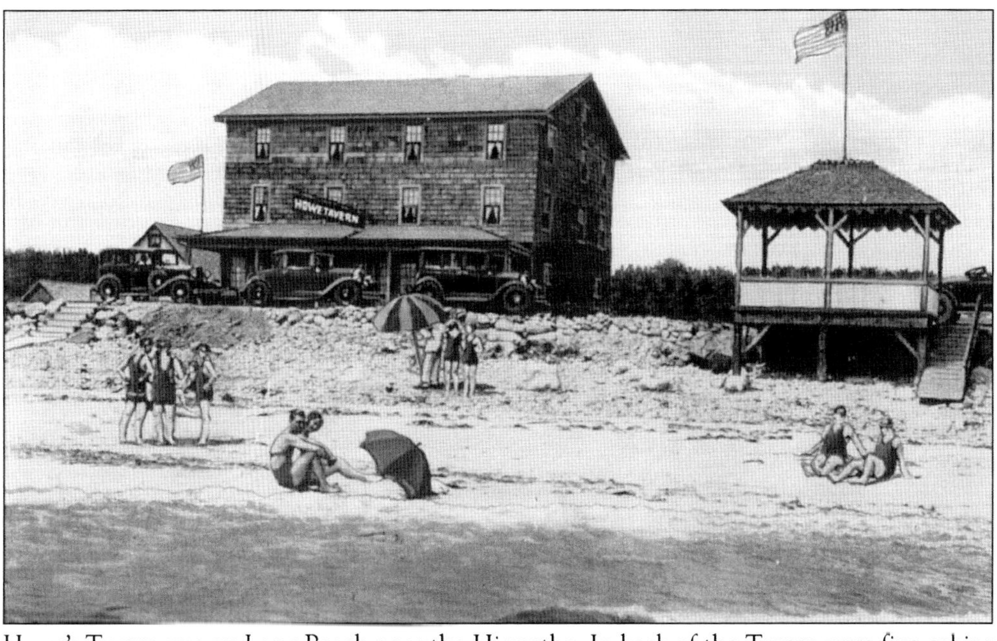

Howe's Tavern was on Long Beach near the Hiawatha. In back of the Tavern were five cabins and a cottage for summer rentals.

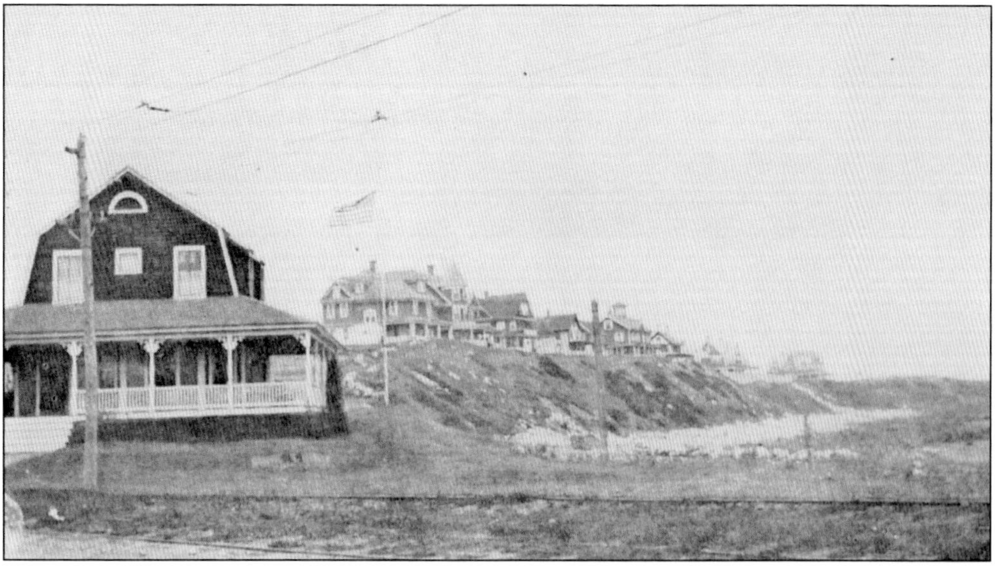
The Breakers cottage near the entrance to Nubble Road. Dover Bluffs is in the background.

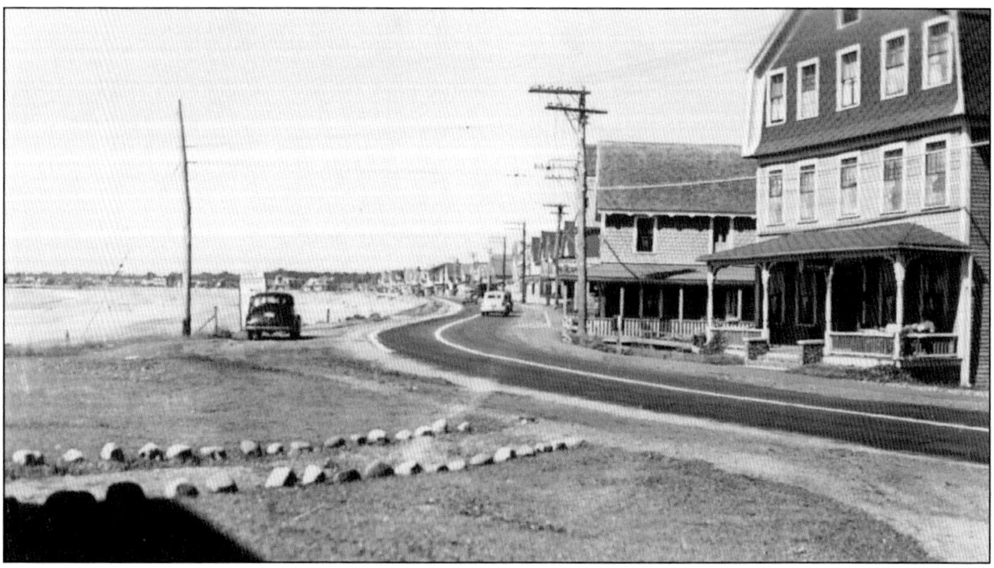
The eastern end of Long Sands Beach as seen from the Breakers.

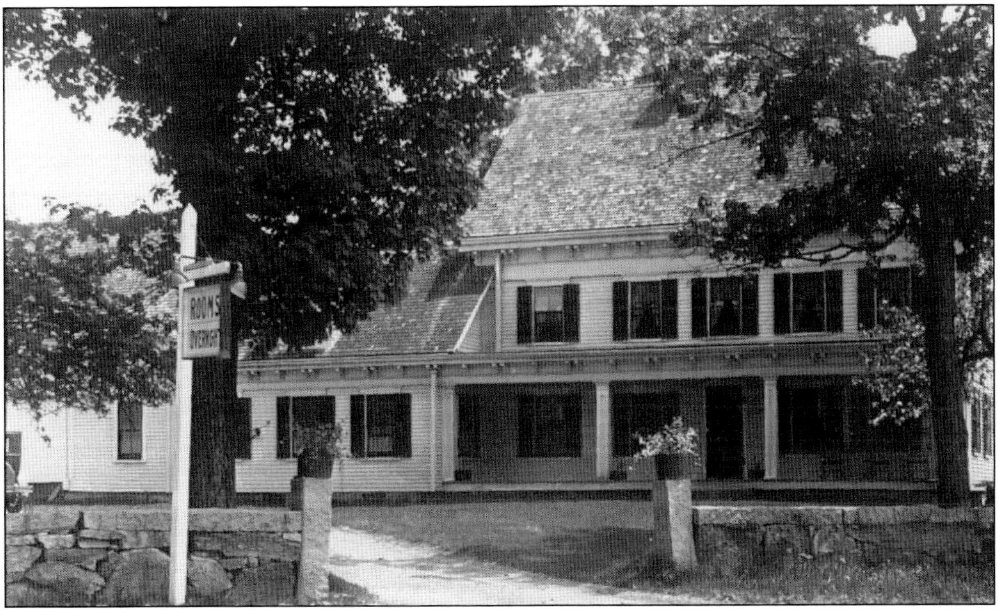


A guest house operated by E.C. Moulton on U.S. Route 1 in Cape Neddick. The increase in automobile traffic stimulated the development of tourist services away from the beaches.

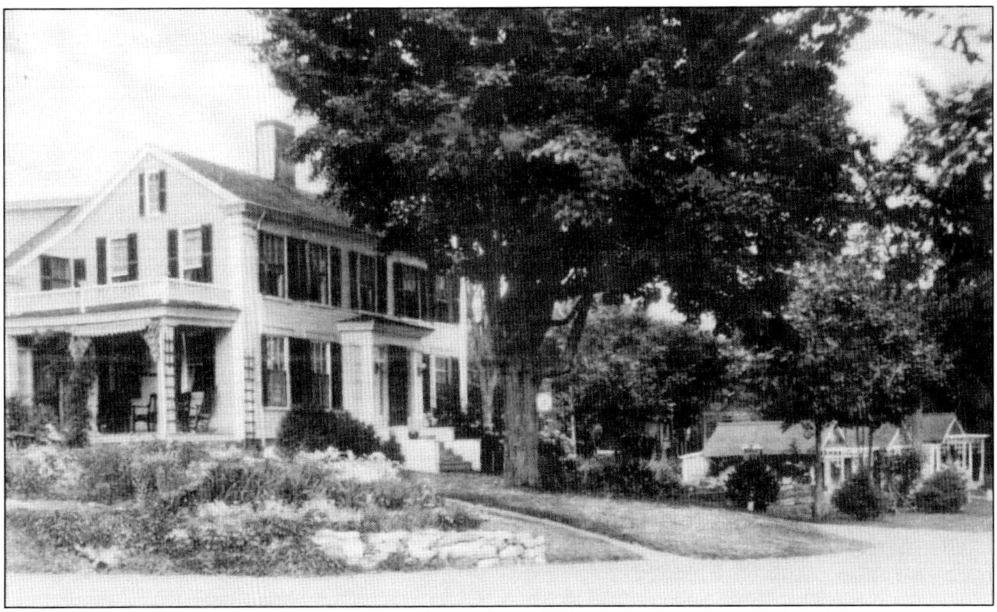

Maxwell's Cabins and Guest House in Cape Neddick advertised hot and cold water, private showers, and beds with innerspring mattresses. Rooms in the house had private baths and steam heat. Meals were also available.

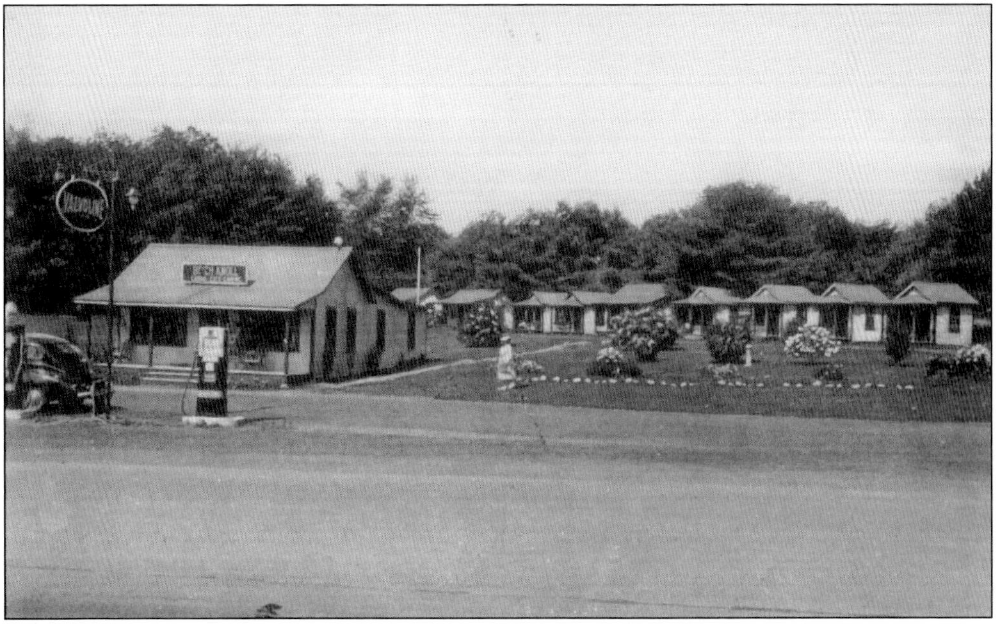

The Birch Knoll Cabins and Camping Grounds were on U.S. Route 1 near the Ogunquit town line.

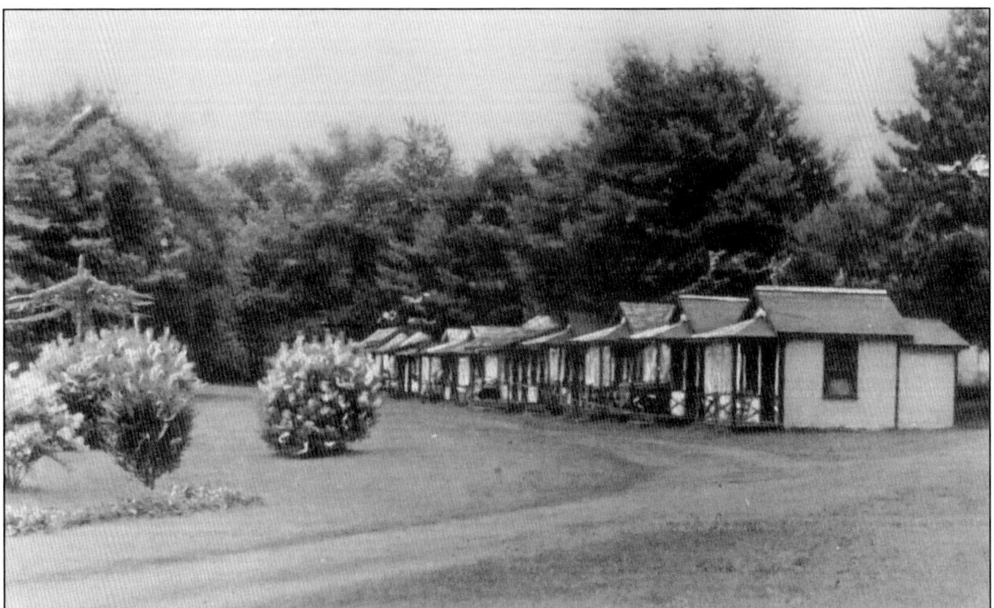

The Birch Knoll Cabins were typical accommodations during the 1930s and '40s. If business was good, a few more cabins would be added at the end of each tourist season. As the number of cabins increased, the number of camping sites was reduced.

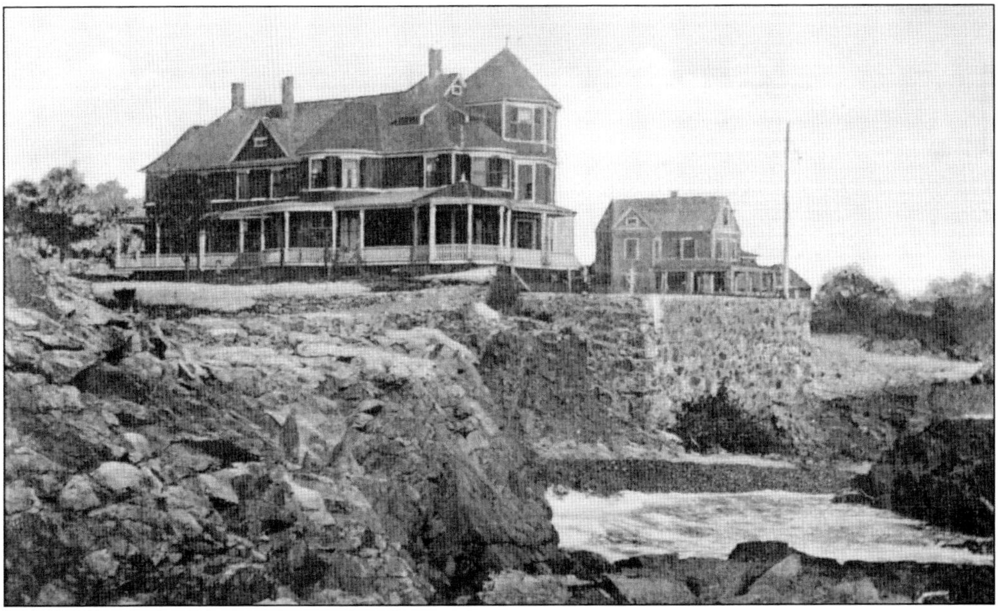

Pebble Beach was at the western end of Short Sands near Dover Bluffs.

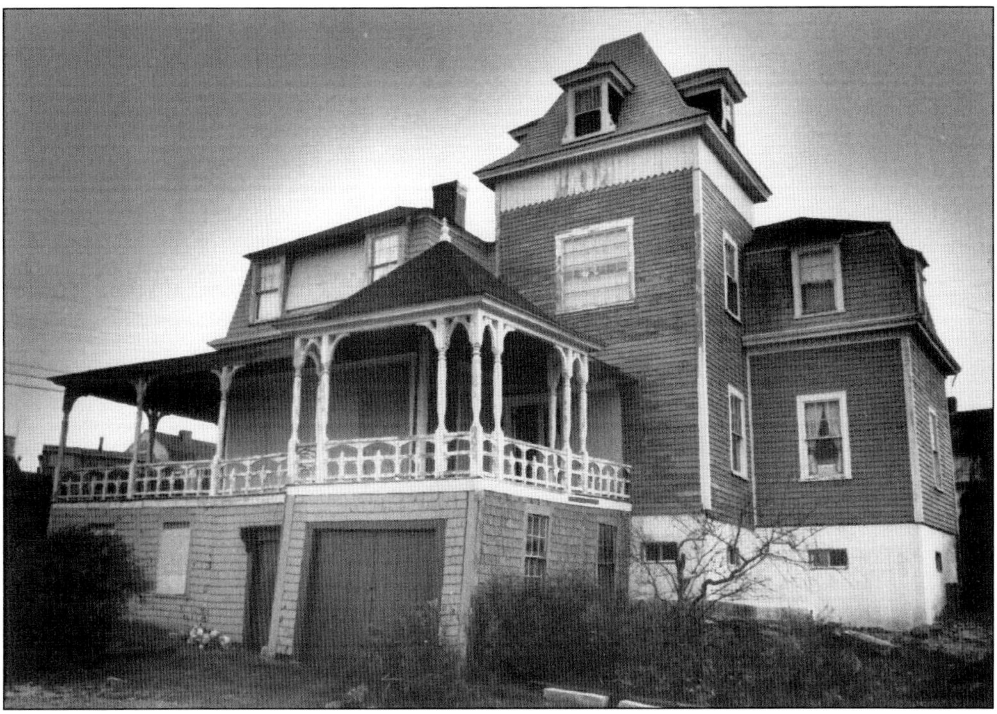

The Governor Sawyer House on Dover Bluffs was owned by a man who was governor of New Hampshire and affiliated with Sawyer Mills in Dover. The building was moved back from the ocean front to the inland side of Nubble Road.

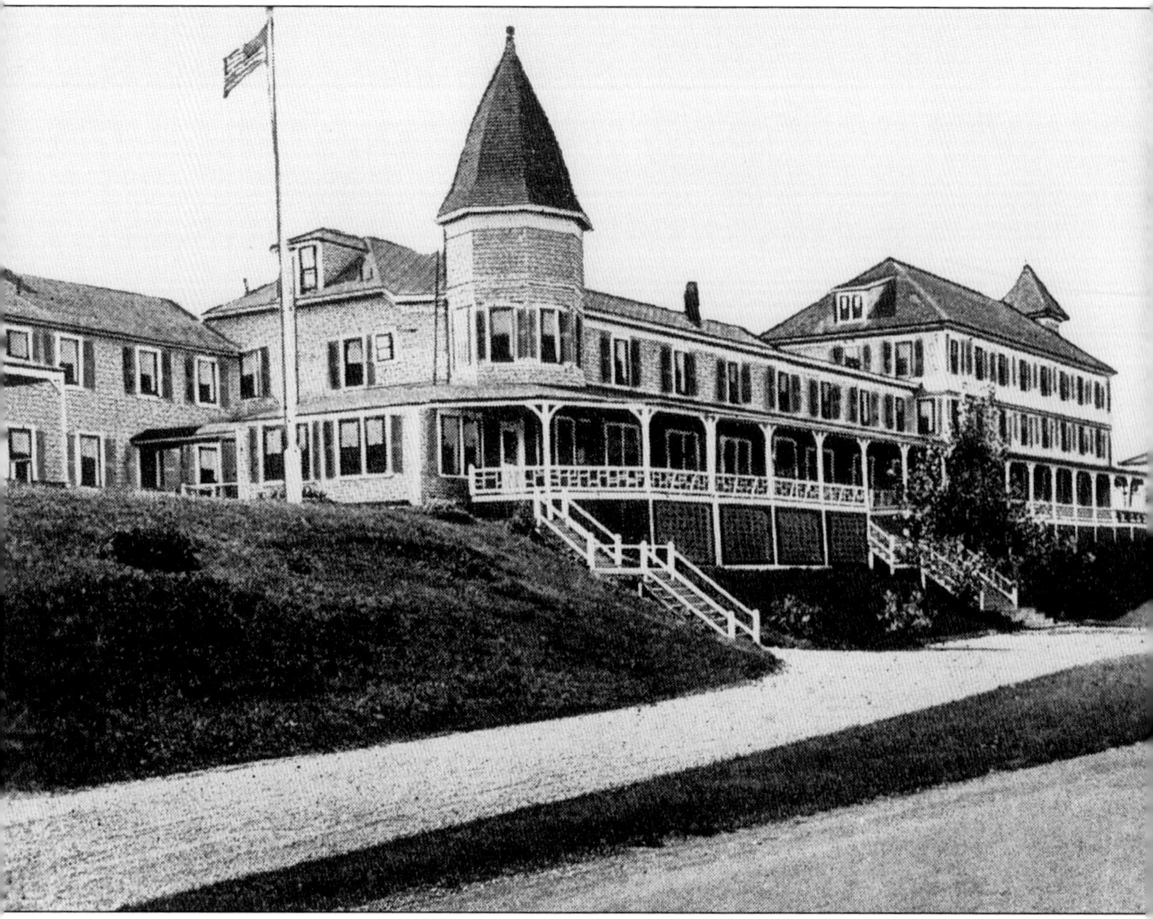

The Ocean House was a York Beach landmark. Located on a ridge overlooking Short Sands Beach, it was owned and operated by the Ellis family for many years. The historic hotel burned on May 20, 1986, while being rebuilt to contain forty-three condominium units.

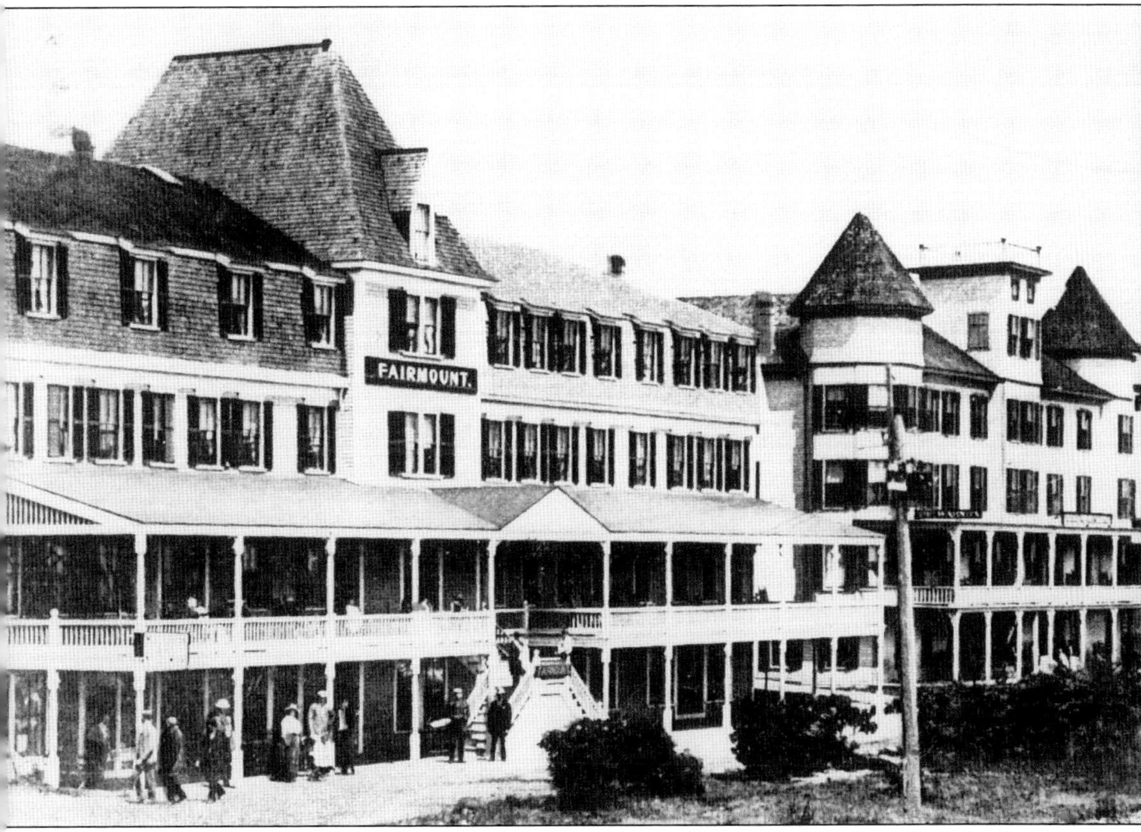


The Fairmont Hotel was one of the original York Beach hotels. It was gradually enlarged to hold 125 guests.

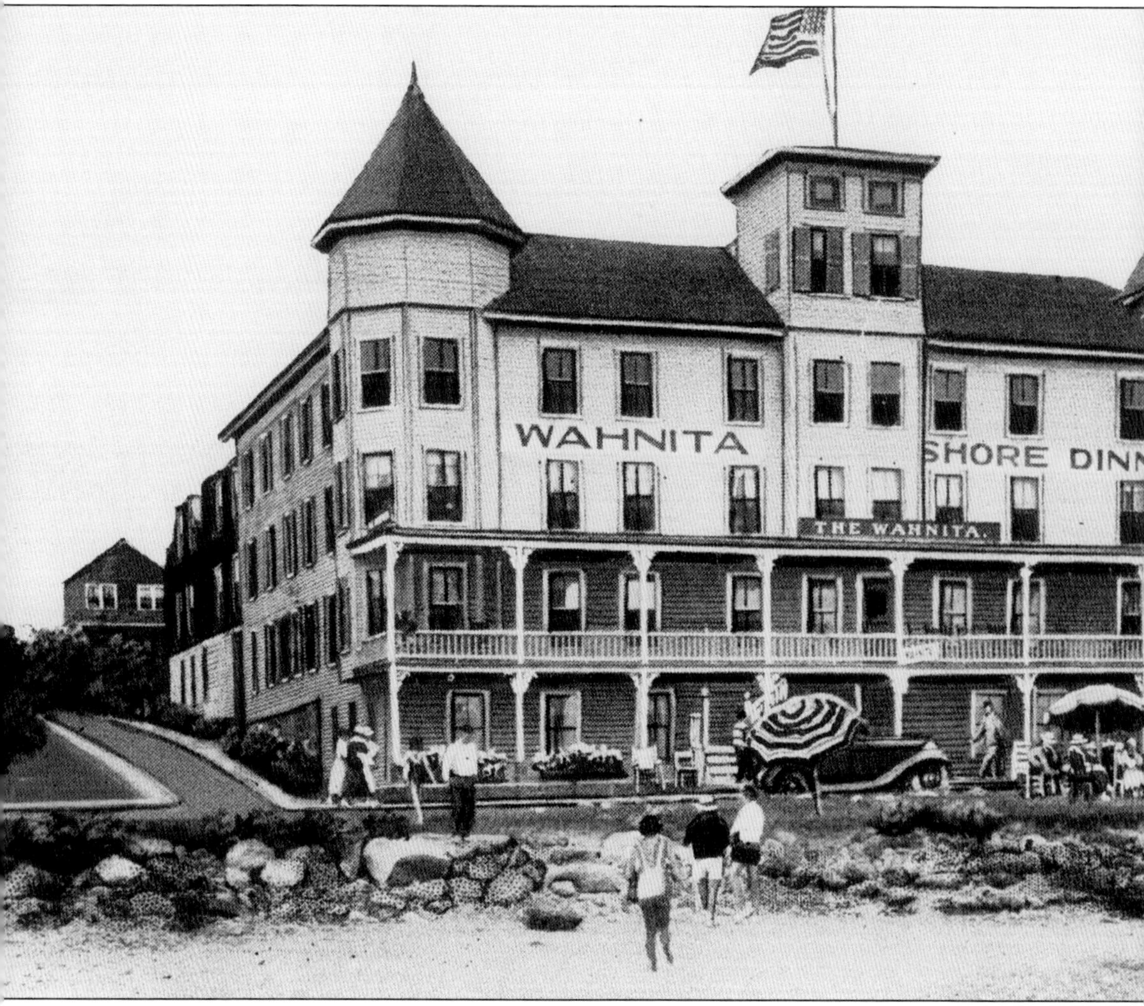


The Wahnita Hotel was adjacent to the Fairmont Hotel. Over the years, the hotel was successively called the Driftwood, the Union Bluff, the York Plaza, the Wahnita, the Driftwood, and the Union Bluff. The original building burned in 1987 but was rebuilt..

# *Seven*

# York Cliffs, Bald Head, and Cape Neddick

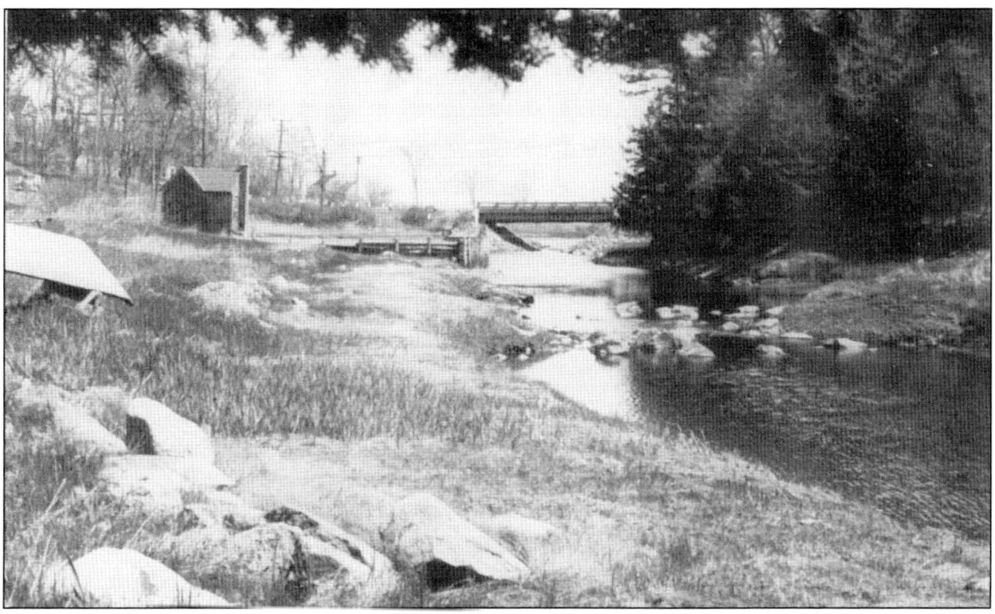

The Cape Neddick River flows from Chase's Pond to the sea. The river once powered many old mills and the mill sites can still be seen from the riverbanks.

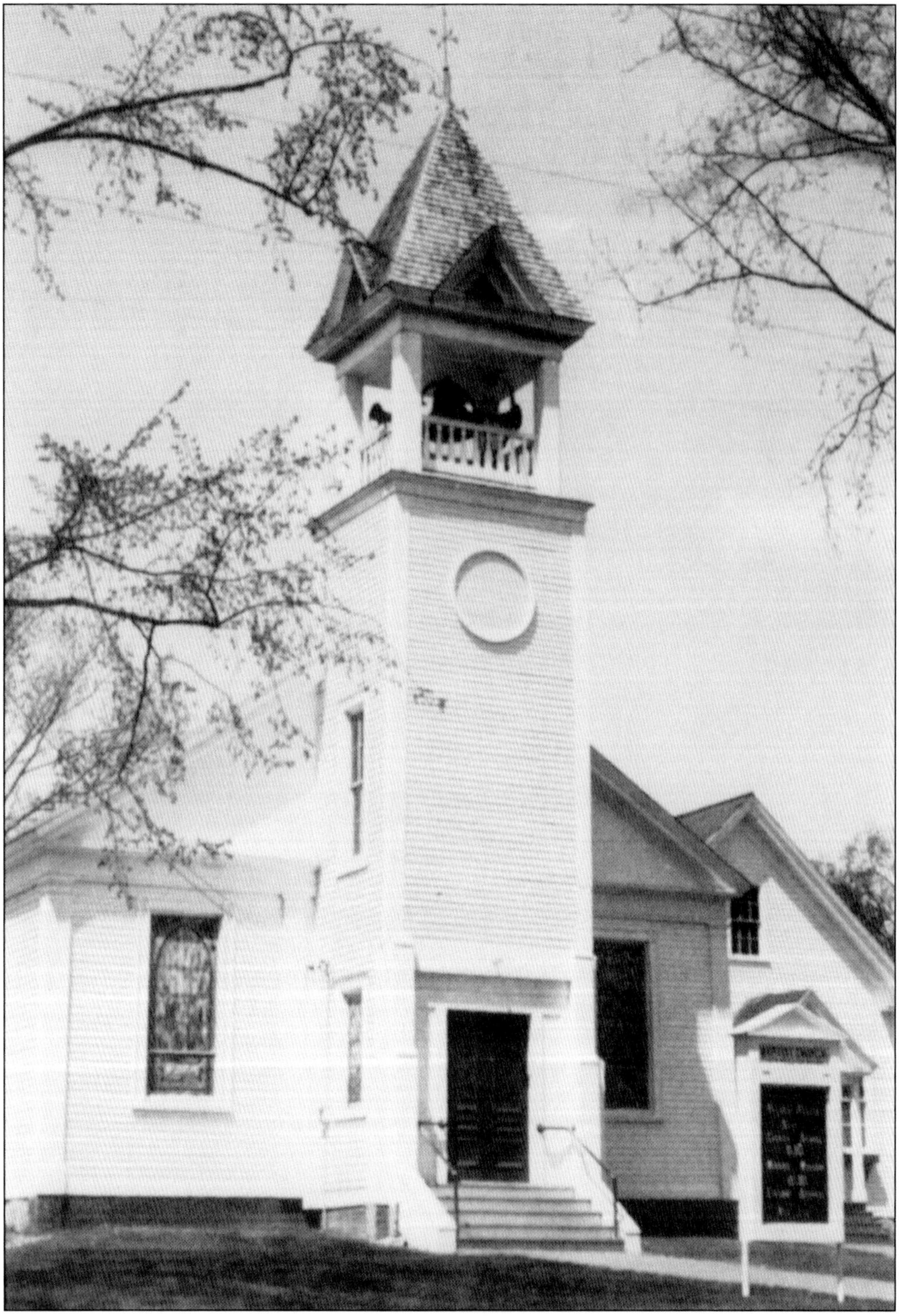

The Cape Neddick Baptist Church was originally built by the Methodist Society. The First Baptist Society of Cape Neddick, formed in 1829, took over the building when the Methodist Society was dissolved.

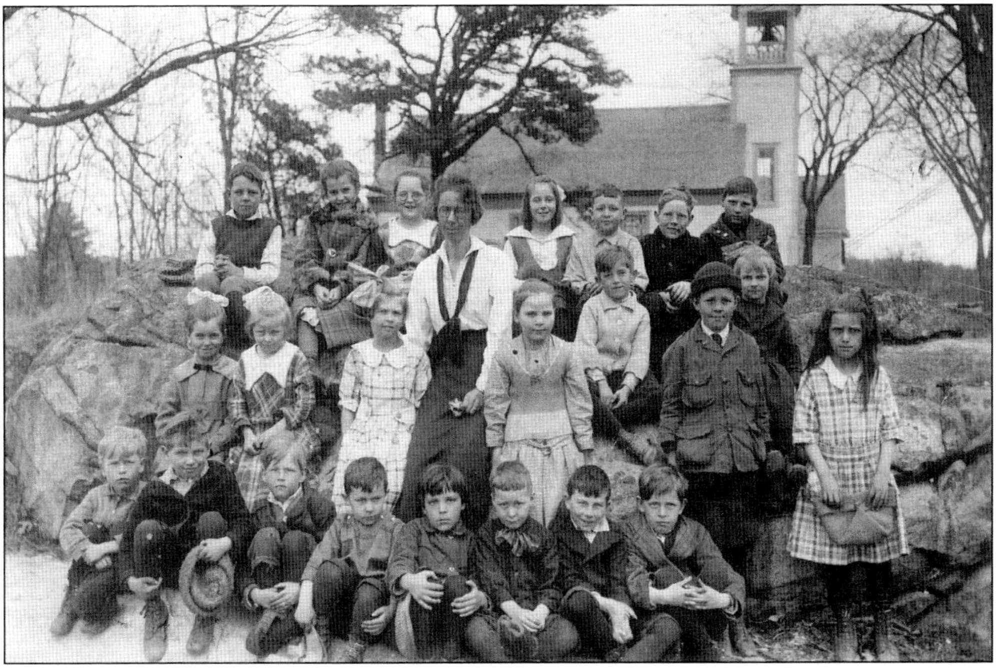

Students at the Cape Neddick School on River Road. The school building in the background is now the annex of the Cape Neddick Baptist Church.

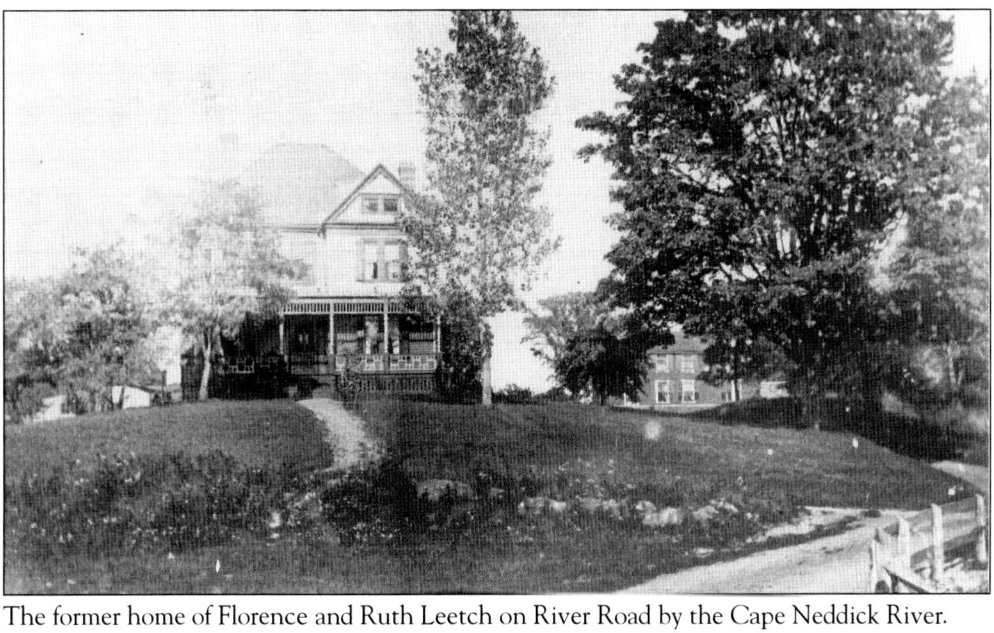

The former home of Florence and Ruth Leetch on River Road by the Cape Neddick River.

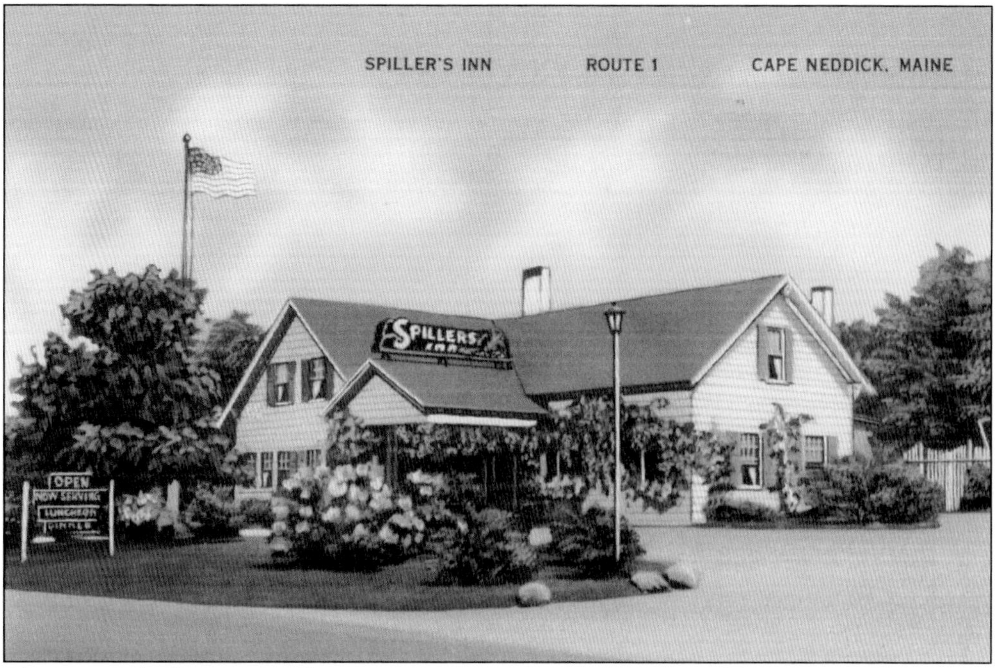


This postcard advertises Spiller's Inn on U.S. Route 1 in Cape Neddick. The restaurant was developed on the site of the Triangle Lunch by Alpheus and Nina Spiller, who opened it in 1930.

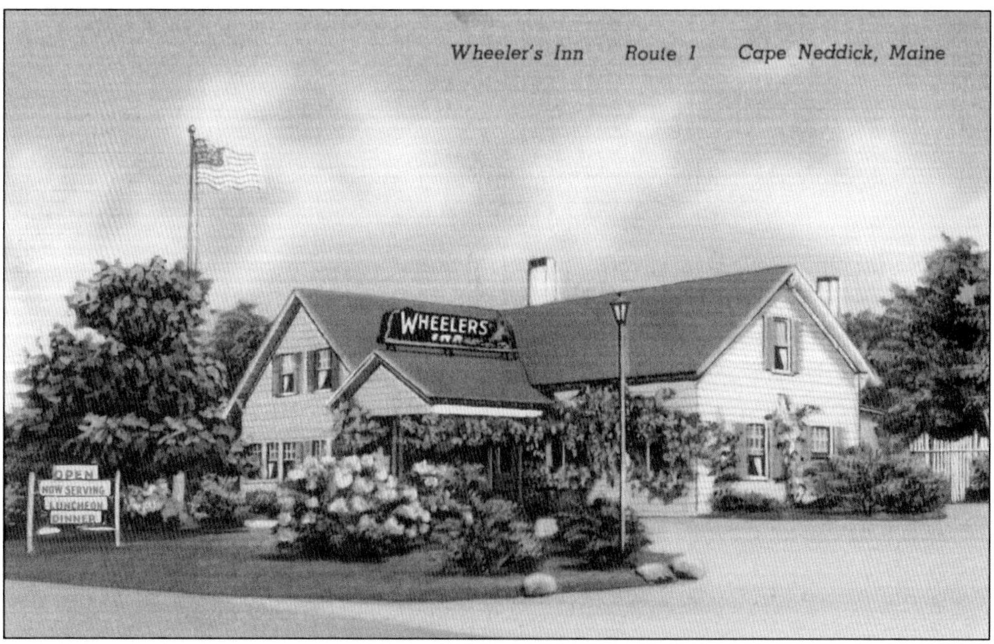


The restaurant became Wheeler's Inn when the Spillers sold it and opened a new restaurant in downtown York Beach. The postcard publisher made few changes to adjust to the change in ownership. It has since become the Cape Neddick Inn and survived a major fire.

Flo's hot dogs are well known to those who travel U.S. Route 1 in Cape Neddick. Flo is shown adding the special sauce that has been enjoyed by thousands of loyal customers.

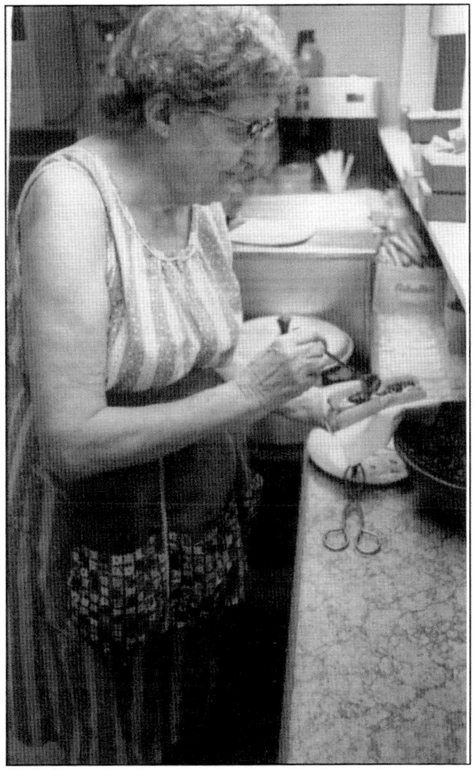

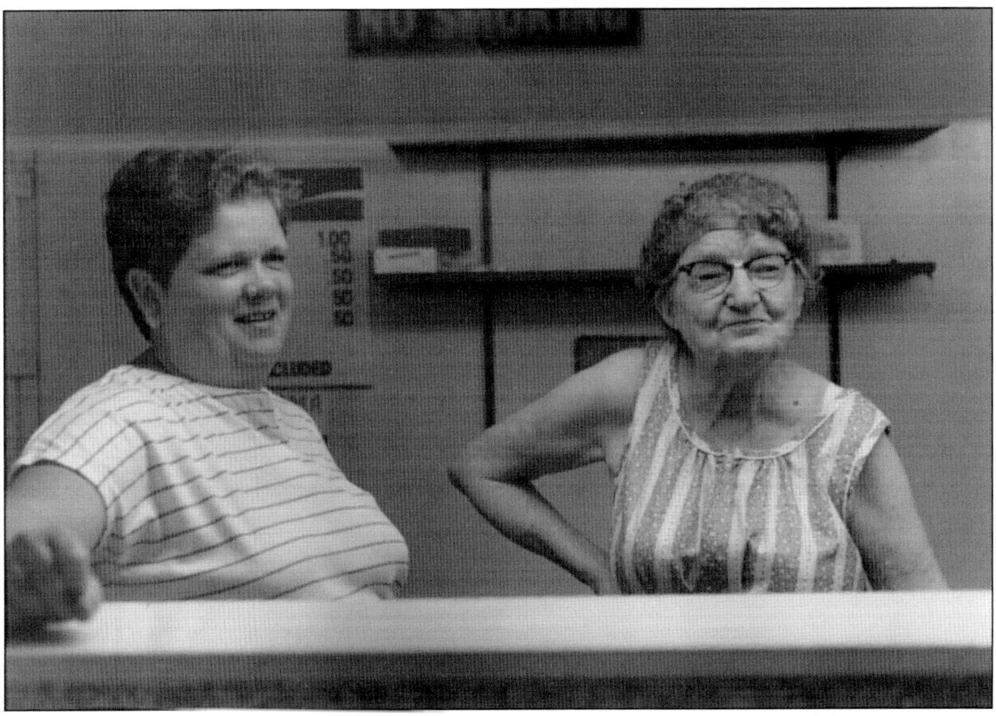

Flo Stacy (right), and her daughter-in-law Gail Stacy, first ask: "How many?" The other details come after the hot dogs are steamed.

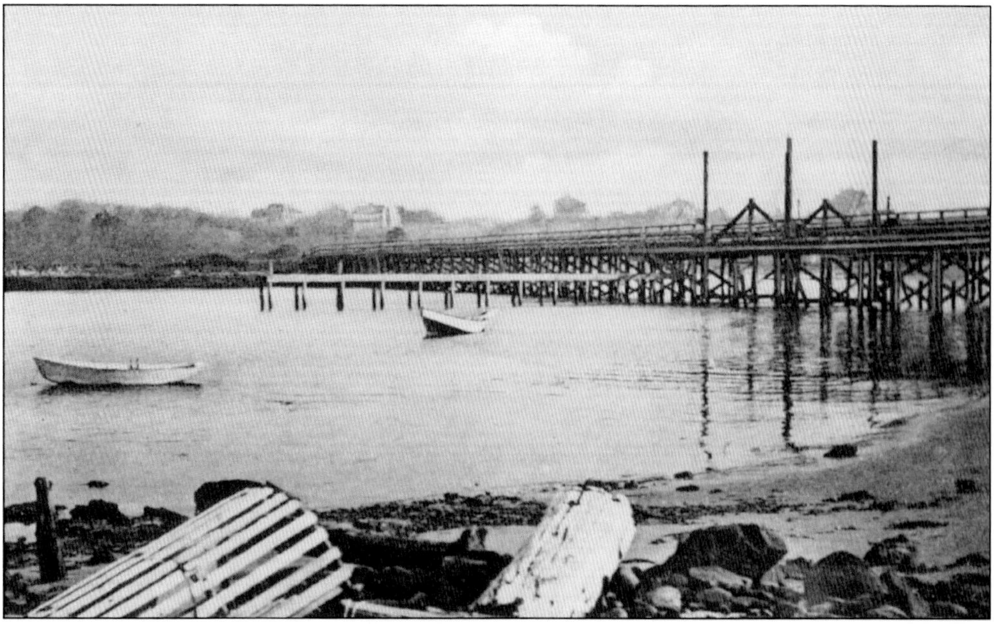

The Passaconnaway Bridge over the Cape Neddick River. At high tide the river matched the entire length of the bridge. The draw was built in halves. Each half was lifted by winches with meshed iron wheels that turned a drum. The chains of the draws were slowly wound around the drum. The apparatus was operated from small platforms, one on each side of the bridge.

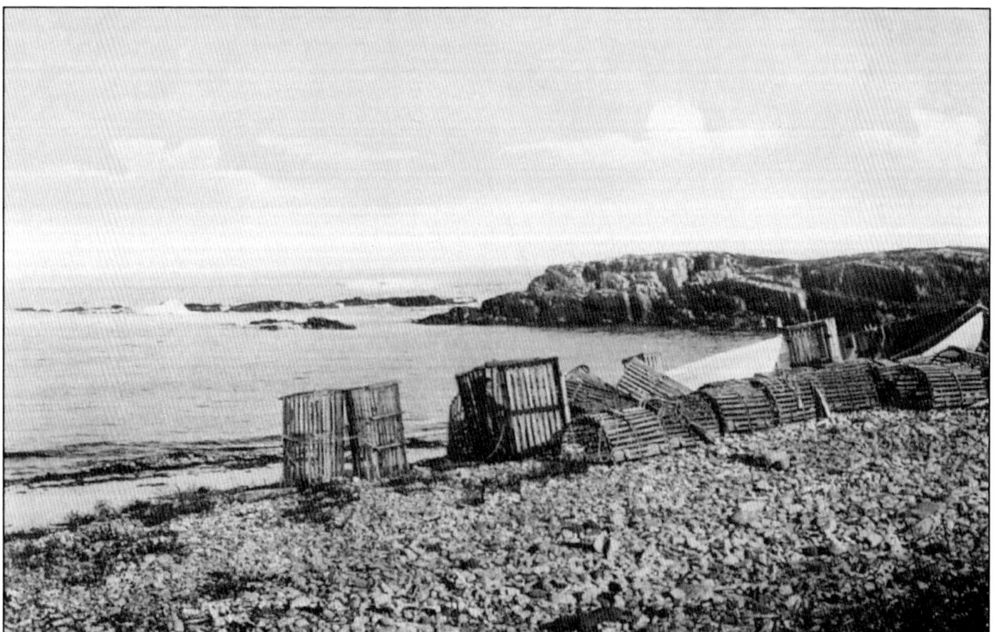

Lobster traps waiting to be claimed line the shore at Phillips Cove.

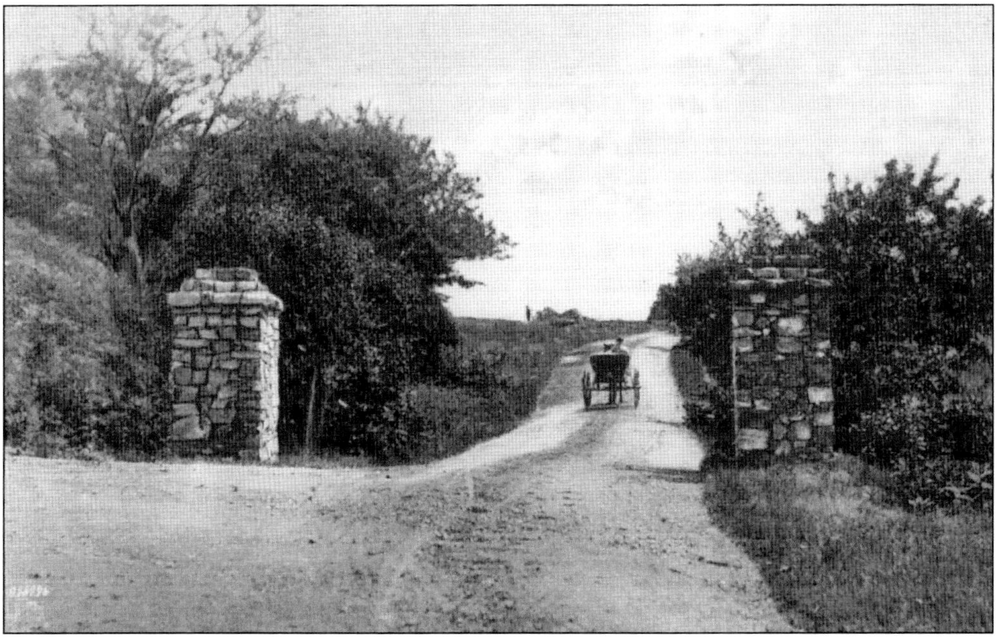

The gateway to the Passaconnaway Inn at York Cliffs.

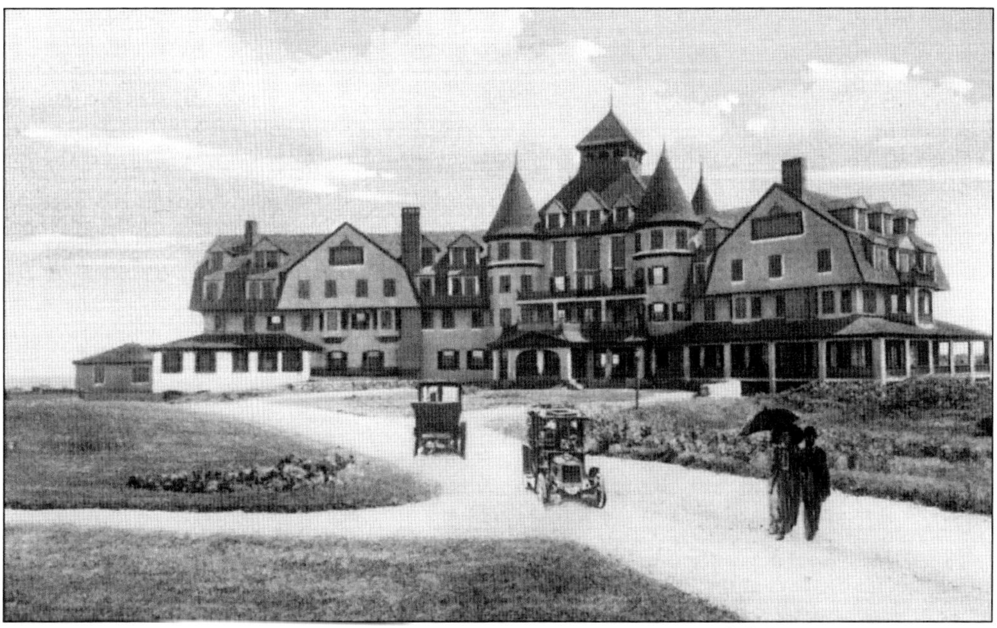

In 1890, a New York City syndicate headed by John, Cornelius, and Adrian Vermule formed the York Cliffs Improvement Company and purchased 400 acres of land at York Cliffs.

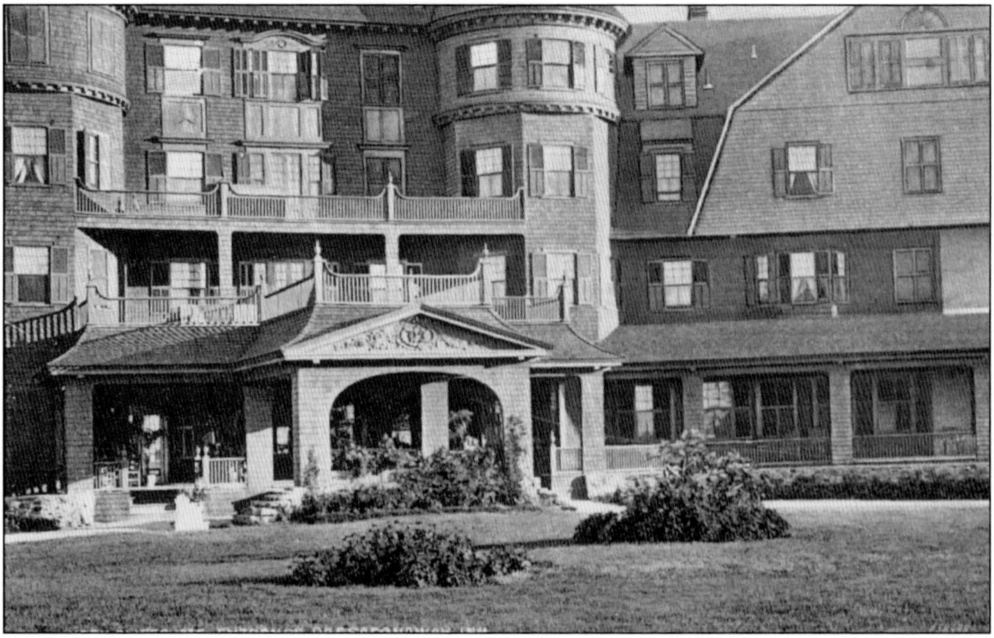

The York Cliffs Improvement Company built the Passaconnaway Inn, which opened on July 1, 1893, and developed plans for an exclusive resort on the Cliffs.

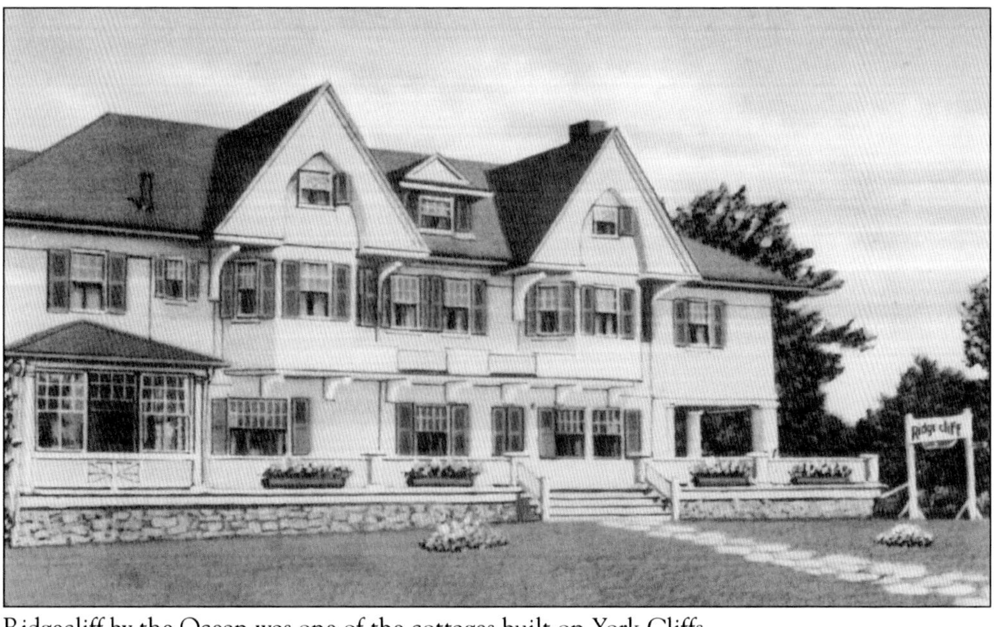

Ridgecliff by the Ocean was one of the cottages built on York Cliffs.

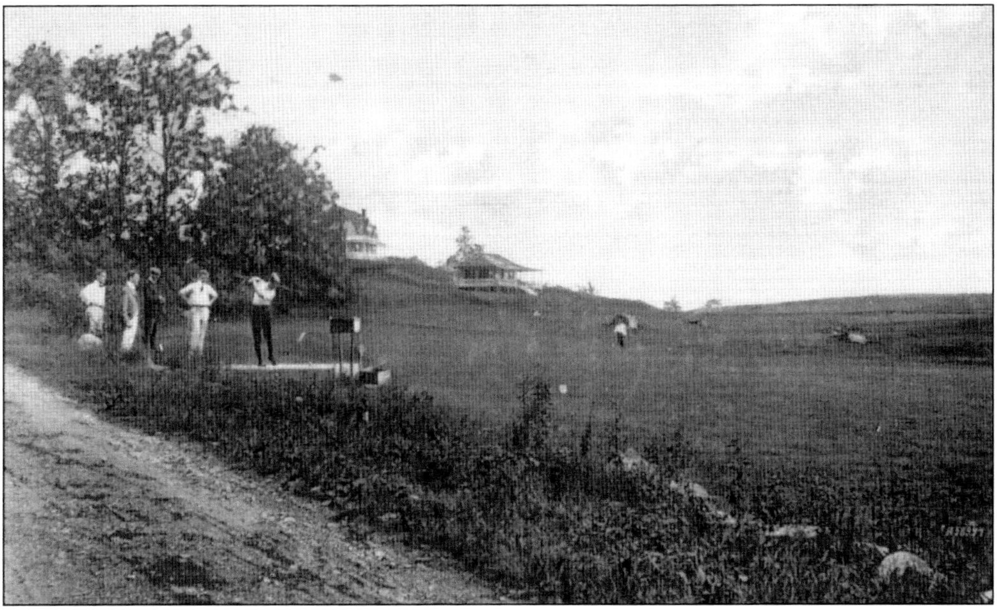

A golf course was laid out for residents of York Cliffs and the Passaconnaway Hotel. Golfers are shown here preparing to drive to a fairway along the river near the mouth of Cape Neddick harbor.

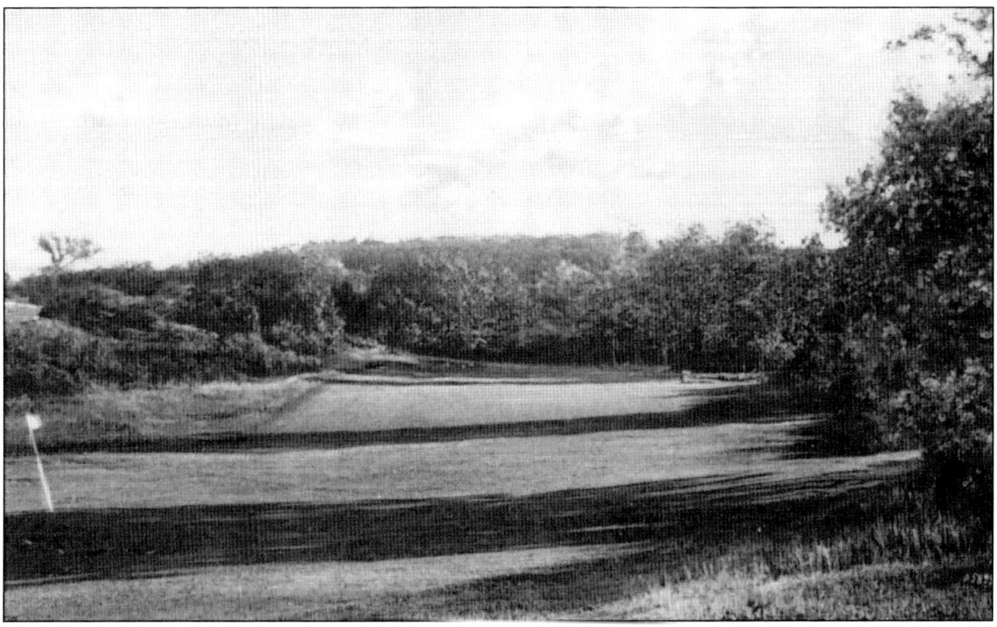

One of the fairways of the golf links at York Cliffs as it looked in 1908.

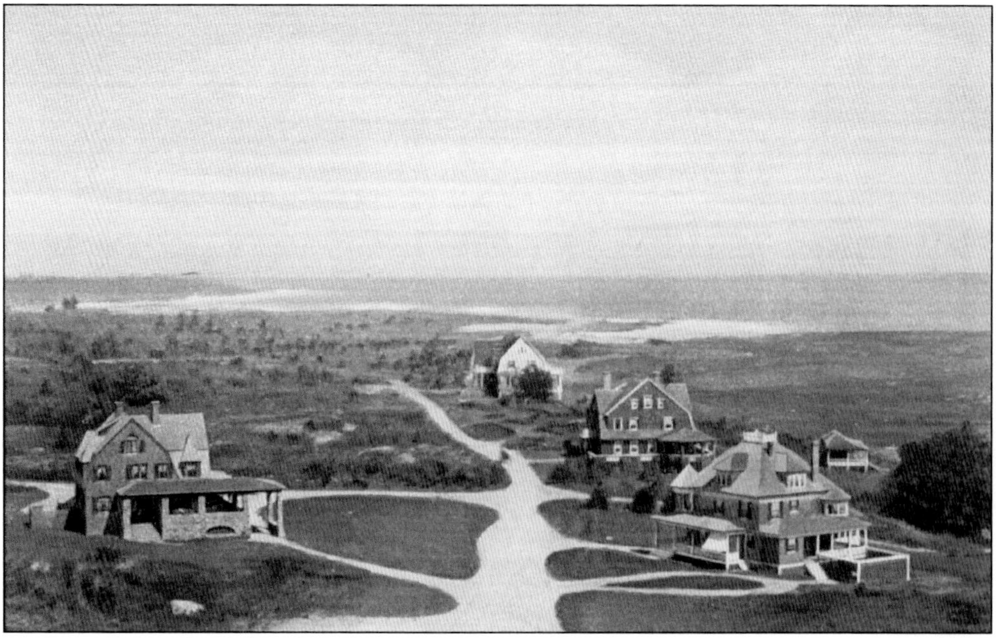

A picture of York Cliffs taken from the cupola of the Passaconnaway Inn looking toward the ocean.

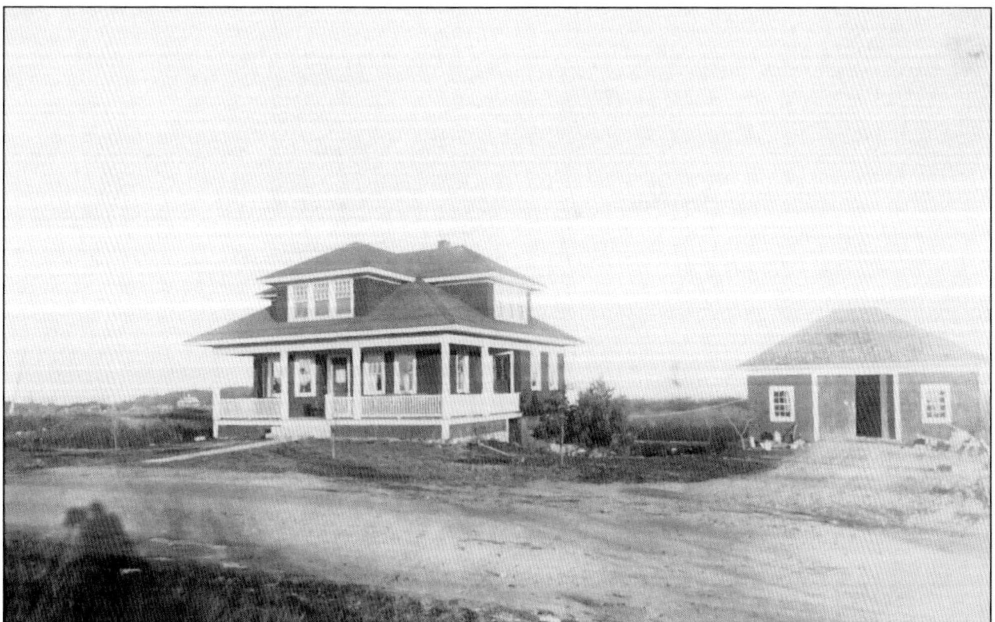

The Edwin N. Walker residence on the Shore Road near York Cliffs.

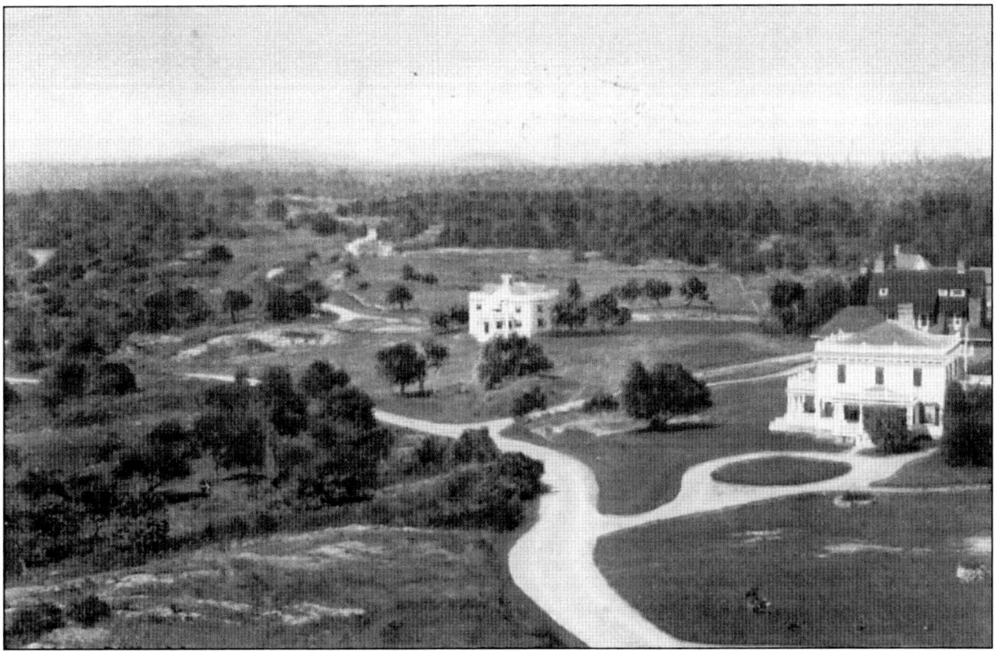

York Cliffs from the cupola of the Passaconnaway Inn. Mount Agamenticus is in the background.

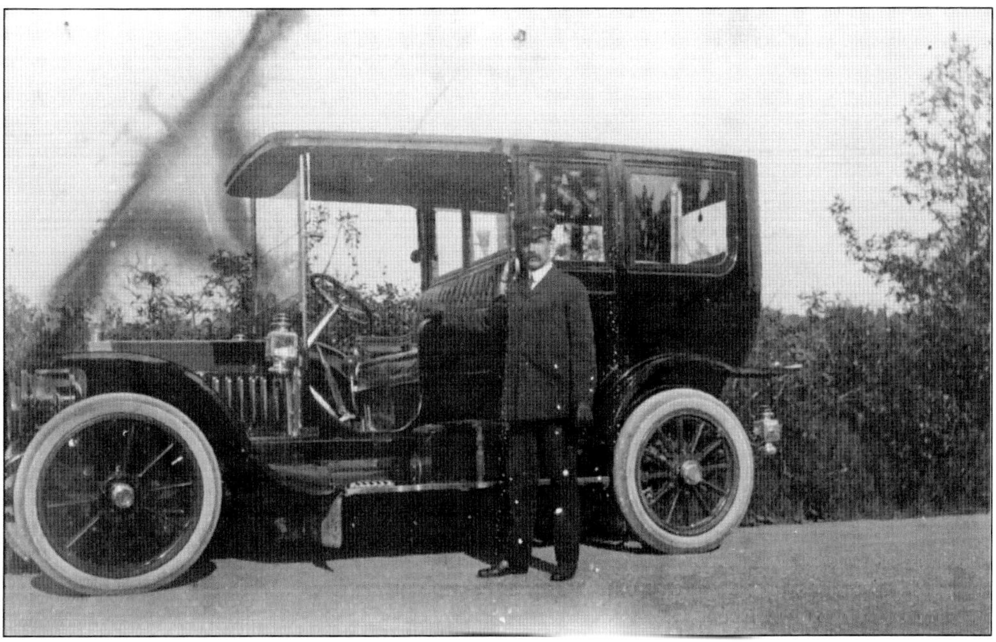

Edwin N. Walker and his vehicle.

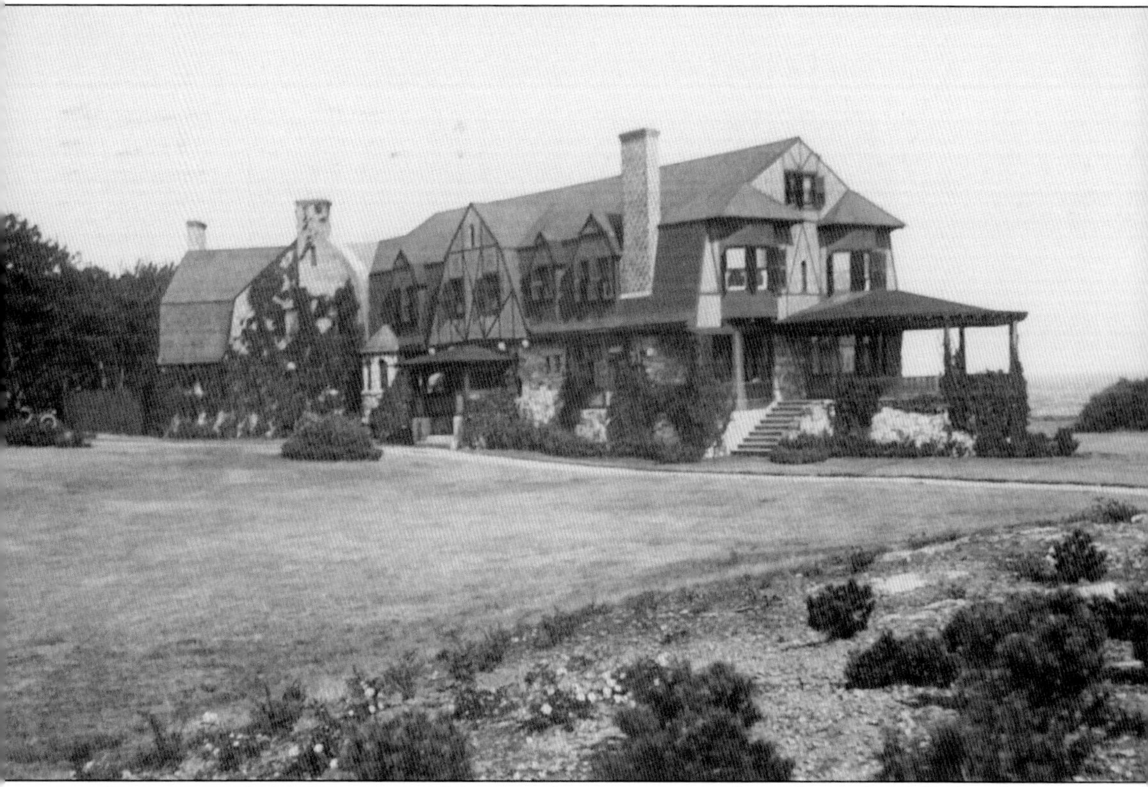

Greystone in 1914. It was one of the first three cottages built in the York Cliffs development and was the home of J.N. Kinney. It was supplied with pure spring water that was pumped from a spring near Chase's Brook.

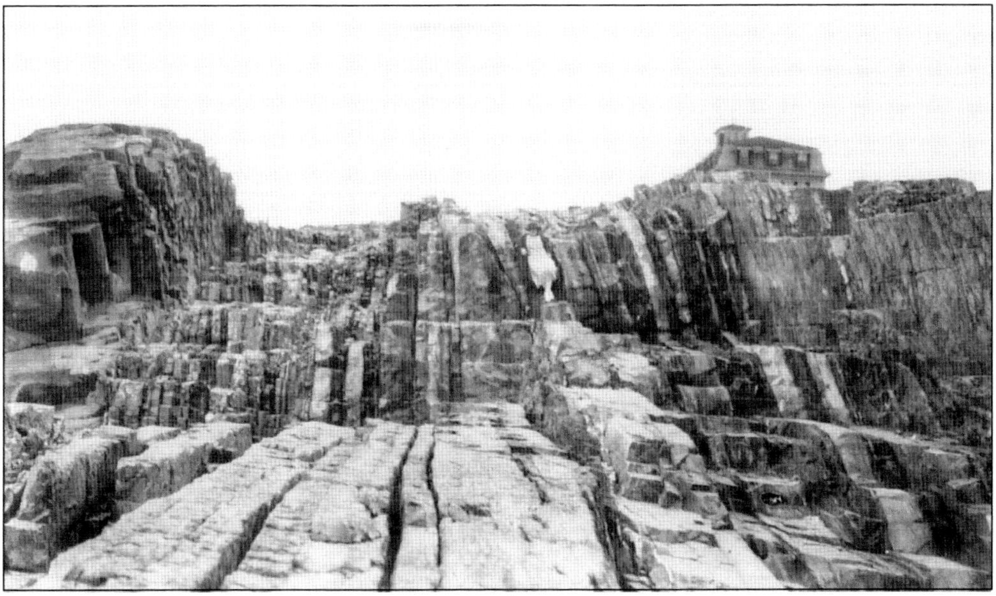
An interesting rock formation at Bald Head Cliff in 1922.

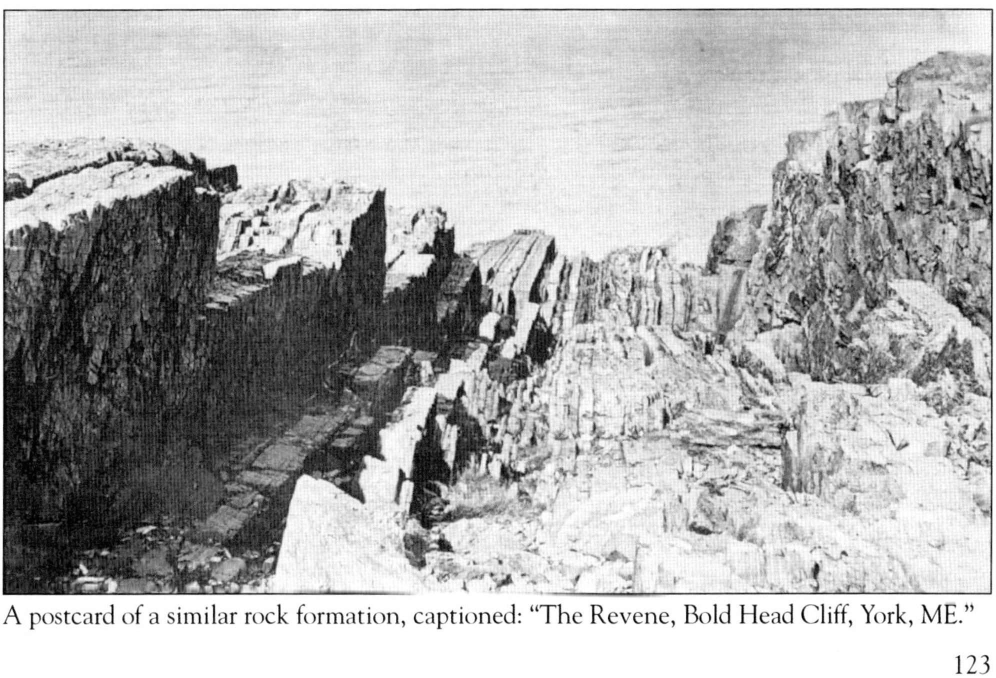
A postcard of a similar rock formation, captioned: "The Revene, Bold Head Cliff, York, ME."

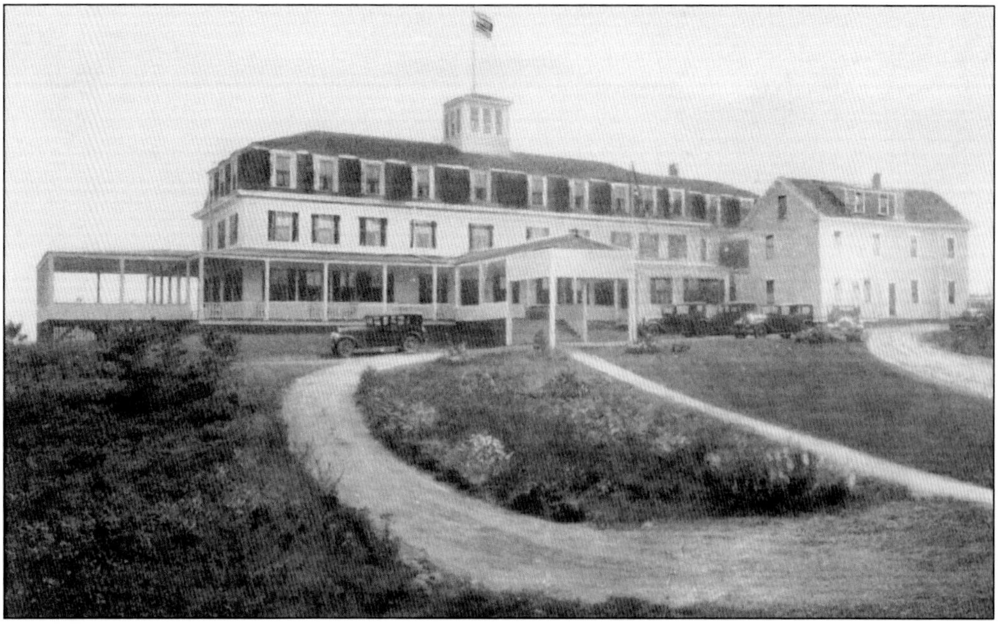

The entrance to the Cliff House at Bald Head Cliff on the Shore Road.

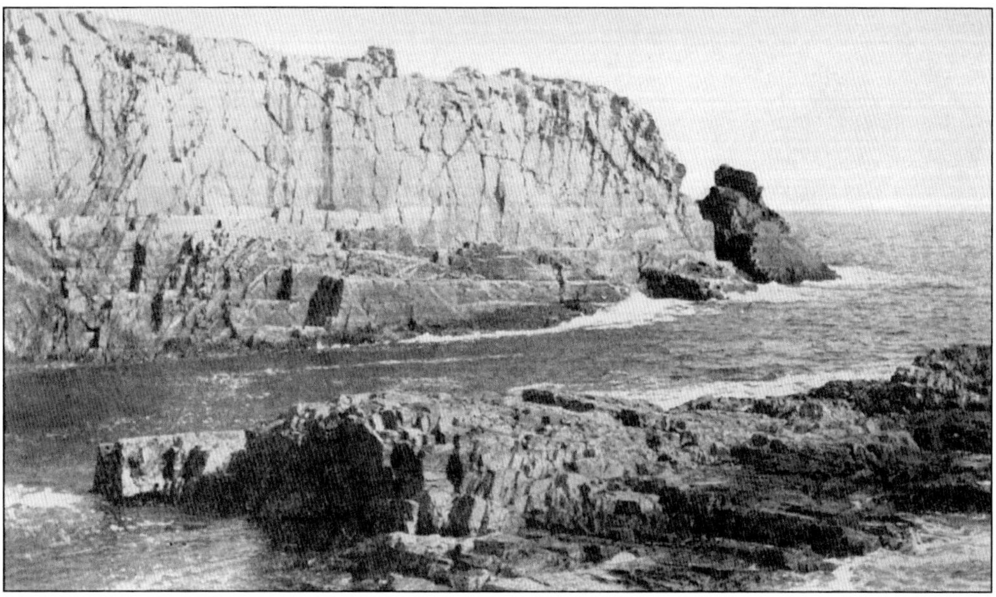

The famous rock formation known as Bald Head Cliff has attracted tourists for many generations.

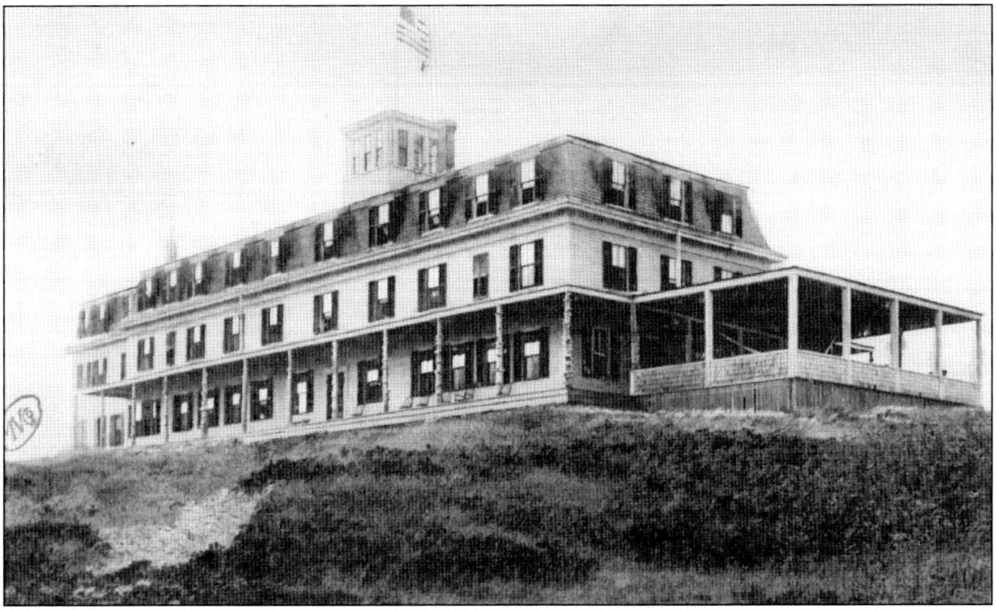
The historic Cliff House as seen from the ocean side.

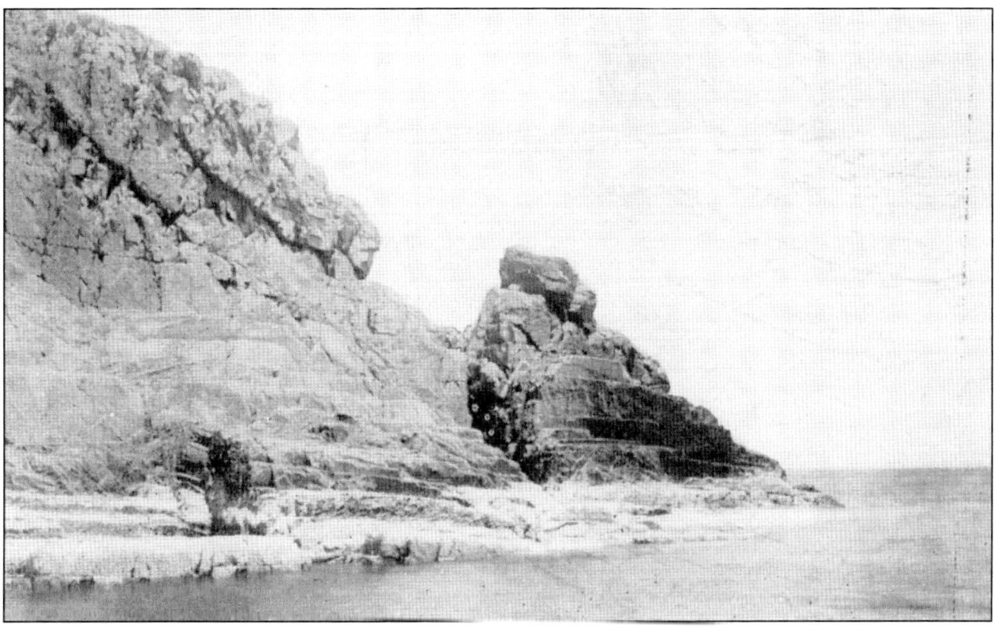
The point of Bald Head Cliff, also known as the Devil's Pulpit.

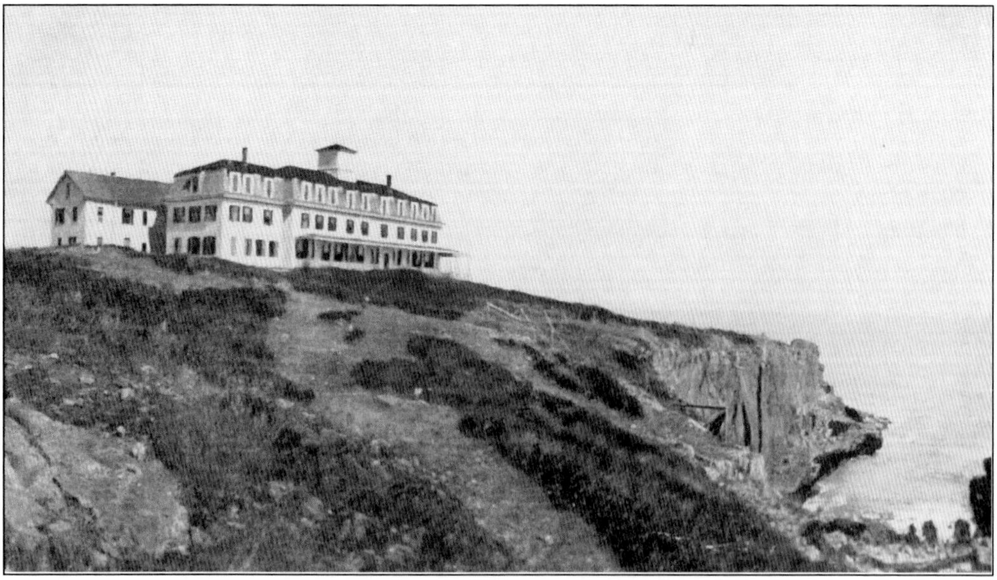

An early postcard of the Cliff House and Bald Head Cliff published by Ko Tsubayama & Company of York Beach.

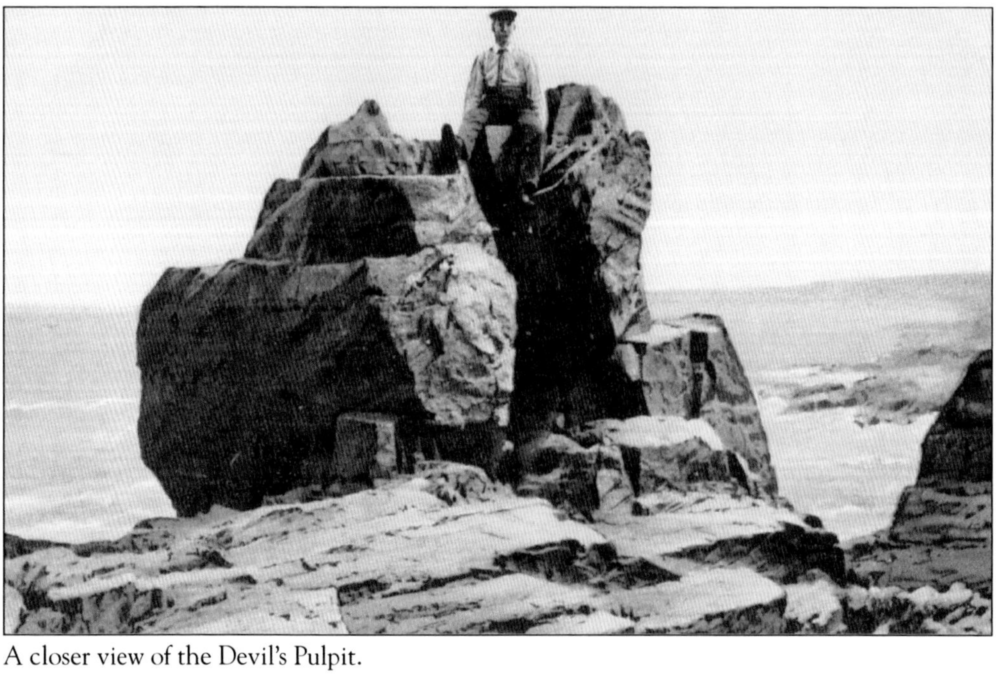

A closer view of the Devil's Pulpit.

The Flume at Bald Head Cliff is featured on this postcard.

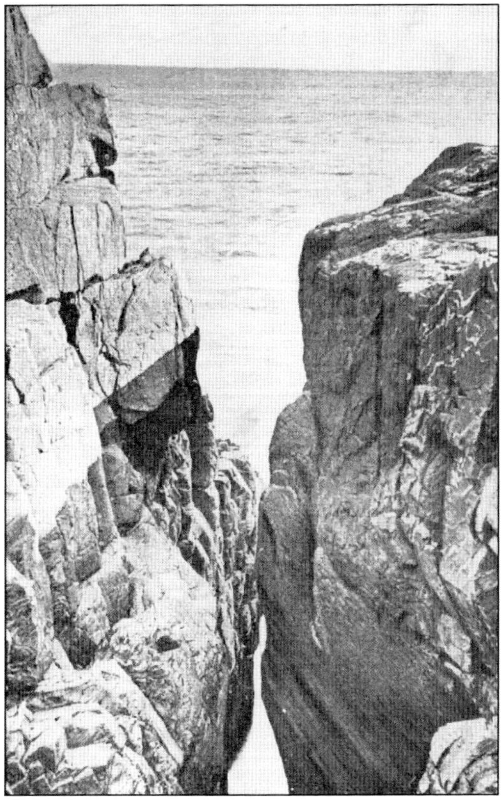

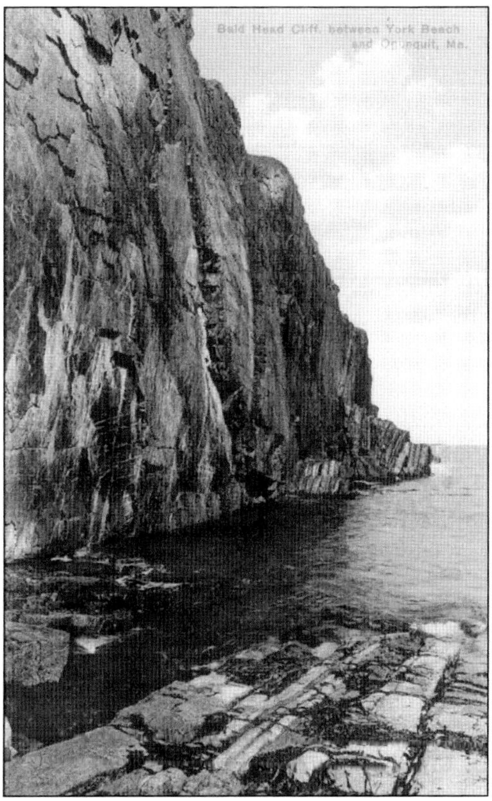


A matching postcard shows the sheai wall of rocks known as Bald Head Cliff.

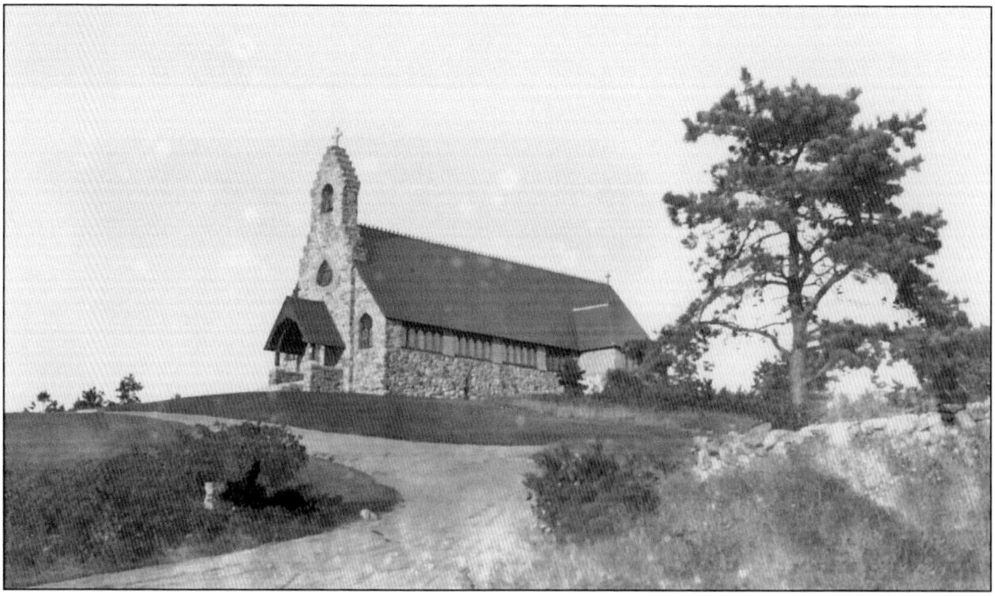

This photograph of Saint Peter's-by-the Sea on the Shore Road was used on a postcard.

# Acknowledgments

Over the years many people have shared their pictures, postcards, and ephemera with me for use in these publications. Many others have provided information about details in those images that were unknown to me, but familiar to them. I am grateful to all of you who have participated in these attempts to assemble the visual history of this community and preserve it for future generations. I have used material from the work of W.N. Gough, the Captain Seavey Collection, and the Wagner Collection. Others who have contributed to this publication are Ethel Freeman, Betty Bridges, Richard Philbrick, David Hilton, Florence and Ruth Leetch, Louise Sodano, Jayne Tillotson, and Howard Moulton. Special thanks to Peter Moore, who contributed many of the key photographs and did much of the research upon which the captions were based.

John D. Bardwell